MW00605577

ALSO BY RICHARD H. UNDERWOOD

CrimeSong: True Crime Stories from Southern Murder Ballads

GASLIGHT LAWYERS

"Rotunda of the Astor House, showing some of the prominent men who dine there." 1899, Content: At the corner of the image, name of the artist (illegible). Printed on border: Thomas F. Byrnes, ex-Chief of Police. Joseph H. Choate. Recorder John W. Goff. Clarence Lexow. Abraham Levy. William F. Howe.

GASLIGHT LAWYERS

CRIMINAL TRIALS & EXPLOITS
IN GILDED AGE NEW YORK

RICHARD H. UNDERWOOD

with foreword by
Gregory J. Davis, MD, FCAP

SHADELANDHOUSE MODERN PRESS
LEXINGTON, KENTUCKY

GASLIGHT LAWYERS
CRIMINAL TRIALS & EXPLOITS IN GILDED AGE NEW YORK

Published in the United States by:
   Shadelandhouse Modern Press, LLC
   Lexington, Kentucky
   smpbooks.com

Shadelandhouse, Shadelandhouse Modern Press, and the colophon are
trademarks of Shadelandhouse Modern Press, LLC.

This book began with an article, Richard H. Underwood, "Mr. Howe's Last
Case," that originally appeared in 31 *Legal Studies Forum* 801 (2007).
This book includes and reprints content from this article with the cooperation
and permission of and grateful acknowledgment to the *Legal Studies Forum*.
All occurrences of the inclusion of such content are documented in the notes.

First edition 2017

LCCN 2017901906
ISBN 978-1-945049-01-9

Endpapers: Map (and detail on an enlarged scale) of New York City
(G.W. & C.B. Colton & Co., 1897) showing a panoramic birds-eye view of
the city, "presented looking east from high above Hoboken and Jersey City"

Printed and manufactured in the United States of America
Book design and page layout by Susan Leonard
Cover design by Matt Tanner

To John Jay College of Criminal Justice,
Lloyd Sealy Library, with a special tribute
to librarians Ellen Belcher, Ellen Sexton,
and Bonnie Nelson

Contents

Foreword

I'm not an attorney, though I have worked intimately with them as a medical examiner/forensic pathologist for over three decades now, in twenty-five states of the Union and in three other nations. In that time, as is true of Professor Underwood in his professional journey, I've become increasingly fascinated by the stories I've encountered—both as a participant and as a listener. When discussing with my medical and law students and resident physicians the similarities and differences of law and medicine, I often think of what I saw years ago on a Central Kentucky horse farm as I drove home from the medical examiner's office one late afternoon: some cows had broken through a fence and were standing opposite some horses across a small stream. The look on the faces of both groups was apparent: "You look a bit like me, but…you're different." So perhaps the same is true for Professor Underwood's and my chosen professions. Different though our approaches may be, the best of law and medicine share the call of stories, whether such stories emanate from our patients, our clients, our colleagues, or our society at large. At their core, it's these stories—be they around a campfire, in a classroom, in an office, at a crime scene, or in a courtroom—that may keep us interested and engaged and that act as a vaccine against burnout, that potential occupational hazard shared by both groups.

Then, as young (and now, as relatively mature) physicians and attorneys, we learned and continue to learn from the examples of others, both as positive and negative role models, and as part of that learning we are absorbed and entertained by their tales. Professor Underwood's chosen stories in *Gaslight Lawyers* are gripping, as they profile *characters*: a word chosen with intent, because their posterity seems larger than life but who, in historical reality, are at times all too human, since they make the same mistakes all humans have made for millennia. These characters, as is true of their mostly less flamboyant modern counterparts, grappled with tasks that had major impacts upon their clients, their greater community, and the way that law is practiced to this day. We have come a long way since the days of his protagonists, and yet we still have a long way to go in acknowledging and dealing with biases that manifest themselves in attorneys, in fact and expert witnesses, and in the interpretation of evidence. As every lawyer and forensic pathologist should realize regarding the "holy trinity" of witnesses, confessions, and physical evidence: witnesses are often wrong, confessions often false, and physical evidence open to misinterpretation.

I share with Professor Underwood his trepidation regarding the seemingly neofascist block architecture of our new Fayette Courthouse complex, in Lexington, Kentucky. Impressive, yes, but with perhaps a wrong impression: to me as a citizen and medical expert who spends a lot of time in courthouses, I yearn for the architecture of the courthouses of old, such as our former courthouse, built in 1898 just a few blocks away—a secular counterpart to a cathedral, a place of gravitas and beauty, reflecting the weight and beauty of justice. If the arc of justice is to be wrought in the proper fashion, perhaps it will be by the students of this remarkable author, learning from and being entertained by his stories, as you will also, in a moment.

Gregory J. Davis, MD, FCAP
Professor and Director, Forensic Consultation Service
Department of Pathology and Laboratory Medicine
University of Kentucky College of Medicine
Former Associate Chief Medical Examiner
Commonwealth of Kentucky

Preface

When I walk by our new courthouse complex in Lexington, Kentucky, I get a bit of a chill. The architecture seems a bit neofascist to me (apologies to its namesake, the late Chief Justice Robert Stephens, Kentucky Supreme Court, who was a friend for some years). The whole, great thing exudes power and social control. That has been the message sent out by courthouse architecture for a very long time. Consider the old Egyptian Revival–style Tombs in New York City (1838–1902), which stood not far from the notorious Five Points neighborhood. And consider its replacements (1902–1941 and 1941–1974), which had a "Bridge of Sighs" (after the original in Venice) over which prisoners went from lockup to courtroom and then back again after learning their fate.

Many sad stories are acted out in these buildings—in the theaters we call courtrooms. Have you stopped to think that, beyond the bar separating the audience of laypersons from the lawyers and parties, there is a stage? There are stage doors, left and right (one may be a robing room and the other a room for the jurors). The judge sits in her or his aerie, looking out and down, much like the lords and ladies would have in their special seating in the Globe Theatre. Courtroom architecture has not changed much over the years.

The period that is the setting for the stories in this book is from the 1870s or so to the early 1900s, the Gaslight Era, when the Victorian Age was yielding to the Edwardian, the gaslight was giving way to the electric light, and the hangman's rope was giving over to the electric chair. On that note, Dr. Allan McLane Hamilton, a character who will make many appearances in this book, made the following observation in chapter XXIII of his autobiography:

> "I had seen men hung years ago in the yard of the Tombs—
> and for the most part these executions were solemn affairs.

Even the ward politician and political healer who had 'gota ticket' were awed, and reverently followed the prayer of the black-robed priests, and everything seemed to be decent and in order; meanwhile scores of white pigeons fluttered on the heads of the condemned men or even alighted on the top of the scaffold. I am sorry to say that the method of electrical execution did not give this impression, and there was a more or less decided feeling that every one thought more of the success of the procedure than that a human being, no matter how wicked, was being sent out of the world with so short a shrift."

Such is progress?

I use the term Gaslight Era loosely. The reader might also use as a reference point the Gilded Age (1878–1889), given its name by Mark Twain and Charles Dudley Warner (a dear friend of Dr. Hamilton), authors of the satirical novel, *The Gilded Age* (1873). This was a time— less than twenty years after the end of the Civil War—of immigration and social upheaval.

At this time most of middle America was still the rural, small town, "Courthouse America" of Edgar Lee Masters's *Spoon River Anthology*.[1] Out West, things were still pretty wild—the 1890 Wounded Knee Massacre and the 1892 Johnson County range war come to mind. In contrast, from the Gay Nineties to 1910, when Mark Twain went out with Halley's Comet, there were great changes in the Big City. While tenements teemed with newcomers who came through Ellis Island, which had opened in 1892, D. H. Burnham's Flatiron Building (1902) "created a bridge between the picturesque world of gaslight New York and the skyscrapers of the aggressive twentieth century commercial market."[2] It was a bustling "city of stores."[3] By 1890, the city's transit system had more mileage than London.[4] By 1895, Edison's electric lights had reached as far as Forty-second Street. In the early 1900s automobiles, motor buses, and taxis would appear on the scene. It was to become the "wonder city of the world."[5]

One associates the times with the rise of masters of industry, like John D. Rockefeller, Andrew Carnegie, J. P. Morgan, newspaper tycoon William Randolph Hearst,[6] and the "big four" newspaper journalists Ervin Wardman (*New York Tribune*), W. J. Kenney (*New York Times*), Richard A. Farrelly (*New York World*), and Charles Edward Russell (*New York Herald*).

But all was not progress. The economy reeled from the Panic of 1893 and would not begin to recover until 1897, when a period of growth would run up to the Panic of 1907. The 1889 Johnstown Flood inspired muckrakers and reformers like Charles Edward Russell[7] to speak truth to power. Russell would help found the National Association for the Advancement of Colored People (NAACP) along with William Edward Burghardt (W. E. B.) DuBois. The horrific Triangle Shirtwaist Factory fire in 1911 would energize the International Ladies Garment Workers Union. Still, with all its horrors, it may seem a rather innocent age to the modern reader. While the Russo-Japanese War of 1905 and Bloody Sunday in Russia, also in 1905, hinted at things to come, nobody was expecting the Great War, which would change everything.

The criminal cases I discuss in this book were tried in this era, when the field of scientific, forensic evidence was only beginning to emerge and when guilt or innocence usually turned on eyewitness testimony. Police methods were crude, and lawyers' ethics on both sides of the "v." were not always what they should have been. Subornation of perjury was common. Judges were often outrageously biased. There were no Miranda warnings and the like, right to counsel was frequently denied, and evidence against the accused was sometimes faked. Cases were tried in the "yellow press," by both the prosecution and the defense.

Because crime science was in its infancy, the guilty actually had a shot at acquittal with the right lawyer; but the innocent were often at the mercy of unscrupulous prosecutors, corrupt police, and hanging judges. Of course, there is certainly plenty of error these days. Even so, there have been changes. Although there are famous criminal trial lawyers today, there are not so many of them and not so many trials. Today we process people through a system driven by draconian sentences which force guilty pleas. Although the death penalty is not as common as it was in the old days, we seem to warehouse a great many more people for long periods of time.

Like the fictional barrister, Horace Rumpole, I "take up my pen at this advanced age"[8] to write reconstructions, not of my own cases but of those of a group of Gaslight Era criminal defense lawyers in New York City. The stories will follow the celebrated exploits—and the fall—of legendary trial lawyer William F. Howe and the rise of two young Jewish advocates, Emanuel "Manny" Friend and Abraham Levy. The stories in this book open with the entrance of Howe, who practiced from around 1860 until his death in 1902. He rose to great heights and then suddenly fell and was replaced by others.

Of course there were other big name trial lawyers in this period. Some of the names may be familiar to the reader. William J. Fallon, "The Great Mouthpiece,"[9] known for his skill at finding that one juror to hang up the process, was resurrected for an appearance in the popular HBO series *Boardwalk Empire*. Earl Rogers became a legend in faraway Los Angeles, California.[10] There was also Max D. Steuer, today forgotten except by a cult following of trial lawyers.[11] All of these advocates have their own biographies, and I will not be tracking their exploits in this book.

As Howe reached the peak of his long career, newcomers tried to make their way defending criminal cases. Friend and Levy appeared, *pro bono*, for the defense in the trial of Ameer Ben Ali (or "Frenchy"), a.k.a. George Frank, accused of a "Jack the Ripper" style murder. The Frenchy case was not the greatest beginning for Friend and Levy; however, with experience these newcomers became quite formidable. Friend and his associates saved Maria Barbella (also referred to as Barberi and Barbieri) from the electric chair. Friend also went on to best Howe in the spectacular, scattered-body-parts Nack-Thorn-Guldensuppe case. Howe never recovered. Friend's sometime partner, Abraham Levy, outlived Friend and emerged victorious in yet another crime of the century (there were a great deal more of these than centuries), the Nan Patterson case.

I discuss a great many other cases and a great many other characters—criminals, judges, prosecutors, detective inspectors, sob sisters, lots of doctors, my favorite alienist, and even a social worker do-gooder or two. Two characters with multiple appearances are Francis Wellman, a Tammany prosecutor who undeservedly (in my opinion) became something of a holy relic after the publication of his *The Art of Cross-Examination*, and the ferocious Judge John W. Goff. The stories conclude with performances of prosecutor William Travers Jerome, who had the reputation—I will let the reader decide whether it was entirely appropriate—as the "Reformer."

My research began some years ago as I was reviewing promising material for a seminar in legal history. One of my friends, a denizen of the local bar and a bibliophile, had given me a copy of Richard Rovere's *Howe & Hummel: Their True and Scandalous History* (1947).[12] Along with Arthur Train's fictional *Yankee Lawyer: The Autobiography of Ephraim Tutt* (1943), about an honest lawyer-hero, and his less well-known *The Confessions of Artemas Quibble* (1924), about a dishonest lawyer-villain, *Howe & Hummel* remains one of my favorites. Rovere's book, which was put together from his earlier articles in *The New Yorker*,[13] made quite a splash when it first appeared, and there was talk of theatrical productions and even a television show based on the exploits of Howe and Hummel.[14] The book is still popular, and it was reissued in 1985 with an introduction by Calvin Trillin and illustrations by Reginald Marsh.

Even today Howe and Hummel are remembered as oddly romantic characters.[15] William "Big Bill" Howe and Abe "Little Abe" Hummel were famously successful and notoriously unethical[16] lawyers who flourished in what Rovere called the "Second Golden Age of the New York Bar." Like many of today's high-profile criminal defense lawyers, they also represented many celebrities, especially those of the show biz set, including P. T. Barnum, Edwin Booth, John Barrymore, and Lillie Langtry. Mark Twain sought their services in a famous case brought by Edward House against Mark Twain to enjoin the theatrical production of *The Prince and the Pauper*. House claimed that Twain had given him the rights to dramatize the book.[17] As best I can tell, the firm actually represented Twain's co-defendant. In any event Twain lost. The evidence showed that House (formerly a friend of Twain) had a contract (a letter agreement) with Twain to write the script for the play and that Twain's repudiation of the contract deprived House of his right to produce and profit from the play. The show went on after a settlement was reached.[18]

Howe and Hummel, masters of self-promotion, were featured in the *National Police Gazette's* "Hall of Fame." According to Rovere, they had a number of newspaper correspondents on their payroll, certainly one or two at *The New York Herald*. Because of these investments, they were able to secure plentiful and favorable publicity. Allusions to Howe and Hummel, and their connection to the criminal underworld, particularly to the empire of the notorious fence and criminal organizer Mother "Marm" Mandelbaum,[19] can be found in such publications of note as Herbert Asbury's *The Gangs of New York* (1927, 1928); and their clients' professional *vitae* fill the pages of Inspector Thomas Byrnes's *Professional Criminals of America* (1886). Critics like Arthur Train believed that Howe and Hummel were actually the masterminds behind much of the crime in New York City. Howe and Hummel held court in colorful offices at ground level on Centre Street, and for a time they handled most of the lucrative criminal defense work in the city.

Howe was a trial lawyer known more for his powerful and emotional summations (he was known as "The Weeper") than for his technical skills, although one suspects that the sometimes faint praise given him by his opponents may have been sour grapes.[20] He was a pioneer of the insanity defense and had considerable medical expertise. Indeed, it was rumored that he may have practiced—or malpracticed— medicine in England prior to coming to the United States.[21] He certainly had a ghoulish side, which served him well in his spectacular murder cases. Big Bill Howe was a giant of a man, who used flamboyant dress as a part of his theatrical courtroom technique. Indeed, he usually appeared bejeweled, much to the delight of the common, and sometimes rustic, jurors.

Little Abe Hummel was the more complex of the two. He was quite cerebral, and he created most of what we would now call Theater Law and practiced it successfully; but he also had a dark side and, with the complicity of numerous young women in the arts, made a fortune setting up and shaking down suckers in blackmail breach-of-promise cases. A small and slight man, he dressed in black—simply but always neatly. It is thought that he was the model for Arthur Train's sinister Artemas Quibble.[22] It is an unfortunate fact of life, a sort of Gresham's law of lawyering, that unethical lawyers tend to drive out ethical lawyers, perhaps because clients favor victory over ethics. But nothing lasts. Big Bill Howe went into decline and died five years after the disastrous conclusion of the Nack-Thorn-Guldensuppe case in Long Island City in 1897. Not long afterward, much like his fictional counterpart Artemas Quibble, Little Abe Hummel was finally run to ground by a crusading prosecutor, William Travers Jerome, convicted of perjury, and disbarred.

Although I am a dedicated fan of Rovere's work, I have done considerable research on some of William Howe's cases,[23] and I have discovered a number of errors[24] in Rovere's history that I think are worth sharing with the reader. As we all know, much of what we think we know is wrong,[25] and much of what is known of William Howe's famous cases is false. Rovere's work is not sourced, and many of his accounts of Howe's cases are surprisingly off base.[26] Still, Rovere's accounts have been passed down uncritically. I write to correct the record, in part because some of Howe's clients were at least as interesting as the man himself.

My reconstruction of the cases discussed in this book are based on newspaper accounts and, in a few cases, on actual trial transcripts. Sadly, over past decades the powers that be in Gotham decided to economize by destroying a number of court records, including the Nack-Thorn-Guldensuppe[27] case. Fortunately the librarians at

John Jay[28] managed to preserve a bit of history, and my research includes transcripts (microfilm on interlibrary loan) of Ella Nelson's famous trial, the Frenchy trial, and a few others.

Included among my stories is the remarkable case of Maria Barbella (a.k.a. Barbieri, Barberi, or Barberri), the first woman sentenced to die in the electric chair at Sing Sing. I came upon the Maria Barbella case while I was researching Howe's last big case, the Nack-Thorn-Guldensuppe murder. During the trial, Nack's lawyer, Emanuel Friend, appeared among the spectators with his most celebrated former client, Maria Barbella, on his arm.[29] Her appearance at the trial apparently caused a stir. According to the press account in the illustrated *New York Herald*, Maria had been convicted of murdering one Domenico Cataldo, faced death in the electric chair, but got off scot-free after a second trial in which lawyer Emanuel Friend and his associates successfully presented a defense of "psychic epilepsy." I had to find out more about this bizarre defense and the lawyers who came up with it.

My search led me to Idanna Pucci's *The Trials of Maria Barbella* (1997). This is a lovely—if somewhat one-sided—account written by the great-granddaughter of Cora Slocomb, the American-born Italian aristocrat who became the Countess di Brazza. The countess came to the aid of the unfortunate Maria in her hour of need. In one sense this was a discouraging find, because I feared that I would be able to add little to Pucci's book-length story; but as it turned out, I did find some interesting new tidbits to share.

The Pucci book is unsourced, which is unfortunate. Reading it, one has the sense that the author had access to original materials—perhaps a transcript of the second trial. I have been unable to locate one, although I did discover a transcript of Maria's first trial, and I was able to locate and rely on a number of other sources.[30] Additionally, while researching the Frenchy case, I had already met Emanuel Friend, and—as previously mentioned—his soon-to-be-famous associate Levy,[31] and their senior partner and mentor House.

Because of my interest in scientific evidence and forensics, I also tried to find out as much as I could about one of the Barbella defense expert witnesses, Ales F. Hrdlicka, MD. Pucci's book has an epilogue which tells us what happened later in the lives of many of the characters associated with the case, but she includes no mention of the fate of Hrdlicka. By following the limited clues, I discovered, among other things, that this obscure young Czech immigrant, a cigar maker turned doctor, would later become the first curator of physical anthropology at the Smithsonian and the author of the theory that held that humans came to America over an Alaskan land bridge from Siberia. I also discovered some curious connections to other historical characters, among them the brilliant Russian polymath Boris Sidis, a protégé of William James and the father of William James Sidis, the unfortunate child prodigy that students encounter in torts class in law school.[32] Maria's second trial was covered by journalist Julian Hawthorne, the son of Nathaniel Hawthorne. One of the prosecution's expert witnesses was Allan McLane Hamilton, MD, LLD, FRS (Edin.), the grandson of founding father Alexander Hamilton.[33]

Maria's story inspired a play by Edoardo Pecoraro, titled *Maria Barberi*.[34] Pucci reports that another play about the case, *Maria Barberi: A Soul on Fire*, a Yiddish language production by Moishe Hurwitz, was successful and was attended by large numbers of Italians "who did not understand a word."[35] A theater placard[36] in the Yiddish theater collection of the Dorot Jewish Division of the New York Public Library, references in German text *Mari Barberi, oder, Dos leben der neshome in holem*. Detail for this item provides the English alternate title, *Mary Barbery, or The life of the soul in a dream*, with a created date of December 18–19, 1896.

I find each of the cases discussed in this book fascinating and entertaining. For more than half of my life I have been a law professor. I am a technician, teaching the fundamentals of trial advocacy, the law of evidence, as well as legal ethics, which many persons in the community must assume is a very short course. I am not a criminal defense trial lawyer. I am also not a credentialed historian. I admit my limitations. I do love stories about lawyers, and I enjoy researching true crime. This is not a work of fiction. I am not making anything up. I have tried to document every point with appropriate citations, along with additional interesting tidbits from time to time, which I have packed into endnotes. I am also looking at the characters who people this book, and their conduct, through an old lawyer's trifocals. I can't help talking about the law and legal tactics and, for that matter, legal ethics. I also hope that the reader will suffer my many digressions. It is hard to pass up any interesting case or character that surfaces along the way. I have tried to keep my discussions linked to one or more of the four lawyers—Howe, Friend, Levy, or Jerome— but sometimes I run off the road a bit. I also try to capture as much as I can about the times—a period of American history about which most Americans know little.

I should also note that some of the material in this book has been on the shelf for a while. This has been a long-term project. Some material, like my account of the Nack-Thorn-Guldensuppe case, was published in law journal format as early as 2007. Such things, and all debts owed to others, are carefully reflected in the endnotes.

GASLIGHT LAWYERS

Chapter One

The Search for William F. Howe: Tall Tales Retold

The solemn silence which had been brooding for fully half an hour over the motley crowd in the Harlem Police Court was suddenly dissipated at 3 o'clock yesterday afternoon. All the figurants in the Mandelbaum[37] case were in their accustomed places, and had ceased to attract more than casual attention, when Mr. Howe made his appearance on the scene. Then it was that a titter was heard at the back of the courtroom, which was gradually extended until it reached the judicial bench, where it could go no further. The cause of this slight ripple of mirth was Mr. Howe's personal appearance, or, in other words, his "get up." The gentleman's suit was of the brightest bottle green slashed with indigo blue, the same combination of color which caused the French dressmaker to exclaim in horror, "Quelle immortalité!" His shirt was of a pink and green draught-board pattern, though this was nearly hidden by diamonds of all sizes. Mr. Howe looked like a Maypole of more than ordinary circumference. He was unconscious of the amusement his appearance caused, or, if he did notice any demonstration, he doubtless attributed it to his excessive popularity. The young girls at the back of the room appeared to consider the lawyer's gorgeous attire immense, if their smiling countenances were a criterion.[38]

William "Big Bill" Howe was a giant of a man, who used flamboyant dress as part of his courtroom theater, much to the delight of the common and sometimes rustic jurors. He was a master

1

of self-promotion, co-authoring with his partner Abe "Little Abe" Hummel a curious tome, styled *In Danger; Or Life in New York. A True History of a Great City's Wiles and Temptations. True Facts and Disclosures*,[39] which was something akin to a guidebook for those seeking sex (and other sins) in the city. The firm of Howe & Hummel also had a number of newspaper reporters on the payroll, which insured that Howe's victories would receive plentiful and favorable publicity.[40] Richard Rovere[41] recounts many of these victories, but in many instances provides little in the way of detail. Some cases were not quite so spectacular after all and have been embellished in the retelling.[42] Sometimes Rovere reports stunning victories that were not victories at all.

Perhaps the most well-known and celebrated of Howe's cases was the murder trial of Ella Nelson. Ella, a widow, was charged with shooting to death her married lover Samuel Post in 1891. Rovere and others have painted it as a case in which overwhelming evidence favored the prosecution. Nevertheless Howe was credited with winning it with a spectacular bit of courtroom theatrics.[43] The loser, Assistant District Attorney Francis Wellman, was bitterly disappointed and was also castigated in the press. After noting that the defense had offered to plead guilty to manslaughter before the trial, *The New York Times* opined, "It is possible that the case may prove of some value in teaching the District Attorney's assistants a little more care in the selection of juries, and not to rely entirely on the fact of having what they deem sufficient evidence."[44]

Here is my summary of the case, pretty much witness by witness.[45]

The prosecution's case rested in large part on the testimony of a young traveling salesman by the name of Nathan Michaels. He was a friend of the victim, Samuel Post. Michaels often visited Ella's flat, with and without Post. Ella took in boarders. On the day of the shooting, Michaels had gone to the flat with Post. The married Post had abandoned his family sometime in the past and had been living with Ella. However, by the time of the shooting, he had moved out. Ella suspected that he was seeing another woman at his new digs, and the evidence showed that she had gone there on at least one occasion to check out his arrangements.

The prosecution's theory of the case was that, on the day of the shooting, Post was leaving Ella to go back to his wife and that Ella shot him in a jealous rage. Michaels provided testimony that he had seen Ella in possession of a gun before and that Ella had said on several occasions in Michaels's presence, and in the presence of her friend Bella Gates, that she would blow Post's head off if she caught him seeing another woman or attempting to leave her for another woman. Regarding the shooting, Michaels claimed that he was in the parlor of the flat, sitting on a piano stool, when Ella confronted Post about her visit to his new address and her suspicion that persons at that location had lied to her about Post's living arrangements. At some point Ella went back to a hall bedroom, whereupon Post announced that he was leaving and went into the vestibule. Ella came out of the bedroom and met Post in the vestibule, where the two talked in an "excited way." Then he saw Post and Ella go into the bedroom. Michaels heard a shot inside of a minute. Post came running out of the bedroom crying out, "Oh my God, I am shot!" as he ran into another bedroom.

Michaels further testified, "Ella came running after him, and the moment she got into the parlor, fired three shots in rapid succession after Sam [Post]. ...After she fired the third shot, she said, 'Now, damn you, I have got you now.'"

When he finished providing this glittering array of incriminating facts, Michaels said he remained sitting on the piano stool for a few minutes and then went downstairs and came back up again. Howe interrupted at this point to comment on the fact that Michaels claimed to have remained sitting on the stool for a few minutes—an odd reaction to say the least.

Following Howe's interruption, Wellman continued his examination at the point Michaels returned to the flat. Michaels said he saw Ella standing over Post with a pistol in her hand. He said he asked her for the pistol, and she said "Let go, Nathan, or I will shoot you, too." Later Michaels volunteered that when he returned to the flat he met Ella at the top of the stairs and she said, "Oh my God, Nathan, I have shot my darling boy." Michaels testified that he then went to find a policeman and a doctor. He found a policeman and reported the shooting—and then he went straight home!

On cross-examination Howe would make much of Michaels's testimony of his own reactions. After seeing his friend shot, Michaels did not go to him but remained sitting on the piano stool for at least a minute, went downstairs for four or five minutes, and then returned. Although his friend had just been shot in the abdomen, Michaels went straight home without making further inquiry as to his friend's condition until the next morning. Howe also got Michaels to say that when he returned to the flat and followed Ella into the room he heard no remarks made by either Ella or Sam Post. Howe's cross-examination also brought out that Michaels had borrowed money from Ella in the past and may still have owed her a small amount. It seemed a minor point.

The next witness was Officer John Thompson, the policeman hailed by Michaels. Officer Thompson testified that he went to the flat where he saw "...a man in a kneeling position, and a lady over him, like hugging him...and in his hand was a revolver." Thompson testified that when asked his name, Post falsely replied that his name was Smith. The officer took the pistol from Post's hand.

By now two other officers arrived, and Officer Thompson went for an ambulance. Officer Thompson on direct examination said that neither Ella nor Sam Post had said anything to him, but on cross Howe got him to say that Ella said, while bending over him, "Sam, my boy, you are not going to die and leave me." Officer Thompson was sure that the gun was in Sam's right hand, and his left was across his abdomen. He saw another officer (also named Thompson) arrest Ella. She was sobbing very loudly. Howe also got Officer Thompson to say that, when Michaels hailed him, Michaels said that "[a] girl was shot by a feller," and he pointed to the flat. The point may have been that, closer to the time of the shooting, Michaels had not really been sure who had done what to whom.

An Officer McDonald testified as to his participation. He too saw Ella kneeling by the body and rubbing his forehead, saying, "Sam, you are not going to die, you are not going to die are you?" Post eventually replied, "Well, I guess I am, a man with a bullet in the center of his stomach don't very often live." Post continued to refuse to give his true name. Officer McDonald asked Ella who shot Post. She did not at first answer but finally said, "I did not do it." With continuing questioning by Wellman, Officer McDonald also testified that Post looked at Ella and said, "You are satisfied now, aren't you?" He also said, "You made a bull's eye." When Ella left the room, Post supposedly said, "Keep an eye on that woman."

Wellman called a police captain who testified that Ella made no answer to questions as to the cause of the shooting or as to who did it. The forensic evidence, such as it was, showed that there was only one wound, to the abdomen, and only one bullet taken from the body. The revolver contained four empty cartridge cases, but Howe properly objected when Wellman tried to get a police witness to testify that the empties appeared to have been recently fired. The testimony was excluded.

Much of the coroner's testimony related to an antemortem statement taken from Post. Oddly enough, two newspaper reporters were present when the statement was taken, and they testified as to what they wrote down. Much of the transcript deals with Howe's efforts to challenge the admissibility of this statement as a dying declaration. Howe would make much of it in his cross-examination. Howe argued that it was not clear from Post's responses to the coroner's questions that Post knew that his death was imminent—that all hope was lost. The judge heard Howe out but ruled that the statement qualified as a dying declaration. The matter was argued in the presence of the jury with the judge telling the jurors to disregard what they were hearing (nowadays we would argue the matter outside the presence of the jury). The statement was admitted. Still, Howe was free to argue that it was not free of ambiguity, that Post may not have been thinking clearly, and that the statement was coached. In any event, the statement was read to the jury.

> I have not been living with my wife for some time and I met this woman, Ella Nelson, and I went to live with her, but as I have a wife and family I made up my mind to lead a decent life, as I held a position of trust, down town. I took a room on 24th Street. I wanted to get some clothes there, of no intrinsic value last night and then told her "I cannot live here." She said: "You can take a room and board here as well as anywhere else." She then said to me "You are not going out" I said "Yes." Then there was a bank [sic] bang and the first shot hit me in the abdomen and I ran behind the door. She said "...you, you are not going away." I then took the pistol from her. Nathan Michaels, a traveling salesman from the Commonwealth Rubber Company was present. She had frequently threatened me before and once fired at me.

Howe called only one witness, Ella Nelson herself. She testified that for a long time she believed Post was a single man and only learned of his family late in the relationship. She testified that she never owned a pistol, although Sam Post had one. She denied threatening him with a pistol. Indeed, she testified that he had threatened her with a pistol before. As regards the shooting, she admitted that they had had words over her visit to his new lodgings, her belief that he was seeing another woman, and his statement that he was going out without her. He had the pistol, not her. They had a scuffle over the pistol and it went off. She denied the truth of Michaels's version and of ever threatening to shoot Post. She said she did not know how the pistol went off, but she heard two shots.

Wellman cross-examined Ella aggressively, but she held up pretty well. She did not know what happened and could not remember anything like four shots. Wellman spent some time attacking her character in suggestive ways. From the questions, it seems that he was insinuating Ella was allowing other women boarders to use the premises for prostitution. He inquired as to her sexual experience with the married Post. Wellman confronted Ella with the suggestion that she had made incriminating statements to her friend Bella Gates when Bella visited her in the Tombs:

> Q. "Don't you remember that the day you were...after you were arrested Bella Gates came to see you at the Tombs didn't she?"
>
> A. "Yes."
>
> Q. "Don't you remember you said to her 'Michaels is the only man who can convict me. Get him out of town.'?"
>
> A. "No sir."
>
> Q. "You said to her, 'Michaels is the only man that can convict me?'"
>
> A. "No sir."
>
> Q. "What?"
>
> A. "No sir."
>
> Q. "Bella Gates, will you stand up, please? Do you deny that you said to her 'Michaels is the only man that can convict me?'"
>
> A. "Yes, I do;...if I said..."
>
> Q. "And don't you know that she then went to Michaels to see if he would leave town?"
>
> A. "No sir."
>
> Q. "Do you deny that absolutely?"
>
> A. "Yes; I don't know it."

Wellman was laying the foundation for calling Bella Gates as a rebuttal witness. The cross-examination continued.

Wellman got Ella to admit that she had once gone to Boston, suggesting that it was to check up on Post's relationship with another woman. Ella countered with an explanation that she was checking up to see what Post might have done with money she had given him to pay off some kind of debt he owed a prior employer. Her story was not altogether convincing. She finally admitted that she was concerned that he was spending money on another woman. She finally gave the name of the woman—V. G. (Grace) Osborne. Wellman then got Ella to admit that she had found a note from Osborne (signed "yours only, Grace") to Post in Post's pocket a month before the shooting. Wellman retrieved the note from Howe's custody, read only the salutation "My darling love," and did not offer it into evidence. This note had apparently been part of the cause for the argument that preceded the shooting. Finally, Wellman made much of the fact that she remained silent under police questioning when she could have explained the shooting as an accident.

Howe did not object to Wellman's allusion to the letter. Indeed, Howe welcomed it, proceeded to introduce the entire, very lengthy, letter into evidence (the reading of it took up nine pages of the transcript), and turned it to Ella's advantage. The letter described in great detail the Osborne-Post affair and her hopes that he would soon get a divorce and that Ella and Post would carry out their plan to go out West together. *The New York Times* would later report that "[i]n describing the scene afterward" Howe said that he related to the jury:

> You must have observed the strength of my position when I tell you that the district attorney had prepared the jury to believe that the man whom Ella Nelson had shot had been weaned from his wife by the murderess on trial, and that by her machinations and threats he had been prevented from returning to the bosom of his family on the very night the shooting occurred. Well do I remember in rounding to the full meaning a sentence to the jury "This man dies with a willful lie in his mouth [in his

antemortem statement] and a written lie in his pocket [that he was returning to a decent life with his family]."[46]

After Howe rested for the defense, Wellman called Bella Gates. She was not entirely cooperative. She admitted that she had visited Ella in the Tombs, but Howe did not let Wellman put words in her mouth. (Wellman had a tendency to lead his witnesses to secure important testimony.) At first Bella said only that "[Ella] spoke of Mr. Michaels as being the only person that was present there." However, she eventually came around to saying that Ella said, "He would be the only one who could convict her or do anything against her." On cross-examination Bella told Howe that Michaels testified falsely when he said that she told him that she had heard Ella threaten the deceased. Wellman then called Robert Gordon, a former partner of Post in the insurance business, to testify that Post owed him nothing. This was apparently intended to counter Ella's tale that she had provided money to Post to help bail him out of an unfortunate situation with a former employer. It is hard to say what effect the rebuttal would have had on the jury.

It is Wellman's version of the case that has survived until now, and this is what he had to say for himself in his memoirs.

> Throughout Howe's final appeal to the jury the prisoner sat with bowed head, covering her face with both hands and sobbing audibly. Just at the close of his speech Howe went behind her chair, and taking her by her wrists forced her hands from her face, at the same time challenging the jurors to gaze into her heartbroken countenance and see if they could possibly find in it anything that would brand her a murderess. Now Howe usually wore very long, sharply pointed finger nails, and as he snatched the woman's wrists he dug his nails deeply into her flesh...[which] caused the woman to utter a piercing scream that could be heard throughout the court house. ... *I was sitting with my back to the prisoner at the moment, and did not realize the trick Howe was perpetrating* [emphasis added]. It would be impossible

to describe the effect this unearthly screech had upon me,
steeled as I was to the manufactured defence that Howe was
attempting to foist upon the jury. It was as if someone had
suddenly put a lump of ice down my back. The jury seemed
completely petrified by it, and I saw the case was over from
that moment.[47]

It is a curious fact that the coverage of this short trial in
The New York Herald made no mention of anything quite so
spectacular.

> Then Mr. Howe began the summing up for the defence.
> His chief effort was to break the testimony of Michaels,
> and upon the contradictions of his evidence with the
> ante mortem statement of Post he dealt with great strength.
> He appealed strongly to the sentiments of the jury and when
> the prisoner repeatedly bowed her head upon her arms and
> shook and shook with emotion the jurymen were evidently
> moved. He asked for a complete acquittal, as the shooting
> was entirely accidental.[48]

The paper did note that Ella "swooned" when she heard the not
guilty verdict. She and Howe were reportedly hoping for a verdict
of manslaughter at best. For its part, *The New York Times* noted,
presumably sarcastically, that "[t]he jury was an average one as to
intelligence."[49]

To find out what really happened, I consulted the trial transcript,
which narrowly survived a housecleaning of New York court
records in the later 1970s.[50] Unfortunately the trial transcript is not
complete. There are no opening statements or closing arguments.
The transcripts end with the trial judge directing "Now, Mr. Howe,
go to the jury." At that time the defense summation preceded that of
the prosecution, and it may have been that the arguments of counsel
were not always transcribed. On the other hand, it is possible that the
closing arguments were lost somewhere along the line. In any event,
when Howe died in 1902, he was praised for his advocacy in several

news articles which mentioned his closing, reporting that he stood behind Ella and pulled her arms apart so that the jury could look upon her, at which point her face was "deluged with tears,"[51] with no mention of a scream. Was this a reporter's accurate memory or just another bit of folklore?

We are fortunate to have one admittedly second- or third-hand report of the jurors' reaction to the evidence:

> A friend of one of the jurors said that he had been told the exact situation of affairs in the jury room. When they retired, an informal discussion showed that seven were in favor of a verdict of acquittal and five one of conviction. Then they sent to the court for the ante-mortem statement of Post and discussed that. Those in favor of acquittal said that it was so indefinite when describing the shooting that it substantially corroborated the statement of Mrs. Nelson that she at no time had possession of the pistol. The testimony of Michaels, who was in the flat at the time of the shooting, was totally disregarded. After returning from supper, the five who had held out for conviction agreed to the acquittal.[52]

Again, Wellman had the last word in one of his memoirs. It all seems a bit too self-serving:

> About midnight, after the jury had rendered their verdict of "not guilty," and were leaving the court house by the main stairway, I followed them and inquired upon what possible theory they had freed the prisoner. One of them answered, "Why bother about it now, isn't it all over?" I replied that I was in a sense acting for them as District Attorney in my attempt to suppress crime and wanted to learn how our juries looked at such cases, in order that I might do better next time. One of the jurors, who had nearly reached the bottom step, looked around and half shouted back at me, "What to hell difference does it make to you?" "Stop where you are, gentlemen, please," I said, Just for one moment until I answer the question. It makes just this difference to me.

I am trying to figure out how it was you convinced yourself
that this woman was not guilty, when just before the trial
began, she had offered to plead guilty if I would guarantee
her a sentence not to exceed twenty years in State's Prison."
This little speech of mine proved a pretty close second to
the lady's scream in its effect on those twelve sheepish
looking men.[53]

Two other trials are frequently cited as evidence of Howe's
cunning and powers of oratory. I was able to locate newspaper
accounts of one and a complete transcript of the other.

The Unger case of 1887 involved a grisly crime. A young Prussian
immigrant named Bohle was rooming with a "sea captain" by the
name of Edward Unger. Bohle had some money, and the evidence
showed that Unger tried to get him to loan it out so that Unger could
start a "butcher's business." A quarrel between the two ended with
Bohle dead and butchered. Unger killed him, perhaps as he slept
on a sofa, by caving in his head with a slung shot or a hammer. He
dismembered the body, put it in a trunk, and had the trunk shipped
to Baltimore. However, the clues were easily followed, and the case
of the body in the trunk was soon solved. "Captain" Edward Unger
was arrested.[54]

The condition of the body when it was examined at the morgue
by Coroner Levy and a Dr. Jenkins was described in ghoulish detail
in *The New York Times*:

[T]he little finger of the right hand was deformed, or at
some time had received an injury, as it was bent and stiff, as
if the tendon had been injured. There appeared to be a scar
on the finger. [These facts tended to identify the body as
that of Bohle.][55] The head had been broken from the trunk
so that three cervical vertebrae were visible. The legs had
been amputated close to the base of the spine, and the feet
were broken off at the ankles. The left arm was severed in
two places at the shoulder and the bone had been broken
by wrenching.[56]

Inspector Thomas Byrnes (more on him later) was very confident: "Although we have not got the head we will prove that Unger killed Bohle...and that the body sent from Baltimore is Bohle's."[57] Howe suggested early on that he would challenge the identification of remains as those of Bohle and threatened to bring one of the severed parts into court, if necessary.[58] Howe's attempts to challenge the identification at the coroner's inquest failed; indeed, his arguments were criticized in the press and were said to have ended in a "childishly unsatisfactory manner." The lawyers and the coroner too were faulted for arguments which "bristled with uncomplimentary personal allusions."[59]

When jury selection began on February 11, 1887, Unger was joined in court by his two daughters (neither of whom lived with him): Annie, who was eighteen years old, and Emily, who was variously described as seven or eight. Both were neatly dressed and attractive. "The little one nestled close to the prisoner as he took his chair, pressing her face against his. When she stepped away from him she was crying. Unger's eyes had also filled."[60] Jury selection was completed by February 14.

> The prisoner was joined by his young daughters on reaching the court room. They exchanged greetings, and the eyes of the women in court, of whom there was a good number, filled sympathetically at the sight of the children's grief. The little one clung to her father when the older had again gained her composure, and during the morning session she leaned against his breast, with his arm around her. Unger had been spruced up over Sunday, and looked much better than when he appeared in court Friday.[61]

This was vintage Howe.

Unger's defense would be that he killed Bohle in self-defense when Bohle assaulted him with a knife and that he dismembered the body in an effort to save his family from disgrace.

This would be a hard sell, given the blood spattered crime scene, and the fact that the victim was much smaller than the defendant.

There was also the problem of his detailed confession,[62] which had been secured by the famous Inspector Thomas Byrnes, who is credited with inventing the "third degree." The prisoner had resisted interrogation, so sure was he that the absence of the victim's head would defeat attempts at identification. But Byrnes wore him down by systematically confronting Unger with the telltale physical evidence—the trunk, and then articles of clothing, and finally seating him on the bloody sofa on which Bohle had died.[63]

Unger took the stand in his own defense, spending a great deal of time reciting his record as a ship's mate and later a captain, along with his exploits during the Civil War.[64] The judge finally had to cut him short and get to the facts of the case being tried. The most interesting part of Unger's testimony had to do with his immediate reaction after the killing, how he hid the body behind the sofa and then tried to sleep with the consequences of his acts weighing on his mind.

> His body was slipping off the sofa and I raised it to the corner of the settee. What had I done? I didn't know. I thought I'd take my own life. I got a razor from the cupboard and was going to cut my throat when I remembered my children. What could I do? Then I thought that if I gave myself up I should be put in prison and there would be no one to keep my children. I looked at the clock. It was 10 o'clock. My boy might come home at any moment.[65] I must hide the body. So I put it behind the sofa.
>
> That night when I went to bed I imagined I still saw Bohle. I jumped up and ran to the room where the body was. It was there. I went out and drank several glasses of whisky. Then I came back. The body was still there. I went to bed again. I tried to think of what to do, but I couldn't. I saw Bohle standing beside me. Again I jumped up, and went to see the body. I can't describe the night I passed. If there's a hell I was there that night. In the morning I was stifling and choking. I went to the Grand-Street Ferry and took the boat to Brooklyn, drinking several times. Then the idea of putting the body in the trunk

occurred to me. I can't realize that I did it. It didn't seem to me that I actually cut the body up. I was stupefied. I know that if I hadn't done it he would have driven the knife into me. I certainly did it. I am a miserable man.[66]

A reporter from *The New York Times* described Howe's summation to the jury in the following manner:

Mr. Howe, in summing up, alluded to the defendant's children, and reminded the jury that they had children of their own in case they had forgotten that fact, and spoke of true love, the truth of affection, and other abstract qualities. He said that Unger could not be found guilty of murder in the first degree because there was no evidence of deliberation and premeditation. He could not be convicted of murder in the second degree because there was no intent to kill.[67]

Other accounts report the following detail:

"Gentlemen, Edward Unger did not cut the dead man's head off. He did not mutilate the body. He did not throw the head from the ferryboat under the paddle wheels. He did not put the dilapidated trunk in a box and send it to Baltimore." Then the lawyer paused. The Court was astonished, for Unger had acknowledged doing each of these things.

It so happened that on Unger's knee there was at that moment sitting his little seven-year-old child, ignorant of her father's peril, running her hand through his grey hair. After his pause Mr. Howe pointed suddenly at the child and exclaimed dramatically:

"Look at that little girl. It was she who cut off that head; she who mutilated that body. It was not Unger. Yes 'twas she, 'twas she; for Unger could not bear the thought of having it said that he, her father, had committed so horrible a deed, and therefore in a moment it occurred to him that he could hide the deed which had been perpetrated, he mutilated the

body. It was the thought of that little girl which caused him
to do it, and therefore I say it was she that did it."

The effect was remarkable.[68]

The jury returned a verdict of manslaughter. Judge Barnett
was incredulous. In sentencing the prisoner to the maximum that
he could for manslaughter—twenty years—he commented on the
"absolute falsity" of the self-defense claim and described the jury's
verdict as "exceedingly merciful."[69] Howe had asked for no delay in
the sentencing, making the observation that the jury were entirely
justified in arriving at the verdict.[70]

Another of Howe's interesting cases was that of Michael
Considine who was tried in 1896 for the murder of John Malone.[71]
The prosecution offered evidence that on the night of the murder it
was snowing heavily, and Malone was walking in a leisurely manner
in front of the St. James Hotel, corner of Twenty-sixth Street and
Broadway, when Considine approached him, asked him for money,
and shot him in the stomach. According to Francis Wellman's telling
of the tale[72] [Wellman was not the prosecutor and was writing years
after the fact], the defense was to be that Considine fired in self-
defense as Malone raised a heavy walking stick to strike Considine.
On the other hand, according to Wellman, Howe supposedly offered
a plea of guilty to second degree murder, believing that the jury
would not accept that Malone would be carrying a cane in a raging
snowstorm, but the offer was rejected. As Wellman's story continues,
at the trial Howe demanded that the district attorney produce the
cane or provide some excuse for not producing it.[73] To his surprise
the prosecutor produced a heavy cane, which was obviously loaded
with lead. The quick-thinking Howe raised the cane high and
brought it crashing down on the counsel table, with considerable
effect on the jury, as well as on the district attorney.[74] Considine was
promptly acquitted.[75]

Lawyer Theron G. Strong recounted a similar story in his
book, *Landmarks of a Lawyer's Lifetime*, which was published in

1914—ten years before Wellman's account. Perhaps Strong was Wellman's source. If Howe actually acted this out, it is possible that he did so in his closing argument, which is not available. The trial record does not include the summations of counsel, which is not uncommon. Nothing else in the transcript obtained from the Lloyd Sealy Library includes the incident reported by Strong and Wellman. However, it does reveal Howe's prowess in both direct and cross-examination.

Howe put his client on the stand. With the aid of some rather audacious—and amusing—leading by Howe, Considine told his tale of self-defense. He had had numerous business dealings with Malone who, if Considine is to be believed, was not an altogether admirable character. As absurd as it sounds, Considine had been induced to invest in a patent that Malone claimed to own—a patent for a "nailless horseshoe."[76] Considine asked for his money back after Malone reportedly sold or mortgaged the patent. When he met Malone, he had expected some accommodation. He reminded Malone of how he, Considine, had given him financial assistance in London. He explained that he, Considine, was now suffering unfortunate conditions. Malone became enraged and responded, "What the hell do I care about your conditions?" And, "You lie, you son of a bitch, I was never penniless in England." And, "Don't say that again, you son of a bitch, or I'll knock your goddamned head off." Malone again threatened to "knock [his] goddamned brains out" as he raised the stick. Considine had a pistol in his pocket and shot Malone in self-defense. The stick was produced in court, and the witness demonstrated how Malone had wielded it. The prosecutor foolishly allowed the witness to repeat all the details during his cross-examination. The heavy cane was introduced into evidence, and the jurors were able to feel its heft.

Howe was a master of sarcastic repartee; one assumes that this was much to the edification and delight of the jurors. Here are some examples:

> Mr. Lewis: "Now, May I ask, Mr. Howe, not to lead him about this as you have been doing now."

Mr. Howe: "Well, if you have any objection to my questions, Mr. Lewis, there is the Court."

…

Mr. Lewis: "There is the cane, Mr. Howe. Do you wish to make any use of it?"

Mr. Howe: "No. Your client wanted to use it. We don't."

Mr. Lewis: "My client?"

Mr. Howe: "Yes."

Mr. Lewis: "No my client is the People."

…

Mr. Howe [to the victim's sister]: "You got this cane from the New York Hospital; didn't you?"

The Witness: "Yes Sir."

Mr. Howe: "At the time your brother was lying there?"

The Witness: "Yes Sir."

Mr. Howe: "The cane that your brother had taken to the hospital, as the last witness described?"

The Witness: "I believe so."

Mr. Howe: "Thank you."

Mr. Lewis: "I wish I had your grace of manner, Mr. Howe."

Mr. Howe: "You will never attain it."

Mr. Lewis: "I am afraid not. I will offer this cane in evidence." [Needless to say, Howe was happy to have it admitted in evidence.]

Howe produced a number of character witnesses to testify as to Considine's nonviolent character, as well as several witnesses to corroborate the defendant's testimony on several points, including the fact that Considine had pawned his watch at Malone's request, as he, Malone, was short on cash to buy passage to London. A man named Jesse Roach testified that he saw the incident: "I saw a man standing up over another man, with a stick in his hand, and he had him by the throat."

A police officer was recalled by the prosecution to testify that when he arrived (across the street) he could not hear what they were saying but that the defendant and victim were ten feet apart, and the victim was backing away when he [the officer] heard the shots fired. He never saw such a stick. The officer was severely and successfully cross-examined by Howe. His testimony could have been given little credit since an orderly at the infirmary where Malone was taken had testified that when Malone was admitted he was still clutching the stick across his chest. Even better, the victim's sister testified that she was given the stick at the infirmary. It should also be noted that Howe had aroused the curiosity of the jurors to the extent that they asked their own questions about Malone's size. The point is that Howe did not win merely because of a lucky break and a stunt.

Chapter Two

The Search for William F. Howe Continues: Stunning Victories That Were Not

Rovere mentions several of Howe's celebrated cases by names that must have been invented by the press—for example, the case of Jacob Rosenzweig, the "Hackensack Mad Monster," and the case of Annie Walden, the "Man-Killing Race-Track Girl." These days, to be a mad monster, one must kill in large numbers and dine on the remains. Along the same lines, "Man-Killing Race-Track Girl" suggests a serial killer who lures her victims to a quiet corner of a racing venue where she castrates and eviscerates them, not necessarily in that order. Neither of Howe's cases was anywhere near as sensational, but numerous writers have picked up Rovere's references to these cases without providing any more details.[77]

"Dr." Jacob Rosenzweig was an abortionist who sometimes practiced under the name of Dr. Ascher. He immigrated in 1865 from Russian-ruled Poland.[78] There is no evidence that he had any real medical training. At the time all manner of quacks plied their trade by paying a tax and advertising their services.[79] The infamous Madame Restell advertised openly and was said to be worth millions in today's dollars at the time of her death.[80]

The hapless Rosenzweig was not a serial killer and apparently was not a particularly skilled abortionist. Miss Alice Augusta Bowlsby, of Patterson, New Jersey, had the bad luck of employing him. He botched the job, and Alice bled to death. Before rigor mortis set in, Rosenzweig forced her five-foot-two-inch body into a trunk to ship it out of town. Authorities speculated that she may have been alive when she was crammed into her container. The trunk got no further than the Hudson River train depot before a baggage agent noticed the tell-tale odor. The authorities soon located the truckman who had taken the trunk from Rosenzweig's office, and Rosenzweig was arrested.[81]

After the body was identified, Alice's seducer, one Walter Conklin, also of Patterson, added to the tragedy by shooting himself in the head.[82] Howe made his appearance in the case on September 8, 1891, requesting bail, which was denied.[83]

When the trial started on October 26, 1891, Howe was sick and Hummel had to take over when Howe's application for a postponement was denied. The prisoner seemed shocked by this development. When Howe appeared on the second day, the prisoner calmed down. In District Attorney Samuel B. Garvin's opening statement, he lamented that the only charge that could be brought under the governing law—a charge for a type of manslaughter— provided a penalty of not more than seven years. The case for the People proceeded briskly—it was an open-and-shut case.[84] Howe's theory was that the body was not that of Miss Bowlsby and that, if it were, her death had been procured by Conklin.[85]

Rosenzweig took the stand and denied participating in an abortion, but his testimony was "incoherent." During the cross-examination Rosenzweig claimed that he was not Dr. Ascher but that he had only taken over that man's office. Then he was forced to admit that he had advertised under the name Dr. Ascher. He denied that he ever performed an abortion and that he had ever performed an abortion on a person named Nellie Willis. The prosecutor completed his impeachment of Rosenzweig by producing William Woodward, a non-practicing physician, who testified that he had been introduced to Rosenzweig as Dr. Ascher. Also, Nellie Willis, witness for the prosecution, was produced to testify that Rosenzweig had performed an abortion on her but that she had had to go to the hospital because his "instrument" caused her to bleed. Howe attacked Nellie's character, but he could not shake her

testimony.[86] Rosenzweig was convicted and given the maximum
seven-year sentence.[87] In their book, Howe and Hummel discuss
the case but make no mention of their participation at the trial level;
indeed, they generally blacken the character of Rosenzweig, their
client. But they do recount a surprising turn of events and Howe's
later victory for Rosenzweig on a point of law.[88]

Although the accounts are confusing, some time after
Rosenzweig's manslaughter conviction, the legislature passed a new
statute making the penalty for crimes such as Rosenzweig's up to
twenty years at hard labor. It seems as though the new statute also
had the effect of repealing the statute under which Rosenzweig was
convicted. Meanwhile, Howe had somehow gotten a ruling that his
client should have a new trial. Howe then argued that Rosenzweig
could not be tried under the new law and, as the old law had been
repealed, "[N]o law existed under which the prisoner could be tried
and convicted."[89] A lawyer named Ira Schafer (his association with
Howe is unclear) argued for Rosenzweig's discharge, and Judge Josiah
Sutherland granted the motion. "[T]he murderer of Miss Augusta
Bowlsby triumphantly left the courtroom a free man."[90]

Another case Rovere makes much of is that of Harry Carlton,
a.k.a. "Handsome Harry." Rovere claims that, in the case, Howe
"very nearly forced the courts to declare an open season for murder."
Ex-convict Carlton had been convicted of murdering a policeman.[91]
Howe argued at sentencing that Carlton could not be sentenced to
hang because, in June 1888, the legislature had passed legislation
that did away with hanging and substituted death by electrocution.
However, the language of the statute also stated that death by electrocution would not become legal until January 1, 1889, and then only
for crimes committed after the date that the legislation was passed.
His point was that there was now no penalty for Carlton's crime.
Rovere writes:

> [T]he startled judge agreed that...he had no power to
> sentence Carlton or any other first-degree murderer...
> and the effect on the community was comparable to that

of Orson Welles' terror fifty years later. ... If Howe was upheld...the courts might be forced to dismiss all first-degree indictments for murders committed in the state between June 4 and December 31, 1888. Indeed, by extension, anyone who killed with intent in the remaining few weeks of the year could kill with impunity.[92]

Was Judge Randolph B. Martine indeed startled? The newspaper reads that he overruled Howe's motion and told Howe to take his argument to the appellate courts.[93] Carlton was sentenced to be hanged February 13, 1889. His case ultimately reached the court of appeals, which ruled against him on October 9, 1889.[94] He was resentenced on October 17, 1889, and was hanged on December 5, 1889.[95]

A choice Rovere mistake is his account of the acquittal of Annie Walden, the "Man-Killing Race-Track Girl." Rovere describes her as having "embroidered a gentleman's midriff with the contents of a six-shooter." He then quotes a partial account of her trial, which he attributes to *The New York Herald*:

> [W]hile Miss Walden, gently encouraged by her attorney, was telling her story in an almost inaudible voice, the third juror cried softly, the sobs of juror nine could have been heard in the corridors, and there was moisture in the eyes of all but one or two of the other jurors. The prisoner's many devoted friends held handkerchiefs to their eyes, and when Lawyer Howe spoke, his voice was full of tears.

Rovere then states that "Miss Walden, too, was acquitted."[96] Unfortunately, the facts are that she was convicted and sentenced to life imprisonment.

The 1891 killing, tried in 1892, was not so simple as Rovere suggested. Annie Walden was the daughter of Rev. Phillip Graham of Almedia, Pennsylvania. The proverbial preacher's daughter gone wild, she struck out at an early age for Philadelphia but then, finding the "Quaker City" too dull, moved on to New York City, where she lived first with a bookmaker and then took up with and married James Walden, a young "sporting man" who spent a good deal of his time at the track. They lived unhappily,[97] and neither appears to have been on good behavior. Annie made claims of being beaten by her husband, "frequently into insensibility," and complained that he was seeing another woman.[98]

The fighting ended in a confrontation in front of the Metropolitan Opera House. Annie shot her husband James twice—the second time in the neck.[99] At the trial she cut an attractive figure, and she was dressed out in mourning clothes. During Howe's address to the jury (apparently his opening statement) she lay in the arms of her aunt and presented a pitiful figure. However, she gathered herself together to tell the story and submit to cross-examination. Annie claimed that she had confronted her husband because he had abandoned her. She claimed that she had taken a gun to the scene to frighten him but that she had not intended to shoot him. She further testified that he struck her and that she could not remember much after that.

Once again, Howe's opponent was Francis Wellman. Wellman's strategy focused more or less on tarring Annie's character.[100] Wellman was still smarting from his defeat in the *Ella Nelson* case, and he later gave this account of the trial (though he did not mention Annie Walden by name):

> I told the jury in great detail what I knew about the prisoner's lawyer, his methods with jurors, and deceptions he had successfully carried out in the various cases we had tried together—all in such laudatory terms of Howe, as an advocate, that even he seemed rather pleased with himself than otherwise. It turned out that I was right in my estimate of that jury. All they needed was to be convinced that the whole defence had been staged purely for its effect upon them, and a quick verdict of guilty followed.[101]

Today's lawyers and judges recognize this as improper argument—prosecutorial misconduct?[102] Contemporaneous sources indicate that these remarks were made:

> Assistant District Attorney Wellman, when he began his address, declared to the jury that he must do some unmasking. He said he had seen the whole scene gone through with in court before, and spoke of Mr. Howe pinching a woman at the proper time when addressing a jury, so that she might make an effective scream. He said that Mrs. Walden had rehearsed just how she was going to act in court. ... He had seen Mr. Howe go through all this acting before.[103]

It appears that Howe missed the boat by not objecting forcefully at the time. He did complain about Wellman's remarks at Annie's sentencing. For his part, Judge George Landon Ingraham responded that he had not heard Wellman make such remarks, although he agreed that it would have been improper argument. In any event, he denied a motion for a new trial and sentenced Annie to life imprisonment.[104] In its report of the sentencing proceedings, *The New York Times* again confirmed that Wellman had made the improper remarks just as Howe had belatedly complained. On the other hand, the paper also noted that, when asked if an appeal would be taken, Howe opined that his client Annie Walden was lucky to have gotten off "as easily as she did" and that a retrial would likely "mean conviction in the first degree."[105] Annie Walden went off to Blackwell's Island. There were hints of suicide[106] and stories of illness, including reports that she was dying of consumption.[107] A petition for her pardon was initiated by Rev. Braddin Hamilton, the chaplain in Blackwell's Island (now Roosevelt Island),[108] but District Attorney DeLancey Nicoll would have none of it, reporting forcefully and negatively to the governor. Six years would pass, and then there was a great fire at Blackwell's Island. It was reported that "Annie Walden, a life prisoner, who has served eight and one-half years for homicide, rushed into the burning quarter of the hospital building and rescued a child."[109]

Commissioner Francis Lantry of the Department of Corrections recommended that executive clemency be granted for Annie and eight other heroic prisoners for their conduct during the fire.[110] Annie Walden was pardoned by Governor Theodore Roosevelt and, accompanied by her father, she returned to Almedia, Pennsylvania. She was then in her early thirties and would have a second chance at life.[111]

Rovere credits Howe as being a pioneer of the insanity defense. Certainly insanity, psychic epilepsy,[112] automatism, and altered states were hot topics in the medical jurisprudence of the day on both sides of the Atlantic.[113] Rovere doesn't provide much detail—just a few anecdotes. He tries to give Howe credit for the "brainstorm" theory of temporary insanity used by Delphin Delmas in the famous Harry Thaw[114] case, but is unconvincing. He then turns to the Alphonse Stephani case.

Alphonse J. Stephani was a wealthy young man who killed his late father's lawyer when the lawyer failed to settle the estate to his satisfaction. Rovere characterizes the case as "another [of Howe's] notable acquittal[s] through simulated lunacy. ... Stephani was not convicted."[115] The Stephani case was covered extensively in the press and spawned much related civil litigation. The case also provides an interesting side story about Howe's botched presentation of the expert testimony of a noted alienist (at this time neurology, psychiatry, and psychology had not become distinct specialties) of the time, Dr. Allan McLane Hamilton.[116] How is it that Rovere failed to notice that Stephani was convicted?

Attempts to simulate insanity were not unknown at the time but were usually unsuccessful. Dr. Hamilton related his experiences with such cases. He reported on the interesting case of Harry Rose, an actor who killed his wife "in a fit of jealous rage."

> After his arrest he promptly indulged in a farrago of ridicu-
> lous nonsense which is said to have convinced his eminent

counsel, Mr. Abe Hummel, that he was "raving mad." This
consisted in offering Hummel "millions," and taking the
diminutive lawyer into a dark corner of his cell and impres-
sively telling him that he would make him "rich beyond
dreams of avarice"; he also did many many other silly things.
A commission[117]subsequently disregarded all this, as well
as the sickly sentimental articles in some of the newspapers,
and Rose was sent to Sing Sing. ... While in the Tombs,
and subsequently in State's Prison, Rose practically established a school for the training of simulators, and ever since
the defense of insanity has been more popular than it ever
was before. My experience with these cases has enabled me
to detect the rules for "fooling the doctors" which from that
time have been handed down from Rose.

According to contemporary newspaper accounts, young
Alphonse Stephani was left a generous inheritance when his father
died, but he wanted more and took advantage of his mother, who had
been named the executrix of his father's estate. Lawyer Clinton G.
Reynolds advised Stephani's mother to bring criminal charges against
her son, but she chose instead to proceed in civil court. The same
day that he was served with process he went to the Wall Street law
offices of Reynolds & Harrison and gunned down the lawyer, after
a short and sharp argument. Reynolds lived for a time and gave an
antemortem statement to the coroner.[118] Stephani's trial began on
March 30, 1890. It was reported that Howe was to be paid $35,000
by Stephani's mother if he "escap[ed] the fatal chair."[119] Stephani's
appearance and demeanor were reported as follows:

Stephani paid no attention to what the witnesses were
saying. His appearance was well in keeping with the defense
of insanity, on which his lawyers rely. His long black hair
fell down to his shoulders, and in that he took more interest
than in anything else, every few moments combing it back
with his fingers. His favorite attitude, when not combing

back his hair, was to sit with his chair tilted back, his hands clasped behind it, and his eyes directed toward the ceiling.[120]

The first witness for the defense was his mother:

> Mrs. Stephani…said that her husband, who died in 1888, was a gloomy man, somewhat peculiar in his manner. One of his brothers had been insane. Her son had been strange from childhood. When only eighteen years old he had become impressed with the idea that she was attempting to harm him, and refused to eat any food which she had cooked. He was abusive in his manner toward her and had once struck her. When a trip to Europe was given up he had attempted to hang himself, and once before he cut himself in another attempt to end his life. He said that he was tired of living. All this had followed a fall from a horse when he was about sixteen years old.[121]

Howe called a former associate of lawyer Reynolds, John H. Bird, who testified that he had observed the defendant acting irrationally; and Howe called a number of medical experts in support of the insanity plea. Nevertheless a verdict of murder in the second degree was returned on April 3, 1890, and, on April 10, Stephani was sentenced to life imprisonment. His mother sought a pardon from Governor Roosevelt, but her application was denied.[122] After serving a year in Sing Sing, "his insanity became so evident to every one that he was transferred to Dannemora [a state facility for the insane]. … He ha[d], despite his psychosis, extraordinary business ability, and…increased his inheritance to a great extent."[123]

In 1914 the wealthy Stephani attempted to prove his sanity and said that he would seek a pardon if the issue were decided in his favor.[124] His action seeking discharge under a writ of habeas corpus was denied.[125] When he died in 1935, he left an odd holographic will[126] purporting to disinherit all persons of blood relationship and creating a foundation to provide income for certain German cities. Probate of the will was denied on the ground that Stephani lacked

testamentary capacity.[127] Litigation over Stephani money fills the
New York law reporters.

Rovere also seems to have suffered from some technical confusion
in his account of the Stephani case. He cites Francis Wellman's book as
giving Howe credit for the technique of "silent cross-examination."[128]
In fact, Wellman was giving himself credit for the technique, and
his anecdote is drawn from the Stephani case. Wellman reports that
Howe placed Dr. Hamilton on the stand:

> Upon calling him to the witness chair…he did not question
> his witness [in the usual manner] so as to lay before the
> jury the extent of his experience in mental disorders and
> his familiarity with all forms of insanity, nor develop before
> them the doctor's peculiar opportunities for judging correctly
> of the prisoner's present condition. The wily advocate
> evidently looked upon District Attorney Nicoll and myself
> who were opposed to him, as a couple of inexperienced
> youngsters, who would cross-examine at great length and
> allow the witness to make every answer tell with double
> effect when elicited by the state's attorney. In accordance
> therewith, and upon the examination in-chief, Mr. Howe
> contented himself with the single inquiry: [Qs and As
> inserted—not in original]
>
> Q. "Dr. Hamilton, you have examined the prisoner at the
> Bar, have you not?"
>
> A. "I have sir," replied Dr. Hamilton.
>
> Q. "Is he, in your opinion, sane or insane?" continued
> Mr. Howe.
>
> A. "Insane," said Dr. Hamilton.
>
> Q. "You may cross-examine," thundered Howe, with one of
> his characteristic gestures. There was a huddled consultation
> between Mr. Nicoll and his associates.
>
> A. "We have no questions," remarked Mr. Nicoll quietly.

Q. "What!" exclaimed Mr. Howe, "not ask the famous
Dr. Hamilton a question? Well, I will," and turning to the
witness began to ask him how close a study he had made
of the prisoner's symptoms, etc.; when upon our objection,
Chief Justice Van Brunt directed the witness to leave the
witness box, as his testimony was concluded, and rules that
inasmuch as the direct examination had finished, and there
had been no cross-examination, there was no course open to
Mr. Howe but to call his next witness![129]

Dr. Hamilton had a somewhat different recollection of the
incident, in his book *Recollections of an Alienist*. In a chapter titled,
"Judges, Juries and Expert Witnesses," Dr. Hamilton criticizes
interrogating counsel who propound complicated hypothetical
questions to their experts—what he describes as "hypnotic questions."
He suggests that this happened in the Stephani case:

> Mr. Wellman in his book upon cross-examination relates
> the sharp move of the District Attorney in the Stephani
> case, who declined to examine me after Mr. Howe had read
> a long, tiresome question which took a half hour to finish,
> fearing and thinking that I would bring out something that
> might help the prisoner. Undoubtedly this was an inspira-
> tion, but can one conceive the attitude of a public prosecutor
> whose duty it is to present *all* the evidence *against as well as
> in favour of the man in the dock?*[130]

Herbert Asbury[131] attributes yet another celebrated victory to
Howe. William J. Sharkey, a Tammany healer as well as a notorious
burglar, gambler, and pickpocket, killed an associate, Robert Dunn.
Dunn was an employee of the City Comptroller's Office but was
also a faro dealer in a New York City gambling establishment.
Sharkey fronted Dunn $600 to operate a faro game in Buffalo.
When Dunn failed to return the money, Sharkey shot him dead
in a Hudson Street bar. Sharkey was eventually convicted and
sentenced to be hanged, but the execution was stayed pending

review.[132] Sharkey was sent to the Tombs to await his fate. He seems to have enjoyed many creature comforts provided by the industry of his girlfriend, pickpocket Maggie Jourdan,[133] but that was not her only contribution. Maggie, with the assistance of Sarah Daley (Mrs. Wesley ["Wes"] Allen), the wife of another well-known felon, managed to pass off female garb to Sharkey during a visit to his cell. Sharkey escaped from the Tombs in this disguise, and some said that he changed clothes at Howe & Hummel's Centre Street office[134] (across from the Tombs) before departing the city. Allen and Maggie were arrested, but only Maggie was tried for her complicity in the escape. Here is what Asbury had to say of the trial:

> Maggie Jourdan was arrested that evening at the home of her mother, 167 Ninth Avenue. She greeted the detectives cheerfully and remarked that she was "the happiest little woman in the world." In due time she was tried before Recorder Hackett in general Sessions Court, and her chief counsel, the celebrated Big Bill Howe, defended her with such persuasive eloquence that the jury disagreed. She was promptly released and the indictment against her was quashed.[135]

Once again, contemporary newspaper accounts seem at odds with the conventional wisdom. Maggie's trial "excited considerable public interest,"[136] so one suspects that her counsel would have been accurately identified. They were named as Ex-Judge Beach and John O. Mott.[137] In the end, there was a hung jury. Perhaps this is what Asbury meant by "the jury disagreed." The jurors deadlocked six for conviction and six for acquittal, although "[o]ne of the six for conviction...was willing to acquit if by doing so a verdict could be arrived at."[138]

Was Howe actively involved in the trial? It does appear that Sarah Daley, along with "Keeper" Lawrence Phillips, was the first party arrested, and she immediately employed Howe & Hummel to represent her.[139] Sarah was released after the case against Maggie was dropped.[140]

Sharkey made his way to Havana, Cuba. Maggie followed him there since he had promised to marry her. However, the drunken Sharkey abused her and finally assaulted her—firing off a revolver, the shot just grazing the back of her head. She returned home, and Sharkey remained in Havana under the alias of Frank Campbell,[141] there being no extradition treaty with Cuba at the time. Asbury's account ends at this point, but there is more of interest.

First of all, Sharkey did not enjoy his stay in Cuba completely unmolested. There is a report that he was actually arrested in Santiago de Cuba, perhaps when he was trying to enter insurgent lines.[142] However, he was apparently released and was never returned to New York. Of even more interest are the further adventures of Maggie Jourdan.

On or about July 27, 1880, John Jourdan, Maggie's "sneak-thief brother," and an accomplice, made off with cash and $40,000 in bonds from the vault of the Middletown Savings Bank of Middletown, Connecticut. They were arrested in November of the same year and were jailed pending extradition.[143] Apparently on account of illness, John Jourdan was transferred to Bellevue Hospital. At some point he was visited by a woman who some thought was Maggie Jourdan, and he disappeared from the hospital. He simply walked out,[144] and he remained at large until August 8, 1884, when he was arrested at a Lexington Avenue residence after some kind of dispute with one Eliza Austin, alias "The Whale," who was the wife or mistress of "Tip" Little, a notorious felon.[145] Eliza claimed that Jourdan had stolen $100 from her. Jourdan claimed an "intimate relationship" with Eliza and that she was making a false claim out of jealousy over another woman. Later, after Eliza had apparently been beaten up by Tip, she changed her story and refused to press charges against John Jourdan. Curiously, John Jourdan was discharged and was not held to account for the bank job![146]

In yet another trial of the century, Howe is sometimes reported to have been the defense lawyer[147] for Carlyle Harris, a medical student convicted of poisoning his secret wife with morphine.

However, Howe did not defend Harris at the trial level. The defense was led by William Travers Jerome, who would later become one of New York City's most famous prosecutors.[148] After Howe's death, Jerome pursued the previously untouchable Abe Hummel on a charge of perjury and had him convicted and disbarred.[149] The active prosecutor in the Harris case was, again, Assistant District Attorney Francis Wellman. The case was a public sensation,[150] since it was well known that Harris had been unfaithful to Helen Potts, his young bride, carrying on with seventeen-year-old Queenie Drew, the daughter of a wealthy Kansas cattleman. It also came out that Harris had performed an abortion on Helen. Additionally there was evidence that Harris had been involved in the operation of an unlicensed drinking and gambling establishment called the Neptune Club. All of this was the sort of character evidence that the defense would strive to exclude. It was of limited relevance and highly prejudicial[151]—and likely to persuade a jury to convict. It is believed that Harris's lawyers persuaded him not to take the stand, for fear that some or all of this would come in by the back door.[152] The case was a circumstantial one, and it was very much a battle of experts. Indeed, Allan McLane Hamilton, MD and alienist, had performed an autopsy on Helen Potts, and he appeared as a witness for the prosecution.[153] Harris was convicted and given the death penalty.

Harris's desperate mother replaced trial counsel with Howe in the hope of securing a new trial, a reversal on appeal, or executive clemency. Curiously, in one sense, this was not Howe's first appearance in the case. He had been unable to resist injecting himself into the goings-on by suggesting to Wellman, his old adversary, that during his summation at the close of the case he should call upon the defendant to accompany him to[154] Helen's grave, where he would hear Helen cry out the verdict that should be rendered against him—a turn-of-the-century channeling of the victim.[155] Wellman did something similar.[156] In any event, one would think that his aid and comfort to the prosecution might have suggested that he was not the best lawyer to take over the case from Jerome, but this was William Howe.

Howe tried to get a new trial by collecting affidavits from various witnesses of dubious character.[157] The firm of Howe & Hummel was known for its reliance on such questionable materials,[158] and it was a perjured affidavit that ultimately brought down Abe Hummel. The thrust of Howe's motion was that this newly discovered evidence proved that Helen Potts was a habitual user of morphine.[159] Howe also attacked defense counsel for failing to call Harris as a witness.

The trial judge, Recorder Frederick Smyth, carefully considered the materials presented but denied Howe's motion.[160] Howe's efforts on appeal and his petitions to the governor also failed. Harris was executed on May 8, 1893.[161]

Many reports on the exploits of Howe & Hummel make much of the firm's representation[162] of the infamous Madame Restell. I have been unable to document the connection, but Restell is a fascinating character, well worth the digression.[163] Restell was the defendant in "one of the longest trials held in the East up to the time of the Civil War,"[164] the "Wonderful Trial of Anna Caroline Lohman, Alias Restell," as it was reported in a pamphlet hawked by *National Police Gazette*, price six cents. This 1847 New York City trial, on charges of manslaughter arising from abortions, lasted eighteen days and caused much excitement—filling "a news vacuum."[165] Restell was not defended by Howe (the trial was before his heyday) but by James Brady and David Graham, who were said to be two of the best criminal defense lawyers in New York City at the time. The jury found Restell guilty only of a misdemeanor in procuring a miscarriage, and she was sentenced to a year, which she served at the prison on Blackwell's Island.[166] She was wise enough not to publicize her customer list, and she reopened her business after serving her sentence. In 1854 felony charges were again brought against her and one George Shackford, who was charged with procuring an abortion for a Miss Cordelia Grant.[167] Although the judge suspected that Restell and Shackford may have arranged for the nonappearance of the witness for the prosecution, he nevertheless dismissed the case.[168]

It was not until 1878 that Madame Restell was finally cornered by the reformer Anthony Comstock. (By then organized medicine had joined up with the clergy to further criminalize and stiffen the penalties for abortion.)[169] She was arrested and would have easily made bail, plunking down $10,000 in United States gold bonds, had a judge not initially refused any bail.[170] She was out of the Tombs in a couple of days. There would be no trial. Shortly after court convened on April Fool's Day, a messenger delivered a note to the judge. The stout sixty-seven-year-old Madame Restell had slipped into a tub of water and cut her own throat from ear to ear.

Howe and Hummel filled five pages of their book with her story, never suggesting that they represented her, and indeed, vilifying her (no doubt hypocritically?):

> It is a strange, revolting story, carrying its own warning and moral, besides furnishing an admirable instance of the unexpected forms in which Nemesis manifests herself.[171]

Chapter Three

The Case of "Frenchy"—Part 1

London Crime and Gossip
A Terribly Brutal Murder in Whitechapel
(from *The New York Times*, September 1, 1888)

Her head was nearly severed from her body, which was literally cut to pieces, one gash running from the pelvis to the breastbone...

Old World News by Cable
Whitechapel Startled by a Fourth Murder
(from *The New York Times*, September 9, 1888)

The Whitechapel fiend murdered his fourth victim this morning and still continues undetected, unseen, and unknown. ...The latest murder is exactly like its predecessor. The victim was a woman streetwalker of the lowest class... Her throat was cut so completely that everything but the spine was severed, and the body was ripped up, all the viscera being scattered about...

Dismay in Whitechapel
Two More Murdered Women Found.
The Night's Work of the Mysterious Assassin
Who Has Baffled the London Police Thus Far
(from *The New York Times*, October 1, 1888)

His last night's victims were murdered within an hour, and the second was disemboweled like her predecessors, a portion of her abdomen being missing as in the last case. ...These make six murders to the fiend's credit, all within a half mile radius.

London's Awful Mystery
The Whitechapel Murderer Still Untracked,
Indignation Against the Home Secretary
and Police...
(from *The New York Times*, October 2, 1888)

The whole police management of the cases, as indeed the system under which they work, is idiotic in the extreme. ... There are any amount of theories published, some scientific, others ingenious, and others stupid...

London's Record of Crime
Another Mysterious Murder Brought to Light.
A Perfect Carnival of Blood in the World's
Metropolis - the Police Apparently Paralyzed
(from *The New York Times*, October 3, 1888)

It was October 3, 1888. All New York City was abuzz over the news of the Whitechapel ["Jack the Ripper"] Murders in London. Who is the murderer? Is it a man seeking revenge upon prostitutes? Is it a wealthy professional, perhaps a surgeon, living the fantastic life of Jekyll and Hyde? Why have the London police not caught the murderer? A reporter for *The New York Herald*[172] interviewed several of the medico-legal luminaries of the city.

First, legendary trial lawyer William "Big Bill" Howe, whom we met in our first two chapters and now described as the "most experienced and astute" defender of murderers, who "has set up the plea of insanity in homicide cases ten times as often as any other explanation of crime," weighed in. Big Bill subscribed to the popular theory that the murderer "is a man who has become insane from brooding over some wrong done to him by one of the class [streetwalkers] to which his victims belong."

As for other legal notables, Recorder (Judge) Smyth[173] was not so quick to advance a theory, noting only that "the heads of the London police must be five feet thick all around. The murderer must have been bathed in blood. They [the London police] cannot for a moment be compared with the New York police."

Justice Truman C. White was also critical of the London constabulary. According to White, "[W]hoever did these murders must have been gory when he left his victims. How is it that the London Police don't track him I can't understand. Seven such murders in succession would be impossible in this city. Inspector Byrnes [who will soon enter the scene as a major player] would have had the man locked up long ago. All this simply goes to show us what a well policed city we live in."

District Attorney John R. Fellows followed suit, announcing "very earnestly" that "[s]uch a state of affairs in New York City would be simply impossible."

Assistant District Attorney Semple was not so critical, suggesting that "[t]he difficulty of apprehending this man arises, no doubt, from the fact that his character is such as to place him above suspicion." A similar view is suggested by a Mr. Robert Todd, described as "an authority on criminal matters." He opines that this was not the work of some common criminal but rather of "some medical crank, whose morbid anatomical ideas [have] led him to commit these fiendish deeds with a view of increasing his stock of surgical knowledge."

Two illustrious members of the medical profession also weighed in on the subject of the "Ripper." First, Dr. Allan McLane Hamilton,[174] whom we met earlier in this book,[175] had much to say. Dr. Hamilton was of the opinion that the murder was "very probably" committed by "a man belonging to a class of insane persons known as piquers. It is a form of insanity manifested by a variety of impulsive desires to do mischief…such as to cut and mutilate."[176] The reporter noted that Dr. Hamilton described the condition as associating a homicidal tendency with a state of sexual aberration—the pleasure of the act being its motive.

That is, "In these Whitechapel cases there are strong signs of sexual aberration in the manner of mutilation. His mental condition at the time he sheds his victim's blood is one of extreme exhilaration." Dr. Hamilton did not think the crime was motivated by a desire for revenge on prostitutes.

Then there was the colorful Dr. Edward Charles Spitzka.[177] Dr. Spitzka was a highly educated physician and a specialist in neurology,[178] serving as the president of the American Neurological Society in 1890. He was the attending physician at the execution of William Kemmler, who was the first person to die in the electric chair, and served as an expert witness in the trial of Charles Guiteau, the assassin of President Garfield. He and his son, Dr. Edward Anthony Spitzka, were experts on the human brain. Indeed, Edward Anthony specialized in the morphology of the brain, and he autopsied the brain of Leon Czolgosz, the assassin of President McKinley. Together, father and son amassed an impressive collection of human brains. Brain collecting was a big thing in those days. Walt Whitman's brain was donated to science. I must relegate Whitman's brain to a note.[179]

For his part, Dr. Edward Charles Spitzka agreed that the conduct of this class of persons is an acting out of a "higher sexual fury." Indeed, he had referred to such persons in his book on insanity, citing examples. A *New York Herald* reporter asked, "How do you suppose he manages to cut the throats and mutilate the trunks of these women without covering himself with blood so as to make detection certain?" Dr. Spitzka replied, "It could be done by making a sudden pass at the throat from behind, but it is a very difficult operation, requiring great patience. This man is probably educated…That he knows something about surgery is, I think, pretty certain."[180]

This was not Dr. Spitzka's only pronouncement on the subject. In 1888 he published "The Whitechapel Murders: Their medico-legal and historical aspects,"[181] in which he speculated, wildly, in my opinion, that "Jack the Ripper" may have been the same person who committed a series of atrocious murders of African-American servant girls in Texas in 1884 and 1885. These murders have since been documented in at least two books and numerous Internet postings.[182]

What did Inspector Thomas Byrnes, who we mentioned earlier was the inventor of the "third degree"[183] and by now a published author with his book *Professional Criminals of America*,[184] have to say at this point? It has been suggested that Inspector Byrnes made a number of comments unflattering to the London police, along with many boasts about how he would have solved the crimes of the Whitechapel murderer in short order[185]—boasts that he might very well have come to regret when the body of an aged prostitute, Carrie Brown, was found mutilated in a room on the top floor of the seedy East River Hotel in New York City. However, the record of Inspector Byrnes's boasts is not that clear.[186] No matter, the press would soon attribute such boasts to him.[187] Byrnes had admirers,[188] but he also had many detractors, particularly in the press.[189]

On April 24, 1891, around nine o'clock in the morning, Eddie Fitzgerald, the night clerk at the waterfront hotel, made his rounds to clear the rooms. Room 31 was locked. Getting no reply from the occupants, Fitzgerald entered using his master key. To his horror he discovered the mutilated body of Carrie Brown, who was eking out an existence as a prostitute and was known as "Old Shakespeare" to the denizens of the area. Her colorful name was attributed to her tendency to quote the Bard when she had too much to drink. In her sixties, Carrie was supposedly the widow of a New England sea captain.[190]

Her body was laying on the bed, on her side with her face to the wall. She was naked from the armpits down, her head and face wrapped in her clothing. She had been disemboweled. A gash extended from the base of the spine, carried upward across her abdomen and reaching a point halfway up her right side. On her back was a lightly carved X, reminiscent of the Ripper murders.

A messenger was sent to the Oak Street Police Station, and Captain Richard O'Connor and his detectives were soon on the scene, with a train of reporters bringing up the rear. On the floor they discovered a table knife with a four-inch blade, the tip broken or ground down to form a sharp point. The key to room 31 could not be found; it was assumed that the murderer had carried it away. Coroner Lewis W. Schultze came down with his own string of reporters. A superficial examination by the coroner led to the conclusion that Carrie Brown had been strangled first and mutilated afterward. The body lay in the room all afternoon, and people climbed the stairs to check it out. At five o'clock in the afternoon, the "dead wagon" took the body away—late, it seems, because Deputy Coroner Jenkins had planned to do an autopsy at three o'clock. He put the autopsy off until the next morning.[191] Captain William McLaughlin and his gang of detectives soon joined the investigation.

It was determined that Carrie Brown was last seen alive by Mary Miniter, an assistant housekeeper, between ten thirty and eleven on the evening of April 23 in the company of a young man whom Miniter described as "about thirty-two years old, five feet eight inches in height, of slim build, with a long sharp nose and a heavy mustache of light color. He was clad in a dark-brown cutaway coat and black trousers, and wore an old black derby hat, the crown of which was much dented. He was evidently a foreigner, and the woman's impression was that he was German."[192]

The man wanted a room, and Miniter claimed that he gave his name as "C. Niclo."[193] She gave that name to the room clerk, Eddie Fitzgerald, and Fitzgerald or a Tommy Thompson made an entry to that effect in the hotel register.[194] Carrie Brown and her companion were assigned to room 31 on the top floor. They retired to the room with a bucket of ale.[195] The same night, a man known as "Frenchy," described as a dark-complected Italian or Frenchman, rented room 33, which was across the hall, diagonal from room 31.

The police ascertained that there were only two doors from which a guest could exit the hotel—one by going through the barroom, which was closed at one o'clock in the morning. No one was permitted to leave through that door after one o'clock. Furthermore, no one could pass out of the hotel by the other exit leading onto Water Street unless Eddie Fitzgerald or some other employee unlocked the door for them. There was a buzzer device connected to this door so that entry and exit could be controlled. There was some thought that the murderer might have escaped out the scuttle to the roof and then down to the street, and there were reports in the press that there were some blood marks on the scuttle.

Inspector Byrnes took over the investigation of the case, and Frenchy was arrested as part of a dragnet, along with a number of other suspects. When arrested, Frenchy had blood on his stockings, on the front of his shirt at the waist, and on his back. It was said that he had a reputation for carrying a knife. He appears to have been implicated by Alice Sullivan and Mary Ann Lopez, two other women of the street. Mary Ann Lopez, also known as "Dublin Mary,"[196] had at one time been Frenchy's lover. It seems that Mary had previously had Frenchy arrested for allegedly biting her arm in a dispute over a dollar bill that Frenchy had given her for sex. Later he would admit scuffling with Mary for the dollar when she refused to perform, but he denied biting her.[197] Witnesses suggested that Frenchy had been seen with the Carrie Brown the day before the murder, but it must be remembered that all of the witnesses who provided information to the police and who testified later at Frenchy's trial were shady characters.[198]

The investigation was not exactly trouble-free.[199] At one point there were two suspects named Frenchy, referred to as "Frenchy No. 1" and "Frenchy No. 2." They were reported to be cousins, and one ex-policeman described Frenchy No. 2 as "light-complexioned... with a light or nearly sandy mustache."[200] There were even two Shakespeares—one of whom was very much alive.[201] Byrnes lost interest in Frenchy No. 2.[202] Indeed, he lost interest in tracking down the mysterious man who had taken room 31 with Carrie Brown. He announced to the press that Frenchy No. 1 was his man.[203] Byrnes claimed to have followed a trail of blood across the hall from room 31 to room 33 and to have found bloodstains in room 33—on the bed and on a chair. Even more startling was the announcement that blood had been found under Frenchy's fingernails.

Dr. Cyrus Edson laid out the trail of blood at the coroner's inquest. The State was represented by Assistant District Attorney Francis Wellman. Levy, Friend & House, a new firm (only House had experience) had been appointed *pro bono* to represent Frenchy No. 1, the prisoner, who was now known, for the official record, as George Frank.[204] Frenchy did not help his case any by making inconsistent statements and what appeared to be outright lies.[205] In any event the coroner's jury said that Frenchy was the murderer.[206] He was indicted on May 18, 1891,[207] and pleaded not guilty. Attending the proceedings was the French Consul, Mr. de Belzac, who pledged to aid the defense.[208]

According to Wellman's memoir, *Luck and Opportunity*,[209] Wellman was not impressed by the case against Frenchy:

> It seems that the police claimed they had traced bloody fingerprints on the corridor walls, which led directly from the scene of the crime to the room that had been occupied by "Frenchy." Also, when arrested, blood stains were found on his underclothes, and his finger-nails were black with some substance resembling dried blood.

> Whenever Byrnes had some pet case he wanted tried he always wished it on me. Naturally, therefore, the "Frenchy" case fell to my lot. At first, I refused point blank, much as I liked Byrnes personally, to handle it. The evidence was very flimsy; in their ardor to help their chief make good his boast, the police might very well have mistaken for human blood ordinary stains on the walls of a lodging house of this character.

> Byrnes was much upset by my refusal and criticism of his "evidence." Finally I suggested that he take steps to find out just where the Shakespeare woman had spent the evening before her death and exactly what she had done. All the police could learn was that she was last seen, alone, eating and drinking at a basement bar where they served a free lunch with the drinks. This free lunch consisted of cheese, dried bread, slices of ham and cole slaw.

> I then obtained from him some of the bloodstained clothing and also the parings from the prisoner's finger nails which

the property man at the police department had been crafty enough to preserve.

These samples were sent to a celebrated chemist in Philadelphia, without the police knowing anything about it, and a detailed report of the resulting analysis was requested.

To my astonishment I received a prompt reply first, that the samples were undoubtedly human blood [technically not correct—that could not be ascertained], and second, that the parings of the finger-nails contained particles of partially digested food which could not possibly have been obtained in any other way than during an operation on somebody's smaller intestine. The report also stated that these samples showed partially digested cheese, bread, and some form of cabbage!

Thus, according to Wellman's own post-trial *critical* review, his doubts about the strength of the police evidence and his reluctance to prosecute the case were overcome through his own undertakings, not through those of Inspector Byrnes. Wellman would, indeed, go on with the show—prosecution of Frenchy for the murder of Old Shakespeare. He would also employ a number of questionable trial tactics in pursuit of a victory for the prosecution, if not for truth and justice.

Before discussing the trial of Frenchy (now identified as Ameer Ben Ali) and commenting on the performance and trial tactics of the prosecution and defense lawyers, I will first refer to some rules of evidence and argument.

By the first decade of the nineteenth century, character evidence—that is, evidence that the defendant was the type of person who would be likely to commit the crime charged—was barred.[210] As Justice Robert Jackson opined in the famous case of *Michelson v. United States*:[211]

> The state may not show defendant's prior trouble with the law, specific criminal acts, or ill name among his

neighbors, even though such facts might logically be persuasive that he is by propensity a probable perpetrator of the crime…it is said to weigh too much with the jury and to over persuade them as to prejudge one with a bad general record and deny him a fair opportunity to defend against a particular charge.[212]

Thus it was and is the rule to this day that the prosecution may not offer evidence of the defendant's character (for example, his reputation for violence) unless the defendant has first offered evidence of his character for nonviolence or evidence of the victim's character for violence in support of defendant's claim of self-defense. In modern practice, such character evidence is offered through a reputation or opinion witness. Only if a defendant places his character or the victim's character in issue does the defendant open the door to counterproof by the prosecution. Moreover, even if the door is opened by defense evidence of a pertinent trait of character, it is not wide open. The prosecution must confine his counterproof to the pertinent trait of character injected by the defendant. That is to say, "[T]he defendant does not open the door to his entire character by presenting evidence on only one aspect of his character."[213] Moreover, a defendant does not put his character in evidence "merely by taking the stand [or] providing general background evidence."[214]

In 1891, when the Frenchy case was tried, both the defense and the prosecution were limited, in terms of introducing character evidence, to testimony by a witness as to the defendant's reputation in the community for the pertinent trait of character. Neither the defense nor the prosecution was permitted to introduce evidence of specific instances of the defendant's conduct.[215]

These rules should be kept in mind when considering the prosecution's opening statement, the evidence and innuendo offered by the prosecution in its case in chief, and the prosecution's closing argument or summation.

The Frenchy trial opened on June 29, 1891, following jury selection. The murder, police investigation, and trial garnered great public interest and press coverage. Shortly before the trial began, the defendant talked to reporters and told them pretty much what they could expect his story to be at trial.[216] Recorder (Judge) Smyth agreed that the jurors would be allowed to view the scene of the murder, but he would not permit the defendant to accompany them.[217] Not allowing defendant to accompany the jury to the murder scene would probably be an error today, but Judge Smyth's ruling was in accord with the law at the time.

The prosecution's theory of the case was that Frenchy (Ameer Ben Ali) had stayed in room 33 and that, at some time in the night after Carrie Brown's male companion had left, he had entered room 31 where Carrie was staying. The thought was that Ben Ali entered the room to satisfy his lust, but at some point he became enraged and had strangled and then mutilated his victim. He then returned to room 33 and left the hotel early in the morning—leaving Carrie's torn and lifeless body in room 31.

Wellman's opening statement began with a suggestion that during the defendant's military service "he was connected in some way with the surgical department of the French army."[218] No evidence was ever elicited to support this innuendo. It was Wellman's attempt to suggest that defendant had the surgical skills of the Ripper.[219] It is improper to refer in the opening statement to matters that will not be supported by admissible evidence.

Wellman then launched into a character assassination of the defendant, alluding to an alleged conviction for theft in Brooklyn, his consorting with low women, and an arrest for begging (he wore splints on his arms to fake injuries, which was a common scam of the day) and vagrancy in Queens County. Defense Attorney House quite properly objected to this.[220] Judge Smyth avoided ruling on the issue, suggesting that he would rule on any evidence presented when the time came, thereby allowing the jury to hear and consider what Wellman had said. House also objected to Wellman's reference in the prosecution's opening statement to a knife that had been taken from defendant after he had been arrested in Queens for begging and

vagrancy. House cited a case, *People v. Everett*, but Judge Smyth was
dismissive. It is an unfortunate fact of life for defense counsel that the
judge is probably a former prosecutor (as Smyth had been). Wellman
then proceeded to lay out the array of facts that he would present,
emphasizing Frenchy's repeated statements when he was arrested,
"'Me do nothing, me do nothing,' at a time he had not been accused
of doing anything," and emphasizing the "blood evidence" and the
expert, scientific interpretation of it that was to be forthcoming.[221]

Defense lawyer House moved that all witnesses except for the
experts be excluded from the courtroom. Judge Smyth granted the
motion. The opening statement for the defense was reserved for later;
it would be delivered after the close of the State's case in chief and the
inevitable denial of a defense motion for acquittal. It was now time
for the prosecution's case in chief. After presenting the testimony of
a civil engineer who had prepared scale drawings of the scene of the
crime, plans of the hotel, and the streets about it, Wellman called a
series of lowlife hotel employees and streetwalkers, detectives, and
assorted police officers. As Edwin M. Borchard would later report on
the case, the lay witnesses, "from the lowest stratum of New York life,"
were called to suggest that Frenchy "had been living a sordid life," that
he had stayed at the East River Hotel before, and that he was known
to wander from room to room at night. "On cross-examination, the
credibility of these witnesses [would be] thoroughly attacked."[222] As
the prosecution presented its lousy crew of lay witnesses, they were
forced to bring out their current or revolving door residence in the
House of Corrections to take the sting out of the expected cross-
examination and would remind the jury during their summation that
in criminal cases one had to do with what was available.[223]

The prosecution got off to a poor start by calling Mary Corcoran,
a hotel housekeeper. Corcoran said that she had seen Carrie Brown
at the hotel the night before the murder, but she did not see her again
until the victim was found dead. Curiously, Corcoran claimed to have
found the body first, which was not in line with Eddie Fitzgerald's
earlier statements to the police during the murder investigation. She

also testified that she saw the victim with a man with a derby but that she never saw her in the company of the defendant.

Corcoran's ineffectual testimony was followed by the testimony of Captain O'Connor, who had been called to the scene when the body was found. He stated that after viewing the body he went to collect his detectives and returned with the coroner. O'Connor also testified as to how police collected the knife at the scene and how they had later examined the defendant and his bloody shirt. He later turned the investigation over to Captain McLaughlin. On cross-examination O'Connor was unwilling to swear that on his first visit he saw drops of blood in the hall, on the chair in room 33, or on the doorjamb of room 33. He agreed that when he arrived around 11:30 a.m. with the coroner there were a dozen reporters in train. O'Connor could not say that on his second visit he saw spots of blood. He did not investigate the scuttle.

The coroner testified that he agreed and that he was followed by eight to ten reporters—some in the room and some in the hall. On the other hand, Detective Michael Crowley testified that he arrived at the scene before the coroner arrived and that he saw blood spots and stains on the doors. Crowley found a candle in room 33 burned down to one-eighth inch from the socket of the candle holder. Captain McLaughlin testified that when he arrived he saw blood spots in the hall between rooms 33 and 31, but he saw no blood on the door to room 31 and none on the knob of room 33. (Actually the doorknobs appeared to be button-like devices.)

Catherine McGovern was called to identify the victim's body as that of Carrie Brown. Detective Jeremiah Griffin, who retrieved the knife from under the victim's thigh, followed McGovern. He acknowledged that at the coroner's inquest he had testified that he had not noticed any blood marks in the hallway until the next day, Saturday, April 25.

Mary Miniter was an important witness. Consistent with the statements she made to police during the investigation, Miniter testified that she saw Old Shakespeare, Carrie Brown, at the hotel the night before the murder in the company of a light-complected man, with a light mustache, about five feet eight inches in height, wearing a derby hat. She said that the man she saw was not the defendant. She gave this man the key to room 31, along with a candle. She also testified that this man and the victim went upstairs with a bucket of ale they had ordered. Miniter did not see this mysterious man leave the hotel.

Then came Eddie Fitzgerald, something of a star witness, who had a revolving door connection to the House of Detention. Fitzgerald cleaned up around the East River Hotel and was an assistant to the bartender. He claimed that he was familiar with the defendant because the defendant had stayed in the hotel with a woman other than the victim a couple of nights before the murder. Fitzgerald testified that the defendant had come into the hotel around midnight, after ringing the Water Street bell, and had paid for room 33 with twenty-five pennies. The defendant also was given a candle and matches. Fitzgerald further testified that the defendant came down around five thirty the next morning, while Fitzgerald was sweeping out the bar area. He claimed that the defendant was walking "sneaky like" with his face to the wall on the way out of the hotel. Fitzgerald added that the defendant was wearing a derby and a long overcoat (which did not appear to be "Frenchy-type" attire). Fitzgerald renewed his claim that he had opened the door to room 31 with his master key and discovered the body. He identified the defendant when Officer Adam Lang came to the hotel with Frenchy in tow and said that the defendant confirmed that he had slept there the night before the body was found.[224] On cross-examination Fitzgerald admitted that he was currently housed in the House of Detention. He denied that he had discussed his testimony with the police, but he admitted that he had done so with the prosecuting attorneys maybe three times. The suit he was wearing was paid for by the district attorney's office.

Fitzgerald was followed by Samuel Shine,[225] the bartender, who claimed to have seen the defendant on Wednesday and again on

Thursday (the night of the murder). He too claimed to have seen the defendant leave at five or five thirty in the morning, wearing a long overcoat. Strangely, Shine could not remember seeing the defendant with a hat.

Then came the gruesome stuff, provided by Deputy Coroner Jenkins, the coroner's physician who did the autopsy.[226] It was Jenkins's opinion that the victim had been strangled—had died of asphyxiation—before being disemboweled. Interestingly enough, cross-examination brought out that he made no examination for spermatozoa. On redirect Wellman made the point that if the cutting had occurred after the heart had stopped beating, there might not have been spurting of blood.

Next up was Adam Lang, the police officer who had arrested the defendant a mere two blocks away from the scene of the crime. Apparently Lang had been present in the courtroom in violation of the separation of witnesses order; however, Judge Smyth brushed off the defense's objection to Lang's testimony. Lang also testified that, when he approached, the defendant was leaning against a wall smoking a cigar—not exactly the picture of a frantic fugitive— and the defendant gave his name as Frank. Lang also testified that a streetwalker by the name of Mary Lopez had previously filed a complaint against the defendant, and that when he asked the defendant if he knew Mary, the defendant said that he had been in an affray with her and had bitten her. He said he had been arrested but got out of it all right. Lang further testified that the defendant admitted that he had slept in the East River Hotel the night before but repeatedly exclaimed, "Me do nothing." Lang confirmed that Fitzgerald had identified the defendant. Officer Richard O'Connor followed Lang and testified that when the defendant was brought to the station house the defendant had admitted that he had slept in room 33.

The next witness was interesting. Detective George Aloncle was called into the case because he spoke French. Aloncle claimed that he was able to converse in French with the defendant. According to

Aloncle, the defendant admitted that he had slept in the East River Hotel the night of the murder but said, contrary to other witnesses, that he had slept in Brooklyn the night before and that he had slept in a basement room on Oliver Street with a woman who was menstruating, which accounted for the blood on his clothing. The defendant called the woman "Salle Vache" (dirty cow). He further testified that the defendant also claimed to have a job at a hotel in Brooklyn. Aloncle was unable to confirm anything that the defendant told him, which would prove to be problematic. He did find out that George Frank had been jailed in Jamaica (Queens) for thirty days.

As something of a preemptive strike, the prosecution called Alice Sullivan, who lived for a time at a Mrs. Harrington's place at 49 Oliver Street, where Carrie Brown had also stayed. She was currently a denizen of the House of Detention. Sullivan claimed that she had been with the defendant in a room at the Oliver Street house on April 23 (the day before Carrie Brown's body was found) and that the defendant had paid fifty cents in change ("three ten-cent pieces, and four five-cent pieces") to have "connection" with her. She denied that she was "unwell" at the time; she was not menstruating. She had seen the defendant with Old Shakespeare shortly before the crime and had heard him say that he was going to sleep in the Fourth Ward Hotel (another name for the East River Hotel). Alice also testified to what would have been the victim's last meal, a free lunch at a saloon, consisting of cold cabbage cut up with vinegar, bread, and corned beef. On cross-examination the jury learned of Sullivan's record for solicitation, theft of a watch, and numerous instances of public drunkenness.

The prosecutor then called Mary Ann Lopez ("Dublin Mary"), who was also a resident of the House of Detention. She was actually Frenchy's former mash. Mary testified she had seen the defendant at Mrs. Harrington's place on Oliver Street and had also seen him before with Old Shakespeare. Curiously, Frenchy had denied knowing Lopez during the investigation but reluctantly admitted at trial that he knew her.

Then came Nellie English. She knew the defendant as George and had stayed with him at the East River Hotel. English said that during the night he would get up six or seven times to creep around and feel the doors to other rooms and listen for occupants. She said he once went into a room where there was a female resident and then came out, apparently without incident. Nellie was followed by a couple of witnesses who said they knew defendant as George Frank.

Did Frenchy have a knife when he took room 33 the night of the murder? At least one commentator has suggested that there was no evidence that he did.[227] This was an issue at trial. When Frenchy was arrested for vagrancy in Queens, he was apparently relieved of a knife by Officer John Connor. Connor had with him in the courtroom a knife of the same type, and Wellman tried to get it into evidence. This knife was the evidence alluded to in Wellman's opening, which had drawn defense's objection. Wellman was trying to argue that the defendant was in the habit of carrying such a weapon, which was similar to the murder weapon. House renewed his objection during Wellman's case in chief, and this time Judge Smyth ruled in House's favor. The knife was excluded.[228]

On the other hand, several fellow jailbirds testified at trial that the defendant had a "blade" while in the jail.[229] So, for what it was worth, there was some evidence—perhaps not all that credible. How much it was worth was a question for the jury. Of course, jailbird snitches are notoriously unreliable, willing to say almost anything for favors. But anyone who knows anything about even our modern facilities knows that all kinds of things can be found behind bars. The defense met the jailbirds' testimony with testimony from the constable who had arrested Frenchy that he had thoroughly searched the prisoner and that he was sure Frenchy had no knife.[230]

Mary Harrington was then called to confirm that she knew Alice Sullivan, Mary Ann Lopez ("Dublin Mary"), and Frenchy. Mrs. Harrington confirmed that the defendant had "connected with" Alice Sullivan and that Alice was not "unwell" at the time—she ought to know because she made up the beds at her place.

Finally the prosecution got to the physical evidence. Detective William Frink testified as to how the "blood evidence" had been collected, including the defendant's fingernail scrapings. An appropriate chain of custody for all the material was established through Frink and other witnesses, including Inspector Byrnes. Frink also stated that, although the scuttle was open at the time in question, it would have been "practically impossible" for someone, once on the roof, to get down to the street. A scuttle on an adjoining roof three feet lower was secured from the inside. The owner of the building checked and confirmed this but admitted on cross-examination that he could not swear that it was secured on the night in question. Chief Prosecutor DeLancey Nicoll took turns with Wellman, presenting the testimony of the prosecution's experts. The array of expert witnesses, all compensated for their time, was impressive.

Dr. Henry Formad, professor of biology and pathology at the University of Pennsylvania, led off. He was a specialist in microscopy. He had been called in by Dr. Edson, chief inspector of the New York City Public Health Department, and Dr. Austin Flint, a physiologist. Dr. Formad testified that he had done more than fourteen thousand postmortems,[231] which some critics of the prosecution have suggested had to have been inflated. Actually, the number was not out of line with the claims of the defense experts. One assumes that the postmortems of the day were relatively cursory compared with the modern autopsy.

Next up was Dr. Flint, and he was no slouch either. A distinguished physiologist, Flint had helped found the Buffalo Medical College (which became the State University of New York at Buffalo), and he became the president of the American Medical Association. Today his name is associated with a murmur ("Flint's murmur") found in cases of aortic regurgitation.

Finally there was Dr. Edson. Nicoll skillfully took Edson through the chain of exhibits, and he too confirmed the findings of Dr. Formad and Dr. Flint.

The prosecution's expert testimony (excluding the coroner's testimony) accounted for 112 pages of trial transcript.[232] The testimony was ably summarized by Dr. Flint in an article, titled "Reminiscences of the 'Frenchy' Murder Case."[233]

Also, Dr. Flint would later summarize the expert testimony in a medical journal,[234] Drs. Formad and Edson being in complete agreement. I have included selected references to transcript pages that support Dr. Flint's summary. Such references, with a few additional notes for the reader, are enclosed in brackets in the summary that follows.

I took up the study of the case June 26, 1891, and became associated with Dr. Edson, then of the Health Department, and with Dr. Formad, of the University of Pennsylvania, who has since died. We examined specimens of the matters [microscopicly, spectographicly, and chemically, Tr. p. 666] taken from under the long finger nails of the prisoner four days after the murder, stains from the flaps of the prisoner's shirt, from the right sleeve of the shirt, from the back of the shirt, and from the left sleeve of the shirt, from the wallpaper on the hall near the door of room 33 [the room Frenchy had supposedly taken], from the door itself, from the floor of room 33, from the prisoner's socks, from a chair in room 33, from the floor between room 31 and room 33, from the bedtick under the murdered woman in room 31, from the stockings of the murdered woman, from a petticoat tied about the head of the murdered woman, and from the sheet on the bed in room 31.

In all these specimens mammalian blood was found, presumably human blood. On the prisoner's shirt, the ticking of the bed in room 33, the woman's stockings and petticoat, nothing but blood was found. In all the other specimens blood was found mixed with more or less unchanged coloring matter of bile, fat globules and crystals, tyrosin[e], cholesterin, triple phosphates, columnar epithelium, eggs of round worms, starch granules, partially digested muscular tissue, and partially digested vegetable matter. The specimens containing these matters included those taken from under the finger nails of the prisoner. [Tr. p. 667–675]

Note that there was no claim of a blood match. The experts did not claim that they could prove it was human blood. [Tr. p. 667]. At the time there was no generally accepted test to distinguish human from mammalian blood, although Dr. Formad had found a way of distinguishing the two by painstaking measurement of blood cells, which he did not undertake in the case. [Tr. p. 699]. His method required five hundred measurements of the corpuscles. [Tr. p. 699]. The experts were basing the logic of their opinions on the "admixture" of blood and the other substances. The admixture was the same. [Tr. pp. 717, 764].

> Before I had become associated in the case, the theory of the experts was that the intestinal matters found in the various specimens came from the large intestine. Indeed, the experts at that time understood that a piece of intestine cut out by the murderer was from the large intestine, containing fecal matter and residue of food, and not from the small intestine, which should contain partially digested matters and unchanged coloring matter of bile. [Before Dr. Flint had been called in, none of the experts knew that a portion of the small intestine had been removed, nor did they know what Carrie Brown had had to eat before the murder. TR. p. 675]. After examining these specimens, I insisted that the matters came from the small intestine [Tr. pp. 675, 727–730]; although I was assured that the records of the post-mortem showed that the large intestine only had been cut. [Tr. pp. 675, 727–730] However, I sent for the actual report of the autopsy and found the record that a portion of the lower part of the small intestine had been cut out, the large intestine being uninjured. Before I had ascertained this I had given a positive opinion that the ileum had been cut. This opinion was exactly confirmed by the official record. [Tr. pp. 727–730].

Dr. Flint then summarized the findings and conclusions he offered at the trial:

> 1. That the specimens examined by me contained tyrosin[e], bilirubin, columnar epithelium, partially digested muscular tissue and vegetable substances [consistent with other testimony as to what Carrie Brown had eaten before the murder], microorganisms, etc.
>
> 2. That the tyrosin[e] and bilirubin must have come from the small intestine, while the other matters might exist as well in the large intestine.
>
> 3. That the tyrosin[e] was produced by the prolonged action of the intestinal digestive fluids upon the proteids of food, these matters being first converted into trypsin peptones and afterwards into tyrosin[e], the change into tyrosin[e] being aided by the action of intestinal microorganisms.
>
> 4. That the bilirubin, which strongly colored the epithelial cells and other matters, was characteristic of the contents of the small intestine.
>
> 5. That the appearances were practically the same in all the specimens.
>
> 6. My opinion that these matters were from the small intestine was based mainly on the presence of tyrosin[e] and bilirubin.

Levy did the heavy lifting when it came to the cross-examination of the state's experts and the presentation of defense expert testimony, which followed the testimony of defendant. Levy had done a good job preparing for the medical testimony, but the prosecution experts proved to be tough nuts to crack. At one point Levy tried to impeach Dr. Formad by asserting that the eminent Dr. Rudolf Virchow once contended that "[n]o one is justified in putting the question of a man's life upon the uncertain measurements of dried blood corpuscles" and that Dr. Formad had incorporated that statement into one of his publications. Dr. Formad responded that Virchow had once held that view but that he had since changed his mind and had told Dr. Formad that just "last summer."[235] Levy correctly used leading questions to try to put words in the expert's mouth that he might then impeach, but all too often it came off that he was setting up straw men.

The prosecution closed its case after its last expert, Dr. Edson, completed his testimony. The defense asked that the court be adjourned so that Levy would have more time to prepare his opening statement and give it the next day. After all, he had been preoccupied with the cross-examination of the State's experts. The judge would not give him a break and required that the opening be presented before any adjournment, insisting that the defense testimony be entered the next day. The judge wanted to wrap things up as quickly as possible.

Chapter Four

The Case of "Frenchy"—Part 2

Defense attorneys Levy and House took center stage. Levy presented the opening statement[236] of the defense. House proceeded with the case in chief and called the defendant to the witness stand. The defense theory of the case was that Carrie Brown had not been killed by defendant Ameer Ben Ali ("Frenchy No. 1"), as the prosecution charged. She had been murdered by the mysterious man who had taken the room with her earlier in the evening. This mysterious man had left "Old Shakespeare" dead, and then he had escaped from the hotel. The defense would also try to convince the jury that the prosecution's expert testimony was too good to be true, the materials examined were surely contaminated, the blood on defendant's shirt at the time of his arrest was explained by his having had sex with a menstruating prostitute the night before the murder, and the fecal matter under his fingernails might be accounted for by his unclean habits.

Lawyer Levy reminded the jurors that, on the evening of April 23, the night of the murder at the East River Hotel, Old Shakespeare's companion was light-complected, with a light-colored mustache.[237] He had a German accent. There was no accounting for when or how he had left the hotel. What efforts were made to find him? What of the defendant? Did he flee? What of the prosecution's witnesses? Were they the type of persons who would even understand the oath they took? When the defendant testifies, compare his testimony to testimony of the "harlots and thieves" produced by the prosecution. The prosecution had suggested that the defendant served in the surgical department of the French Army, but there was no truth to that— indeed no evidence had been introduced to support the suggestion.

The defendant had never been in prison before, except for the unfortunate episode in Jamaica (Queens), and the constable who had arrested him and had taken him to the jail refutes the testimony of the jailbirds who claimed he had a blade while in the jail. The defendant had no motive for committing the crime. Finally, the defense would present its own experts to refute the experts for the prosecution.

The defense actually led off by calling the defendant to the stand, after introducing the testimony of the constable who had searched him and who swore that, at the time of the arrest, the defendant had no knife. Then the defense round of the much-anticipated battle of the experts over the blood evidence began. To counter the impressive testimony of the prosecution's experts, the defense presented Drs. Rush Huidekoper, Justin Herold, and Paul Gibier, along with Professor Henry A. Mott. Could Huidekoper, Herold, Gibier, and Mott perform as well as the expert witnesses for the prosecution? Could their testimony plant a seed of reasonable doubt in the minds of the jurors—doubt that Frenchy could be the murderer? Would District Attorney Nicoll's cross-examination of these experts only make the prosecution's case stronger? Could this be a case of the experts canceling each other out?[238] What would be the jurors' impression of Frenchy the witness? Would the defense's decision to call the defendant to the stand prove to be a wise strategy?

First, I'll set out the gist of the defense experts' testimony. Then, I'll discuss the defendant's testimony and performance.

The defense was at a disadvantage because there was no money. The defense experts had to be obtained on a *pro bono* basis. They were well-qualified but not as impressive as those for the prosecution. The press characterized them as "not so confident as the others."[239] Press reports also commented on the public's anticipation, as well as the perceived significance, of the battle of the experts.[240]

The first expert for the defense was Dr. Huidekoper, a physician who had graduated in the same class as Dr. Formad[241] and who had served as the physician to the Philadelphia coroner prior to Dr. Formad's tenure in that role.[242] Dr. Huidekoper also claimed to have done 1,500 human autopsies. However, the prosecution poked at him because he was now a professor of veterinary medicine. The prosecution also made much of the fact that Huidekoper was only thirty-seven years old, and for the past six years he had only treated horses, cows, and dogs.[243] Indeed, District Attorney DeLancey Nicoll's cross-examination, asking Dr. Huidekoper the names of the horses and dogs that he had treated, was sufficiently abusive for Judge Smyth to intervene and move things along.[244]

Dr. Huidekoper questioned the strength of the prosecution's evidence because the blood could have been tracked around by police officers and reporters, and he also played the contamination card.[245] He testified that tyrosine could be made artificially[246] and claimed that bilirubin could be found in urine.[247] Additionally he asserted that columnar epithelial cells could be found in the feces and menstrual blood[248] and in the fallopian tubes and uterus.[249] All this was consistent with the defense contention that the blood evidence could have gotten on the defendant's clothes and under his fingernails by his intercourse with a woman in menstruation and from his unclean toilet habits. Huidekoper also presented the theory that the wounds were probably made by a left-handed person.[250] His testimony was contradicted by the prosecution,[251] and there was no effective follow-up by the defense.

The prosecution's cross-examination drew out that Huidekoper had never before testified on bloodstains and that he had not personally examined the specimens in question but was relying on the findings of Drs. Flint and Formad.[252] Additionally Huidekoper did not challenge Flint's and Formad's findings but only their conclusions,[253] saying that he could not "swear" to the accuracy of their conclusions, as the prosecution experts had boldly "sworn."[254] Furthermore the transcript reveals that the jurors were permitted to ask questions. Indeed, they popped off quite a number of times. During the examination of defense expert Dr. Huidekoper, the inquisitive and seemingly frustrated Juror #3 (he was the one who would later ask the judge to adjourn before the jury instructions and deliberations[255] so that the jurors could enjoy the Fourth of July holiday) asked, "Has it come to this that great men differ in their opinions?"[256]

Dr. Paul Gibier of the Pasteur Institute in New York City testified that the substances that were so important to the prosecution's theory could be found in some cases of diarrhea (catarrhal diarrhea), in the first stages of cholera, and in substances in a state of putrefaction (putrefying blood and intestinal contents).[257] He also said that the presence of such substances might be accounted for by the defendant's intercourse with an unclean woman.[258] Gibier too, was unwilling to "swear" that the specimens originated from the same source.[259]

Dr. Justin Herold, who claimed to have done between 2,100 and 2,200 autopsies and who had testified in murder trials, gave similar testimony[260] and joined with the others in saying that he would not be justified in stating that all the specimens came from the same source.[261] Herold was of the Bellevue Hospital Medical College. His testimony was followed by that of Henry A. Mott Jr., an analytical chemist and the grandson of the famous surgeon Valentine Mott. Henry Mott testified that the specimens relied upon by the prosecution and the critical tyrosine, bilirubin, and epithelial cells could have come from menstrual blood.[262] The prosecution attacked Mott's testimony because he was not a doctor and had had little experience with the microscope.

More important than the battle of the experts was the poor performance of the defendant when he was put on the stand. Calling him to the stand was surely a mistake on the part of defense counsel. Throughout the defendant's testimony, it was clear that his command of English was extremely limited; but it also seemed that he would dodge questions which he probably understood.[263]

Wellman later made the following observations:

> [The defendant was] a huge specimen of a man fully six feet-five in height, when he took the witness stand in his own behalf…he could not speak any language but Armenian [sic].

[At the] first question put to the prisoner by Charles Brook,[264] his lawyer...the man rose up in apparent fury, shouted in his own language, gesticulated wildly, waved his hands above his head and created such a stir that it took several minutes for his counsel to quiet him down.[265]

Even Dr. Formad would opine that the defendant's performance on the stand probably had a greater effect on the jury than the medical testimony presented by the prosecution.[266] One can tell that the reporters had the same impression from the following headlines in *The Sun*, July 3, 1891:

"GOOD MEN, DON'T HANG ME"—AMEER BEN ALI FRANTIC ON THE WITNESS STAND—His long arms swing in Appeals to Allah, and in a String of Weak and Wild Contradiction of Himself and Everybody Else—Screaming Out in Arabic that he is Innocent...[267]

The interpreter was not effective (putting his performance in the best light), which complicated the presentation by the defense.[268] Lawyer Friend did the direct examination of defendant, and Friend's inexperience showed through. Wellman acted toward Friend in a rather imperious manner.[269]

Wellman's cross-examination was aggressive, and at times he attempted to inject inadmissible evidence, suggesting by *innuendo* that the defendant did not care a thing about his wife and children back in Algeria.[270] Judge Smyth sustained defense objections, but this may not have removed the odor of skunk from the jury box. The prosecution also attempted to paint the defendant as someone who may have had some surgical knowledge, alleging that he worked in the hospital where he was treated for his wounds.[271] This was obviously an attempt to allude to "Jack the Ripper." Wellman did not offer any real evidence for that, and one wonders if there was any good faith basis for the suggestion.

He [Wellman]spoke in a bantering way. The cross-
examination was very long, and the man [the defendant]
was tangled up dozens of times. He contradicted himself
time and time again. Whenever he was cornered he would
tell some story, and he did not seem to care one whit whether
it jibed with his other stories or not.[272]

Indeed, the defendant proved to be his own worst enemy.
He would contradict almost every witness and even contradicted
himself. He denied knowing Alice Sullivan, dismissing her by
suggesting that he had sex with some other woman; he could not
say where. He reluctantly admitted knowing Mary Ann Lopez
("Dublin Mary") and denied that he had bitten her, contradicting
what he had supposedly told Officer Lang during the police
investigation. When confronted with his ability to speak French,
the defendant denied being competent in the language. Wellman
bored in with Detective Aloncle's contrary testimony. Wellman insisted
that defendant say "Salle Vache," but the defendant claimed to be
unable to pronounce the words.

As a reporter for *The New York Times* put it:

The evidence, while not as strong as to Frenchy's connection
with the murder, was unfavorable to him, because of the
explanations of his movements he had made to detectives
and then contradicted.[273]

The most startling event in the trial was described by Wellman:

I saw it was useless to cross-examine [false, Wellman's cross
was lengthy and ruthless] so I concluded I had better try for
a repetition of the scene we had just witnessed [apparently
alluding to the aforementioned excitement during the
direct]. I therefore handed him the knife which had been
left behind in the room where the body was found and asked
him to show the jury just how he had used it the night of
the murder. Again the prisoner jumped to his feet, and

brandishing the knife in his right hand, shouted and called on Allah and all the Gods in Christendom to witness his denials. He worked himself up into such a fury that it looked at one time as if he would surely end by heaving the knife at me. Nobody, of course, could make out what he was saying, but guilty or innocent, it was apparent to everyone that it would not be safe to let such a wild man go free.[274]

Wellman told a similar story in a later memoir:[275]

I handed him the knife that had been found in his bedroom and asked him to show to the jury just how he had plunged it into the woman's abdomen while she was sleeping. I anticipated just what and did happen. The prisoner stood up in a perfect frenzy of excitement and, holding the knife in his outstretched hand high above his head, called upon Allah as witness to his innocence. He worked himself into such a pitch of excitement that I expected any minute he would spring at me, standing only six feet from him, and plunge the knife into any part of my anatomy that he could reach. He presented the picture of a veritable madman capable of such an assault as the police had accused him of.

Of course he was convicted. Whether guilty or not, he had proven himself to be unsafe to be allowed at large.[276]

Wellman, the prosecutor, did not seem to care too much about the distinction between guilt and innocence, nor did he seem to care much for the salutary effects of the rules of evidence. He seemed to be extremely proud of his stunt.[277]

The trial transcript indicates that something like this actually happened.[278] Given the excitement, the court reporter may be forgiven for not getting everything down.

By Mr. Wellman:

Q: "Was this your knife (showing the knife to the defendant)?"

Mr. House: "One moment. That knife [not the murder weapon] has been excluded, and I object to its being shown to the defendant."[279]

The Court: "He asked him if it was his knife."

A: "This knife—I brought it with me from Para[guay], Brazil."

By Mr. Wellman:

Q: "And they took it away from you didn't they?" (Objected to)

(Excluded)

Q: "And after they took the knife that you brought from Brazil away from you, [wasn't that just excluded?] didn't you supply yourself with that knife?" (Knife in evidence shown)

[Notice how Wellman has ignored the judge's ruling about the other knife]

A: "This is not my knife—so help me God it is not, this one."

The Court: "Take that knife away from him, please."

A: "They arrest me. I don't know what for. They arrested me innocent four times."

Q: "Innocently, they arrested you four times?"

A: "Yes, Sir. Four times I was in jail for nothing innocently."

The Court: "Now, will you just tell him to stop?"

The Court: "Gentlemen, I will give you a recess until a quarter past 2. You will be here at a quarter past 2, promptly, and you will observe the statutory admonition that I have given you heretofore."[280]

After the defendant and the defense experts testified, something odd, but not necessarily important, occurred. Wellman had attempted to attack the defendant's credibility by suggesting that he had been convicted of larceny—felony theft from the defendant's friend's store in Brooklyn. House objected on the ground that, although the defendant had been arrested, he pleaded guilty to petty or misdemeanor theft and had been discharged without serving a day. House argued, to no avail, that the attempted impeachment was improper under the rules of evidence. Now the defense did something unusual. Lawyer Friend called lawyer House to the stand.[281] Ordinarily it is improper for a defense counsel also to testify as a witness. Perhaps an exception was justified, but no one seems to have questioned this tactic. What did House have to say? He testified that he had gone to Brooklyn to check for records relating to the Brooklyn arrest. There he found a record and copied it. Wellman alluded to the best evidence rule, which requires that the original of a writing be produced, but then he waived any objection. House testified that the complaint was made by "George Frank" (adding to the confusion about names in this case) and not the defendant's friend or relative (again, it is very confusing) Jen Ali. Furthermore, House found no other record that indicated that there was any conviction. Wellman and Judge Smyth seemed to resist the possibility that anything could be concluded from House's efforts.

After the defense rested, the prosecution called three rebuttal witnesses, and it is at least arguable that they were not true rebuttal witnesses, a point that defense counsel argued (correctly, it seems to me) but lost.[282] Dr. Flint was called to reinforce his earlier opinion and to testify that nothing the defense witnesses had said would make him change his opinion.[283] Then Eddie Fitzgerald was recalled to the stand to testify again about the candle found in Ben Ali's room.[284] Fitzgerald had done an experiment with a similar candle that reinforced the testimony of Michael Crowley, who had testified in the prosecution's case in chief. It had taken an hour and five minutes for this candle to burn down to resemble the candle found in room 33—burned down to within an eighth of an inch over the socket. Again, the point was to suggest that defendant's tallow candle had burned for more than an hour—that he had not immediately gone to bed but had stayed up for some purpose. Finally, William Frink, the officer who had taken the defendant's fingernail scrapings, was allowed to state that when he took the scrapings the defendant's fingernails were very long and that they appeared to be the same length now at trial.[285]

As was the custom in New York at the time, the summation or closing argument for the defense preceded that of the prosecution.

Lawyer House did the honors for the defense.[286] He painted the defendant as a poor, friendless foreigner who lacked funds for his counsel or his experts. House felt it necessary to deny rumors that wealthy benefactors had contributed money in the hope of discrediting Byrnes. He moved on to focus on the victim's mysterious companion. The State had made no effort to show when this mysterious companion had left the hotel or by what method. Then House got to the crux of the blood evidence. Whoever had done the deed would have been drenched in blood. There would have been buckets of blood. So why did the police go diagonally from room 33 to room 31—because of a few (four, five, or seven) spots in the hall? And when they found the defendant, he was hanging around a nearby liquor store, only two blocks away from the scene of the crime, arms folded in a careless, negligent way. He had made no effort to flee or to clean himself up. He had been "turned in" by a prostitute with a grudge. His expression, "Me do nothing," was innocent and natural enough—hardly an admission of guilt. The victim had lost all her blood, but all the prosecution had was blood on the defendant's shirt and on his underwear, which would have covered his private parts and which could be explained by his contact with a menstruating woman. The link between a knife and the defendant was based on the testimony of jailbirds and had been refuted by the constable, Officer James R. Hiland, who had searched him before locking him up. Surely Officer Hiland was more credible than jailbirds. The defendant had no motive to kill Old Shakespeare, and he had no reason to even know that she was in room 31. The prosecution's scientific evidence was dependent on claims relating to the contents of the victim's small intestines. But the prosecution's experts would not even swear that the blood was human blood, and they had nothing to say about the blood on the defendant's back and stockings because there were no intestinal contents there. The telltale tyrosine and the like could be otherwise accounted for—the tyrosine by the fact that the blood samples were putrefied. You could admit all that the State proved, yet all of it did not prove that defendant had murdered Carrie Brown.

The prosecutor's summation was delivered by District Attorney Nicoll himself. It began, strangely enough, with what was almost certainly a reference to William Howe's recent (June 21, 1891) triumph over Wellman in the Ella Nelson case.[287]

> [It] is the duty of the prosecution officer, as it is the duty of the defense, so it is the duty of the jury...to be governed entirely by the evidence and the just inferences to be drawn from it, without being distracted from the performance of their sworn duty by any considerations of sentiment, or by any other appeals to prejudice or passion.
>
> There have been instances in the administration of justice in this County, and one of them, at least, not far remote, where, in spite of the clear and positive evidence of guilt adduced against the prisoner, and yielding, as I believe, solely to those human and tender sentiments which sometimes fill the breasts of jurors, they permitted themselves to depart from the lessons which the evidence in that case taught, and to discharge a person who was manifestly guilty. That illustration, which must be still fresh in your minds, at least justifies me in urging upon you again that our duty—yours and mine—concerns itself only with the evidence which has been laid before you, and that we ought not to allow ourselves to depart from it on account of any other considerations, however honorable or humane they may be.
>
> But, if sentiment were ever to enter into the discharge of the duty of jurors, certainly this is no case for indulging in it.[288]

Nicoll then launched into his argument, which today, at least, would be branded an exercise in prosecutorial misconduct. In the Frenchy case Wellman and his boss, DeLancey Nicoll, took every effort to allude to defendant as a wild, uncivilized foreigner who might be expected to commit the crime for which he was charged, not only violating the character evidence rule but also inciting bias and prejudice against the defendant.[289]

The defense had called no character witnesses. There were probably none to call since the defendant was very much a stranger in a strange land. There were allusions to his honorable service in the French army (he was wounded twice), but that did not put his character in issue.

Here are excerpts from the summation delivered by Nicoll, and the reader is invited to find the many violations of the rules of evidence and the law of closing argument—which seem apparent.

> And now, gentlemen, to the proofs.
>
> Let us, in that frame of mind, approach a study of the evidence in the case, as the prosecution have laid it before you.
>
> The first, and the most natural question, which the mind of the juror asks with regard to a person charged with a crime, is:
>
> Is this the kind of a person, is this the kind of a man who would probably have committed an offense of this character?
>
> That is, do the history, habits and character of the defendant afford an inference that he was capable of committing an offense of this description.
>
> Therefore, we naturally approach a consideration of the history, the habits, and the previous character of defendant to find out whether or not it appears satisfactorily to the mind that he was a person who could have or probably would have committed an offense of this description.

Now, here was a man, born in a valley in Algeria, an Arab by birth, of no education, imbued with all the spirit of the Mohammedan religion, and the fierce and ferocious habits of his native land. That is a circumstance which naturally enters into our calculations at the outset. "Is this a man," we say, "who was born in a different country, a civilized country, educated, his morals cultivated, his passions restrained, his habits ordered by law?" Why no. We find that this man is a man who is himself half savage, who belongs to a savage tribe in Algeria, to whom human life is cheap, and who does not take the same view of the sanctity and value of life that we do, who have none of the respect for law that we have, or that any civilized community has, whose religion teaches him that the life of an infidel, one who is not a Mohammedan, one who is neither a Hebrew or a Christian, is of less value than that of a true believer. [Besides making an appeal to bias and prejudice, Nicoll is essentially testifying as a self-qualified expert.]

And so we start from the history and pedigree of this man with the presumption that the defendant is just the kind of man who would probably have committed an offense of this description, and not only that gentlemen, but this particular Mohammedan or Arab seems to have lead a particularly vicious life. With the exception of a few years, when he says he was in the French Army in Algiers, fighting with some natives in revolt, we have no account whatever of his life in Algeria. Nor could I gather any idea from his evidence as to when he first came to this country. It seems to be incredible that even a man of this character could not remember how many winters or summers had passed since he had been in America, even though he took no note of the flight of time by the usual methods. But he could not even remember that, and all we are permitted to know of him from his own statement is his arrival in the City of Brooklyn, and his association with another Arab, named Jen Ali. And there we actually find him, gentlemen, engaged in robbing and defrauding his own countryman, who had taken him in when he came to this country, and pleading guilty, in a Court in Brooklyn, of having robbed this man of the contents of his little shop.[290]

We then find him wandering around Jamaica, where, under the pretense of a fracture of his arm, he is inducing some persons, out of sympathy, to give him now and then a few coins. We then find him lodging as a vagrant for thirty days in the Queens County Jail, from which he is discharged, on the 12th of April, with $1.25 in his pocket. And then again we find him in the locality around Water Street, where these unfortunate women congregate, indulging to an inordinate extent his passions for women of that class. Now, that seems a very natural thing, because this man was of dark skin, and these were white women, and however atrociously repulsive they might appear to us, I believe it is a fact that cannot be disputed, that men of that complexion put a higher value upon a woman with white skin than white men would. But, at all events, we find him spending his entire days and nights consorting to an inordinate extent, with these wretched prostitutes around the 4th Ward Hotel, without any means of livelihood, without doing any work, or probably attempting to do any work, banished from the society of Jen Ali, in Brooklyn, whom he had robbed, ready for anything which might turn up where, he thought, with his low cunning, that detection was improbable; taking one woman, on Wednesday night, to the East River Hotel, and consorting with another woman, named Alice Sullivan, the next morning, at 8 o'clock, and spending every cent evidently, which he had taken from the jail upon these women.

Nicoll then restated all of this argument in summary form:

[W]hen all of these things are considered, it seems to me that he is precisely the kind of man whom you would expect a crime of this sort to be committed, and that we start with a strong presumption and inferences, to be drawn from the character, habits, and history of the prisoner.

Stephanie Pistello, photographer, Robert F. Stephens Courthouse Complex, Lexington, Fayette County, Kentucky, 2017 (1)

Tombs Prison, New York City, circa 1896 (2)

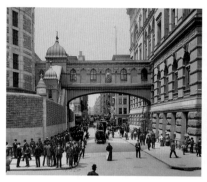

The Bridge of Sighs, New York City, circa 1905 (3)

Carlo Ponti, photographer, "Ponte dei Sospiri (Bridge of Sighs)," Venice, Italy, circa 1890–1899. The Bridge of Sighs connected the prison to the Doge's Palace above the Rio di Palazzo. (4)

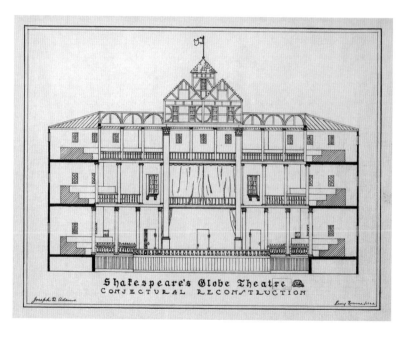

Joseph Q. Adams, Henry Roenne, Shakespeare's Globe Theatre, detail view, conjectural reconstruction (graphic), 1922 (5)

Albert B. Shults, *Immigrants landing at Castle Garden*, 1880 (6)

Jacob August Riis (1849–1914), photographer,
"Children's Playground on Ellis Island (roof garden)"
(the children of detained or waiting immigrants), circa 1900 (7)

Jacob August Riis (1849–1914), photographer,
"Court at No. 24 Baxter Street," circa 1890 (8)

"The Former Offices of Howe & Hummel,
Centre and Leonard Streets, New York, City Showing Their
Proximity to the City Prison, The Tombs," circa 1886 (9)

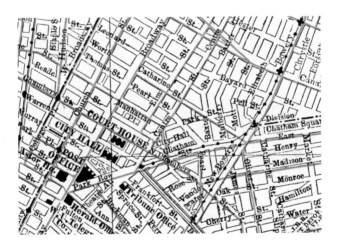

Detail on an enlarged scale from a street map of the business
portion of New York City (Rand, McNally & Company, 1892)
showing Leonard and Centre Streets, North Chambers Street,
and the locations of the courthouse, the city hall, and the office
buildings of two of the major newspapers of the day, the *Tribune* and
The New York Herald. The old Tombs is located on Leonard Street,
and the infamous Five Points intersection is located where
Baxter Street and Park Street cross. (10)

Assessment of the situation, handwritten by Dr. Adams,
New York Hospital, dated February 18, 1891, based on his observations
upon his arrival at the scene of the crime in the Ella Nelson case.
Dr. Adams's handwritten document includes statements that
Samuel Post made to Dr. Adams at the scene of the crime and
at the hospital before Post's death. (11)

Annie Walden's handwritten letter, dated November 4, 1891, to
her father-in-law, Jeter Walden, sent from the Tombs during her
imprisonment for the murder of her husband, James ("Jimmy") Walden,
outside the Metropolitan Opera House, New York City, on October 31,
1891. In the letter Annie pleads with her father-in-law to visit her in
prison, expresses her love for Jimmy, and says she dreams of Jimmy every
night and that "he comes to [her] smiling." (12)

Penitentiary, Blackwell's Island, 1853 (13)

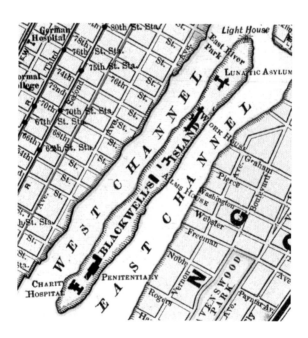

Detail on an enlarged scale from a map of New York City
(Rand, McNally & Company, 1892) showing
Blackwell's Island and the location of the penitentiary
and other facilities on the island (14)

Above left, a young and dapper Dr. Allan McLane Hamilton (15); above right, Dr. Edward Charles Spitzka (16); center, Recorder Frederick Smyth (17); below left, and District Attorney DeLancey Nicoll (18), as they appear in *Notable New Yorkers of 1896–1899* (Moses King, 1899); below right, Assistant District Attorney Francis L. Wellman, as he appears in *First Citizens of the Republic* (L. R. Hamersly, 1906) (19)

The road of the rough: Recorder Smyth's Court of General Sessions,
New York City, 1893 (20)

"I NEVER SAW THAT KNIFE."

As captured by an artist from *The Sun*, "Frenchy" on the witness stand
with the knife during the trial of Ameer Ben Ali, alias George Frank,
alias "Frenchy," for the murder of Carrie Brown, July 3, 1891 (21)

Matteawan State Hospital, Matteawan, New York, circa 1892 (22)

City of New York
                    ss:
County of New York

          Henry Berbenich, employed as clerk by the Board of Health,
being duly sworn deposes and says:

          That in the year of 1891, I was a resident of the City
of New York, being then engaged as a stock clerk by the firm of
A. Friedlander & Co., 377 Broadway, New York, and that some time
after the murder of one Shakespeare was in company with some
friends in a club room at 106 Second Ave., when a reporter, whose
name I don't recollect, made a statement in my presence, that he,
with other reporters had made several marks with blood, in the
room of "Frenchy", so as to make it appear that it was a regular
Jack-the-Ripper murder, and in order to write a sensational story
about it.   I understood by the statement made at that time by
this reporter that there were no blood spots in "Frenchy's" room,
before these were so made.

Sworn to before me this
28th day of May 1901   Henry Berbenich
Chas Muhlenberg
Notary Public

Affidavit dated May 28, 1901, of Henry Berbenich, a clerk
at the Board of Health, suggesting that the blood evidence in the
"Frenchy" case had been planted by reporters, from the pardon file
for Criminal Prisoner/Defendant: George Frank,
1891 Request for Pardon to Governor Odell (23)

Bain News Service, publisher,
Jacob A. Riis, circa 1900 (24)

State, City and County of New York; Ss:

JACOB RIIS, being duly sworn, says; I am a reporter on the Evening Sun, a newspaper published in New York City, and have been since April, 1891; on Friday, April 24th. 1891, being at the time detailed at Police Headquarters, I heard of the murder at the East River Hotel in New York City, since known as the "Shakespeare murder;" and went at once to the Hotel, arriving there about *noon*; on that day. I examined the place carefully, viewing the room where the murder was committed and the other rooms on the same floor; and noticed no blood spots on the floor between the room where the murder was *afterward said to have been* committed and that occupied by Ben Ali or "Frenchy," who is now serving a life sentence after conviction of the crime; nor did I see any blood spots on the outside or the inside of the door of the room *said to have been* so occupied by "Frenchy," or inside of such room; and to the best of my knowledge and belief there were no blood spots on the floor of the hall or in or around the room *said to have been* occupied by "Frenchy" on the night of the murder.

Sworn to before me this 8th day of March, 1901.

AH Bradley
NOTARY PUBLIC,
NEW YORK.

Jacob A Riis

Affidavit dated March 8, 1901, of Jacob Riis, reporter at the *Evening Sun*, debunking the blood evidence claimed by the prosecution to have been found at the scene of the crime, from the pardon file for Criminal Prisoner/ Defendant: George Frank, 1891 Request for Pardon to Governor Odell (25)

As captured by an artist for *The World*, Maria Barbella
in the courtroom on July 18, 1885, when she "was sentenced
to die in the electric chair" (26)

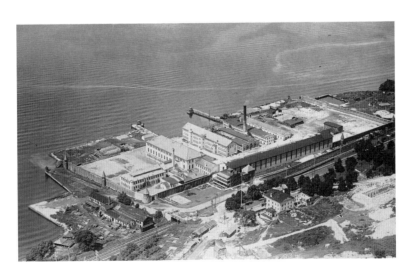

Bain News Service, publisher, Sing Sing prison, circa 1900 (27)

Harris & Ewing, photographers, Dr. Ales Hrdlicka (28)

Theater placard, *Mari Barberi, oder, Dos leben der neshome in holem.* Additional title: "Mary Barbery, or, The life of the soul in a dream." Thalia Theatre, 1896 (29)

An interesting composite by an artist for the *Los Angeles Herald*, which includes sketches of the victim, the killers and their tools, the cottage at Woodside, and the gruesome oilcloth mentioned in the text of the discussion of the Nack-Thorn-Guldensuppe case, November 14, 1897 (30)

Illustration, "Four round set-to between Howe and 'Manny' Friend,"
the *New York Herald*, November 13, 1887 (31)

Artist's sketch from the *New York Herald*, made during the trial
of Martin Thorn for the murder of William Guldensuppe, showing
Judge Wilmot Smith (*left*), Martin Thorn (*center*), and Thorn's counsel,
William F. Howe (*right*), November 10, 1897) (32)

But they have said, in the course of this trial, that he was a mild and gentle preacher. [This was a gross exaggeration.][291]

Well, he did not deny that he bit Mary Ann Lopez in the arm, in order to get a dollar bill away from her. He says he scratched her, and she claims he bit her, and showed the bite. Therefore it appears that, in a contest with a woman, he gave himself up to his passions to such an extent that he actually bit her in the arm, for the purpose of taking the dollar away from her. [He had given her a dollar for sex, and she declined but tried to keep the dollar. He wrestled it back from her.[292]] You saw him, as he appeared on the witness stand, wild and excited, fierce and mad at times, and yet all the time retaining his self-possession, having sufficient low cunning to be able to steer away from the admission of circumstances, which, as I shall show you, he knew would necessarily connect him with this offense.

From all that we have heard of him, and all that we have known of him, and from what we have seen of him, and you have heard him testify, from his assaults on other women, from his extraordinary passions and desires, his lawless appetite, does it not strike you, and is it not a strong inference with which to start in this case, that he was exactly the kind of man who would have committed an offense of this character?[293]

Lawyer House, the oldest and most experienced member of the defense team, was exhausted. There were no objections interposed by the defense at any time during the prosecution's summation.

The jury returned a verdict at ten o'clock in the evening[294] on July 3—they would get their Fourth of July holiday. The verdict was for murder in the second degree.[295] The lawyers on both sides of the "v." were disappointed. Reporters for *The Sun* described District Attorney Nicoll as "quite cast down." Byrnes was at first disappointed but by the time he reached Police Headquarters he seemed to be satisfied. When asked if he thought Ben Ali was

Jack the Ripper, he first declined to give an opinion, but then he could not resist and suggested that he had a statement proving that Ben Ali had been in London when some of the Ripper's murders were committed. He said that it was not necessary to introduce his documentary evidence in the trial.[296]

On July 10, 1891, Frenchy was sentenced to life imprisonment. House made a motion for a new trial and a motion for arrest of judgment—both of which were denied. A notice of appeal was filed, but I have found no record of further proceedings.[297] Ameer Ben Ali was sent to Sing Sing. Not long after, he was transferred to Matteawan, a hospital for the criminal insane.

From the start, the conviction raised some eyebrows. In an editorial, questions were raised about the performance of the defense counsel and about the expert testimony.

> The expert testimony on blood stains and nail scrapings was a very slender and uncertain line of evidence for connecting a man on trial for his life with the crime. The verdict was an inconsistent one, for the one thing certain is that the crime committed was one of murder in the first degree, and the accused was guilty of that or he was guilty of nothing…Even such a wretched specimen of the human species as this Algerian ought not to be sacrificed on insufficient evidence merely to demonstrate the infallibility of our detective system.[298]

Nicoll and Wellman may not have been all that satisfied with second degree murder,[299] but they put on a brave face. Wellman opined in a memoir, "My friend Tom Byrnes had made good his boasted superiority to Scotland Yard, of which, by the way, he was always very jealous."[300]

Commentators have made much of the blood evidence—it was actually not a blood match but a correspondence of the "admixture" of blood and other substances [Tr. pp. 717, 737, 764], according to the prosecution's expert testimony. However, in my opinion, this evidence probably did not account much for the conviction. That the jury found only second degree murder suggests a compromise verdict. The jurors were thought to have been interested in wrapping up the case and going home for the Fourth of July.[301]

On July 13, 1891, District Attorney Nicoll was informed by Governor Roswell P. Flower that an application had been made for the pardon of Ameer Ben Ali. Governor Flower requested an abstract of the evidence that had been presented at trial but did not reveal who had initiated the application for a pardon. When asked who had made the application, House responded that he did not know. "Frenchy is crazy," he said, "and he is better off where he is than were he at liberty."[302]

On May 24, 1901, ten years after the conviction, an article appeared in *The New York Times* stating that a lawyer by the name of Ovide Robillard had forwarded an affidavit to the new governor, Governor Benjamin Odell, stating that a prominent citizen had come forward with evidence in favor of Ameer Ben Ali. Robillard was interested in the case thanks to the French Consul. The affiant stated that he:

> [C]ame to employ on his place [in Cranford, New Jersey] a laborer named 'Frank,' whom he had secured from Castle Garden...On the morning after the Shakespeare murder he went to his barn, and there was warned by one of his help not to go near the man 'Frank,' as the latter had been out all night and was asleep, having acted exceedingly ugly. Five days afterward the affiant says Frank left his employ, and upon sending a servant into the man's room to clean it [the servant found] a key of the East River Hotel room, the place where the murder occurred, the number on the key being the same as that of the room in which the woman was killed. Besides the key, a bloody shirt was found... The man Frank was apparently a sailor, and he spoke broken English.[303]

The affiant gave various excuses for not having come forward sooner. In addition to the efforts of the French Consul, newspapermen Jacob Riis and Charles Edward Russell[304] were also instrumental in securing the pardon.[305]

A statement of the grounds for the pardon (still under the name of George Frank) can be found in the *Public Papers of Benjamin B. Odell, Jr.: Governor/State of New York*.[306] Unfortunately there is no evidence that a formal investigation was undertaken.[307] The grounds for the pardon cited Ben Ali's likely innocence. Governor Odell noted the newly discovered evidence relating to the laborer in Cranford and the discovery of the missing key. He characterized the prosecution's evidence as "weak and inconclusive" and alluded to the illogic of a verdict of murder in the second degree as indicating "doubt in the minds of the jurors." More startling was his dependence on affidavits of a number of "persons of credit," including Jacob Riis, who claimed that they had been to the *locus in quo* shortly after the murder and before the coroner's arrival and that there were, at that time, no blood spots on the floor, none on the door of room 33 (inside or outside), none in room 33, and none on the floor of the hallway around the prisoner's room. This evidence was consistent with trial testimony that there were no stains on the knob or panels of the door of the murdered woman's room.[308] The suggestion was that the blood evidence relied on by the prosecution was accidentally deposited by the crowd of reporters sometime after the affiants' visits, perhaps at the time of the removal of the body by the coroner. Or could the evidence have been planted to make a case against a scapegoat? It is surprising that there was no mention of the fact that these persons of credit could have come forward at the trial.[309]

When asked about the pardon, now Ex-Superintendent Byrnes stated: "The records show that I landed him, and the records show too, what his personal record was. I haven't got the time to go into the details of his career."[310] Byrnes's biographer notes that after Ben Ali's deportation, "No investigation into the prosecution…was ever conducted, and the immaculate reputation of Chief Inspector Thomas Byrnes remained untarnished. Although his technique of attempting to tie Ben Ali to the crime through blood samples was flawed, the process remained a prototype for future forensic practice."[311]

Wellman later wrote, without mentioning the pardon, which he surely would have known about:

> I was relieved to hear a little later that Frenchy had been transferred from the regular prison to the insane ward and still later had been deported to his native land. Of course, he never should have been allowed to enter this country in the first place.
>
> It was such cases as this that caused some people to talk of me as a cold, relentless prosecutor. Nothing could have been further from the fact. True, I put my whole soul into a case when I was certain that the defendant was guilty. But I can solemnly affirm that I never tried to convict any prisoner if I had even the slightest doubt in my own mind of his guilt.[312]

Was Ameer Ben Ali guilty or innocent? He was certainly not Jack the Ripper. Nor is it likely that the real killer, whoever he might have been, was Jack the Ripper. For one thing, the butchery lacked the medical precision attributed to The Ripper's "canonical five."[313] I will leave to others the many Ripper questions.[314]

As to the question of the guilt or innocence of Frenchy, it turns out that there is more than the brief outline of evidence in the Odell papers. A pardon file survived and has been preserved,[315] including copies of the affidavits mentioned by Governor Odell and more.

There are two affidavits from George Damon, who had employed the mysterious laborer in Cranford, known to him as "Frank." In the affidavits he tells of his discovery of the key and a bloody shirt, his subsequent "investigation," and his reasons for not coming forward sooner. His story is supported by the affidavits of his employee Charles Brennan and that of Damon's longtime acquaintance, John Lee.

There also are the affidavits of the now-famous Jacob Riis who was then a reporter for *The Sun*; of Robert Gordon Butler, the editor of that same newspaper; and of Frederick Barber, the editor of *The Telegraph* who also was then a reporter for *The Sun*—all to the effect that the telltale blood was not there when they arrived at the scene of the crime at the time the body was first discovered. Butler claims in his affidavit that he told lawyer House that Barber and another reporter for *The Sun* named Chamberlain could testify to the absence of the blood but that House did not call them as witnesses.

Even more startling is the affidavit of Henry Berbenich, a clerk for the board of health, who claimed that a reporter said in his presence that the reporter and others had planted some of the blood marks in Frenchy's room to provide an opportunity to write a sensational Jack the Ripper story.

Francis Coleman, another reporter for *The Sun*, provided an affidavit reporting that Deputy Coroner Jenkins, who had performed the autopsy, had not been altogether forthcoming at the trial about what he knew. Specifically, it is suggested that Jenkins told him that he found undigested food in the stomach of Old Shakespeare that could not have been there for more than an hour and a half and that, from this, he concluded that she was dead hours before Frenchy arrived at the hotel. Coleman claims that Jenkins did not feel that he could "volunteer" this information "under the circumstances," but he would so testify if questioned during his examination. Coleman goes on to claim that he sent a letter to House providing this information but that House did not pursue the letter. Jenkins's response to a subsequent inquiry by new District Attorney Eugene Philbin, whose investigation is noted below, seems evasive. I do note that there was some testimony by Jenkins about the contents of the stomach,[316] but the cross-examining lawyer was Levy.

Of further interest is a note in the *Bulletin of the Pasteur Institute* for the quarter April–June 1897, providing support for Dr. Gibier's trial testimony regarding possible sources of tyrosine and contradicting the testimony of the prosecution's experts that it could only be found in the small intestine. Also instructive is the summary of all the evidence compiled by new District Attorney Philbin. He noted some evidence from Mr. James Jennings, the hotel proprietor at the time, suggesting that the key now produced may not have been from the hotel after all (he could not verify this himself because the hotel building had been renovated after a fire). Philbin concluded that although "the verdict in question was found upon legal evidence fully warranting the same, yet the proof [at trial] was not so conclusive as to render the claim that after all the defendant was not guilty of the crime an absurd one."

Lawyers all know that affidavits are not worth much as evidence, because, while submitted under oath, they are mere hearsay if offered for the truth of the matters asserted in them. But governors are not bound by the rules of evidence. It is not hard to see why Governor Odell acted as he did.

Another mystery remains. In researching the fate of Ameer Ben Ali, I discovered an article in *The New York Times* archive, titled "Frenchy's Second Victim—A Convict at Matteawan, Assaulted by the Murderer of 'Old Shakespeare,' Likely to Die." The article states that "while in a murderous frenzy, he struck William Greef, a seventeen-year-old convict, on the head with a heavy oak potato-masher...'Frenchy' has been considered a model prisoner. His motive cannot be learned, except that in a moment of thirst for blood he struck the boy from behind."[317] I have found no other commentary that acknowledges this interesting report.

Dr. Formad died on June 5, 1892, at the age of forty-five. He had cut himself during an autopsy and developed blood poisoning which so weakened him that he succumbed to *cholera morbus*[318]— that is to say, he died of septicemia. This was a very high risk for nineteenth-century pathologists. Indeed, Ignaz Semmelweis, who discovered the etiology of childbed fever and who came up with the controversial solution to the problem—that doctors should wash their hands before examining patients—made the connection after the death of his friend Jakob Kolletschka. Dr. Kolletschka was a professor of forensic medicine at Vienna General Hospital. He often conducted autopsies for forensic purposes and did so in the company of students.

Apparently a student accidentally cut him with a knife that had been used during an autopsy. Semmelweis recognized that the disease that had caused his friend's death was identical to the childbed fever that had killed so many maternity patients.[319]

Frederick Smyth died of pneumonia on August 18, 1900, in Atlantic City. After serving as recorder (allowing him to sit as a trial judge), he was elected to a position of justice of the New York Supreme Court (a trial judge position—the high court of New York is the court of appeals). His obituary[320] listed some of his experience as a jurist, particularly his role as judge in the famous Carlyle Harris case.[321] It also mentioned that he had assisted in the prosecution of William Walker, the "filibusterer" who had, for a short time, ruled Nicaragua. Walker was something of a polymath, holding degrees in medicine and law. After practicing medicine in Philadelphia for a short time, he moved to New Orleans to practice law and became a founding partner of the newspaper *The Crescent*. In that role he hired a young poet named Walt Whitman, whose brain we encountered earlier in our story.[322] As the Smyth obituary noted, Walker was known to the public as "the Grey-Eyed Man of Destiny." As far as I can determine, what the prosecution alluded to was Walker's second trial for violation of the US neutrality laws. At the time Smyth would have been an Assistant United States Attorney under John McKeon. Walker was acquitted. (He was tried and acquitted three times). He was executed by a firing squad in Honduras on September 12, 1860. That's the kind of thing that can happen to folks who try to take over other people's countries.

Chapter Five

There Was Something About Maria

[T]he girl...wielded a razor with a hand of iron. [323]

The case of Maria Barbella (a.k.a. Barbieri or Barberi), officially *People v. Barberi*, is the story of an Italian immigrant who took a razor to her lover's throat on April 26, 1895, in a saloon at 428 E. 13th Street near 1st Avenue on Manhattan's Lower East Side. Maria was the first woman sentenced to die in the electric chair at Sing Sing. She escaped that fate after a second trial in which her lawyers presented a psychiatric defense. This is my contribution[324] to the legal history of this fascinating case.

The victim of the crime, Domenico Cataldo, had a bootblacking stand at the intersection of Elm and Canal streets. Maria was the daughter of a tailor and resided with her parents on Elizabeth Street. She would pass Cataldo's stand on her way to work, and that is how Cataldo made her acquaintance about a year and a half before his death. He wooed her with promises of marriage and finally seduced her, possibly with the use of drugs, alcohol, or a combination of the two. For a time, she took up residence with him, still hoping that he would fulfill his promise to marry her. On the morning of the homicide, Cataldo flatly refused to marry Maria and, after a spat during which she locked them both in their flat for a time, he managed to leave and go to a nearby dive where he would meet his fate.

A short time later, Maria and her mother arrived and urged Cataldo to fulfill his promise of marriage. Cataldo suggested that he might if Maria's mother gave him $200.[325] Apparently Maria and her mother left, but then Maria returned. She had taken a razor from a trunk and concealed it on her person. She once again demanded that he marry her, and Cataldo replied, "Do you think I would marry such a girl?" When she persisted, he taunted her saying, "Only pips marry!" or "Only pigs marry!"[326] At that moment Maria drew the razor across his throat. He staggered as far as Avenue A before dropping and bleeding out. Witnesses testified that Maria wandered, seemingly indifferent, toward a grocery where she washed her hands in a bucket of water near the shop window and then went into the building where she and Cataldo had been living. There she cleaned up, changed from her bloodstained clothes into her nicest clothes, and put on her best hat. She sat on a chair near the window and waited for the police. When the police arrived, Maria said, "Me take his blood so he no take mine. Say me pig marry."[327]

Maria had the bad luck of drawing Recorder John W. Goff as her trial judge. Goff has been described as "cruel and sadistic."[328] Lloyd Paul Stryker said, after appearing before Goff, that "as I gazed up at the bench I felt like some fourfooted denizen of the jungle that suddenly stares into the cold visage of a python."[329] Newman Levy, Abraham Levy's son, who also appeared before him, reports that "[w]hen he charged a jury in a criminal case, it sounded something like this: 'Whst, whst, whst, GUILTY!...Whst, whst, whst, GUILTY!...Whst, whst, whst, GUILTY!' It did not matter if the jurors understood anything else he said; that one word uttered with the explosive force of a rifle shot was burned indelibly in their minds."

Being indigent, Maria also had no choice of counsel. Judge Goff had that call, and he appointed Amos Evans, a little-known lawyer who may have had political connections with the judge and appears to have been beholden to him, for some reason. Evans was assisted by Henry Sedgwick. It was his first case. According to Idanna Pucci's *The Trials of Maria Barbella*,[330] Evans and Sedgwick met with Maria only once before the trial. They interviewed her in the Tombs one evening. Perhaps they did not view her case as being that important to them. They did have an interpreter with them, Benedetto Morossi. Pucci makes much of Morossi's limitations, as well as Maria's limited English. The meeting was a short one. It appears that after Maria explained her history with Cataldo, his refusal to marry her, his taunt, and her actions, they packed up and left. She would not see her lawyers again until the day of the trial.

Defense counsel may have improvised the defense during the trial. To the extent it can be ascertained, the defense was to the effect that Cataldo was the victimizer and Maria the victim. The defense opening statement was given after the close of the State's case. Sedgwick announced that Cataldo's *modus operandi* was to seduce women with promises of marriage, which would later be broken. Cataldo was a depraved and lascivious character who had provoked the attack.[331] Goff interrupted the opening, insisting that Sedgwick had gone beyond the facts of the case.[332] After the opening, Evans moved to have the charge of first degree murder dropped, but Goff denied the request.[333]

Maria took the stand in her own defense, but her testimony was presented with difficulty—in part because of the need for translation and in part due to her own limited understanding of the proceedings. After she told the story of her relationship with Cataldo and the events leading to his death, the defense wanted to call other witnesses to provide similar testimony. Judge Goff would have none of it.[334] He refused to allow the testimony for a variety of dubious reasons—it was inadmissible evidence of the victim's character, it was cumulative, and it actually made things worse for defendant. Indeed, all of this was initiated by Judge Goff, the prosecution only objecting later when defense counsel renewed efforts to get the evidence in.[335]

Judge Goff's charge to the jury was as unfavorable to the defendant as he could make it. Before giving the charge, he commented that "[a] jury has nothing to do with mercy. The law knows no distinction of persons. The law does not hold women less responsible than men. The female sex is sometimes used as a cloak for the most horrible crimes."[336]

The jury was out for only an hour and a half before announcing a guilty verdict, and it was reported that Maria showed no emotion, even after the verdict was explained to her.[337] A few days later, Maria appeared for sentencing. Her new defense counsel, Frederick House, moved for a postponement, but Goff opined that he had no discretion in the matter and pronounced the death sentence.[338]

News of the death sentence turned the case into a national *cause célèbre*. Philanthropist Mrs. Rebecca Salome Foster[339] and expatriate American the Countess di Brazza (Pucci's ancestor)[340] hired the firm of Friend, House & Grossman[341] to appeal Maria's conviction. Foster and the Countess di Brazza also organized a petition drive seeking clemency from Governor Levi Morton.[342] This was the beginning of a war between the sexes—fought out in the editorial pages.[343]

Letters crying out for clemency were countered by letters from male correspondents urging the governor not to interfere.[344] One whined that a man, Filippo Giampata, had gotten five years just for stabbing but not seriously injuring a woman "against whom he really had exactly the grievance which…Barbella only says she has against the man whom she murdered."[345] Another complained of the cost of housing her in Sing Sing and the cost of special prison matrons to attend her. "She gets better treatment and food than the other convicts. [I]t is ridiculous to let the case drag along the way it has."[346] Critics likened her case to that of another woman, Chiara Chignarralli, who had been sentenced to death for shooting down her husband. Her sentence was commuted to life imprisonment after a plea that she was dying of consumption. It was argued that Maria was benefitting from the same undeserved "maudlin sentiment":

> There seems to be but one code of honor among Italians
> of the lower east side, and all violations must be wiped out
> in blood. Consequently the sympathies of these people are
> extended without [unreadable] to the girl who wielded a
> razor with a hand of iron.[347]

One letter writer suggested that all of the emotionalism supported an argument against "the extension to women of the suffrage" and criticized the double standard that would free a woman but not a man. "It is a distinct infringement of the principle that what is sauce for the goose is sauce for the gander."[348]

A most fascinating response was sent in by a woman from Cape Cod, alluding cryptically to the *Brown* case in Kentucky, in which a husband was acquitted of the murder of his wife and her lover on the theory that such vengeance was justifiable. This Brown affair was presumably the now obscure case arising from the killing of Archibald Brown, the son of the Governor of Kentucky, John Young Brown. He had been carrying on with Mrs. Nellie Bush Gordon, the wife of Fulton Gordon, a member of a prominent Louisville family. Gordon caught up to the pair at Lucy Smith's "house of assignation" in Louisville, Kentucky, and gunned them both down. The trial judge dismissed the case at the close of a preliminary hearing, issuing the remarkable opinion that "[the defendant's] action will teach adulterers and the adulterous when they ply their infamous calling, they are standing upon a precipice over an abyss into which they are in danger of being dashed at any moment."[349] The Brown case was not pressed further. So much for the sauce rule. The *lex non scripta* sometimes proves mightier than logic and evidence.

From the other side of the gallery, calls were made for assistance for Maria's family,[350] and mass meetings were organized by Americans of Italian birth.[351] Two people actually claimed that they were willing to die in her place![352] Sob sister[353] columnists stoked the emotions of the public,[354] pointing out that Cataldo was a cad who deserved his fate. Henry Blackwell, a woman's rights activist, wrote that "if every man who seduces a child of fifteen and leaving her no practical alternative but suicide or a life of prostitution, were promptly put out of existence, the morals of the community would be vastly improved."[355] Another piece stated, "The woman suffragists have also taken the occasion to enforce some of their principles upon public attention,"[356] attributing to Susan B. Anthony:

> My opinion is ever and always against murder, whether by the individual or the State, but especially am I opposed to the State's murdering a young woman who can not understand our language and for a crime that is condoned

in a man, young or old, with scarce a reprimand. The law refuses to punish the man, who, under promise of marriage robs the woman of her chastity. But when the forsaken creature takes summary vengeance the New York law consigns her, without judge or jury of her peers, to a most ignominious death—whether by electrocution or hanging—for women in the State of New York have no political peers among men save those inside the State prisons, the idiot and lunatic asylums.[357]

This piece also included a statement attributed to Mrs. Mary A. Livermore, favoring a pardon:

A jury of women would have acquitted Maria Barberi. I would have acquitted her. A man shoots down his wife's companion, and though a form of arrest and trial is gone through with, it is but a form, for the man is acquitted, and the public says that it is alright. When a woman undertakes to avenge her innocence she is condemned to death. I for one can not blame Maria Barberi. If the law will not protect women—and it won't—they must protect themselves. I would have done what she did myself. I say now, as I have always said, that if a man had the temerity to ruin a daughter of mine I would strike him dead without hesitation. He would not occupy the same planet as me. The Governor should pardon her.[358]

The governor played it safe: "There will be no occasion for action in the case on my part until after the appeal which has been taken is decided in October."[359]

Frederick House, the senior partner of the firm, argued the appeal.[360] The opinion of the New York Court of Appeals[361] took Goff to task for a variety of errors. He had been, as we would say today, overactive. He was chided for improperly excluding witnesses who could corroborate Maria's history with Cataldo, injecting improper comment in his jury instructions which intruded on the province of the jury, and allowing and participating in protracted cross-examination in which the same question was repeatedly asked and answered—by the "suggestion and direction of the court." The justices alluded vaguely to other unspecified rulings "difficult if not impossible to defend." The court focused on the fact that Maria had been convicted of first degree, or premeditated, murder.

> If [Maria] inflicted the wound in a sudden transport of passion, excited by what the deceased then said, and by the preceding events, which, for the time, disturbed her reasoning faculties, and deprived her of the capacity to reflect, or while under the influence of some sudden and uncontrollable emotion, excited by the final culmination of her misfortunes…the act did not constitute murder in the first degree.[362]

The court further noted an important disadvantage, also emphasized in Pucci's account of the first trial—Maria's lack of English.

> Her testimony was delivered in a foreign tongue and reached the jury only through the medium of an interpreter; and, in that process, it may have lost much of the fullness and force which a narrative always derives from being transmitted directly to the court and jury in their own language.[363]

This disadvantage was compounded by Goff's refusal to allow in the testimony of other witnesses as to the relations between Maria and the victim. The appellate court held that this testimony was admissible on the crucial question—Maria's state of mind. Goff had kept all that out. The court observed that Goff's notion that the excluded evidence was actually injurious to the defendant was bizarre: "[I]t is not apparent how [this] hypothesis could have been seriously entertained."[364]

[I]t is plain that the case was tried upon the theory that the
relations of the parties, prior to the morning of the homicide, had no bearing upon the question of deliberation and
premeditation, and that was the principle upon which the
evidence referred to was excluded. This will be made plainer
by reference to the charge of the learned recorder to the jury.

[Goff had charged the jury that] "You are only called upon
and expected to determine, by your verdict, what was the
condition of the defendant's mind at [the time of the attack];
and the only way in which you can determine such condition,
and the only way known to law and to reason, is by the acts
of the defendant at that time; and by those acts and from
those acts you may infer the operations of this defendant's
mind. ...These instructions excluded from the consideration
of the jury all the facts and circumstances preceding the
homicide, and of which that act was but the culmination.
This part of the charge renders the ruling excluding the
corroborating proof intelligible, but we think that both the
ruling and the charge were in these respects erroneous."[365]

So Maria was granted a new trial on the theory that the excluded
evidence was admissible to negate premeditation and to defeat the
charge of first degree murder.

When Warden Omar Sage was told of the action of the court
of appeals, he was greatly relieved. He did not look forward to
officiating at the execution of a woman, and his wife had taken a
great interest in Maria, teaching her to speak and read English. It
took some time for Maria to understand the meaning of the news
from Albany.[366]

Maria's case was one in which delay was to work to the advantage
of the defendant. While in the Tombs prison awaiting her second
trial, Maria was attended by a Matron Smith. She also received
the continuing attention of the Countess di Brazza. Just as Maria's
second trial began, "Gathered About Town" in The New York Times
included a report portraying Maria as industrious, as she kept busy

knitting gifts for her many supporters.[367] Also included in this piece was a review of a New York City performance by the celebrated Cherry Sisters, whose hideous stylings were the subject of a famous defamation case which established the critic's right to fair comment:[368]

> "The Cherry sisters do not represent such an unusual type," said the man who saw the entertainers—that word is the only one which covers their varied accomplishments—on their first night.
>
> "Why, you would not have to go any further than—well, say, Flatbush," he remarked nonchalantly, "to duplicate them." It is hard on Flatbush. But then, the critic knows the place only by reputation.[369]

One might say that they, too, were pioneers in the area of women's rights; but they were really terrible performers.

Maria's English would greatly improve while she waited for her second trial. Moreover, Hearst's *Journal*, in a spectacular turnabout, would come out in support of a novel defense offered by her new lawyers—Maria was the product of a degenerate family and suffered from psychic epilepsy, which had caused her to cut Cataldo's throat while under the influence of an epileptic frenzy.

Chapter Six

There Was Something More About Maria

Madonna Mia! is still her cry;
But mark her vacant stare.
There's madness in that glaring eye.
The madness of despair.[370]

Many Victorian and Gaslight lawyers, including the notorious William F. Howe,[371] turned to psychiatric defenses, often to manipulate the truth. Insanity, psychic epilepsy,[372] automatism, and altered states were hot topics in the medical jurisprudence of the day on both sides of the Atlantic.[373]

The second Barbella trial would present a classic battle of such experts. The prosecution presented the testimony of a number of experts, including Dr. Hamilton; the defense presented four. I'm particularly intrigued by the testimony of Dr. Ales Hrdlicka, who was only twenty-eight years old at the time of the trial. He would provide the scientific-looking data supporting the defense experts' opinions that Maria was not responsible for her actions.

Ales Hrdlicka immigrated to the United States in 1881 and received a medical degree from the Eclectic Medical College of the City of New York in 1892.[374] He entered private practice and received some additional medical training at the New York Homeopathic Medical College. Hrdlicka developed an interest in the work of Cesare Lombroso, the Italian criminologist, and anthropometry, which involved measurements of the human body, human variations, and their application to the study of the insane. In the third edition of his treatise, *Criminal Man* (1884), Lombroso opined on the links between atavism and degeneration, his theory being in part that generations of sick people would pass down their mental abnormalities and that each generation would get progressively worse.[375] He went on to define a type of criminal, "the Epileptic Criminal (*delinquente epilettico*). In this kind of criminal, criminal epilepsy, disguised as psychic epilepsy, and moral madness characterized by unidentified epileptic seizures appear together."[376] These sorts of theories were discredited early in the twentieth century but had some following in the day.[377]

In 1894 Hrdlicka joined the staff at the State Homeopathic Hospital for the Insane in Middletown, New York.[378] His involvement with legal proceedings began with his testimony in the Barbella case. Later he would obtain positions at the New York Pathological Institute (1896/7–1899) and then at the American Museum of Natural History (1899–1902), and he would become curator of physical anthropology at the Smithsonian (1903–1943). In 1895 he wrote a paper, "Contribution to the General Pathology of the Insane (Physical Examinations and Measurements),"[379] in which he described himself as being among the class of scientists who would establish "on the principles of heredity and related natural laws, the facts that certain psychical abnormalities are in very close and more or less steady relations with certain physical abnormalities."[380] Hrdlicka acknowledged his debt to Cesare Lombroso.[381]

Dr. Hrdlicka was the first of four experts called by the Barbella defense. According to Pucci, Hrdlicka presented a forty-page report to each juror, although he did not read it to them.[382] Much of the presentation was directed by defense lawyer Edward Hymes, who had joined the team because of his experience with insanity cases. On the other side of the "v." was veteran prosecutor John F. McIntyre.[383] The draft of the hypothetical question presented to Hrdlicka was delivered to court in a satchel by a "boy," and it took two hours to read![384] It was as much a premature closing argument as it was a question.

The other three experts would testify that at the time of the infliction of the wound upon Cataldo, Maria suffered from a spell of psychical or psychic epilepsy. Dr. Hrdlicka's opinion, based on his voluminous history of the Barbella family members and on his detailed anatomical measurements of them, was to the effect that Maria suffered from hereditary infirmities that manifested themselves physically and psychically and that the sum of the effects of this hereditary predisposition amounted to a form of epileptic condition. Furthermore, the condition was not, strictly speaking, the disease of epilepsy but more of a persistent epileptic inclination which, under special circumstances, was capable of some form of epileptic manifestations.[385] Adding all of this to the testimony of Maria and other witnesses, he opined:

> [T]here was an aura, or at least aura like symptoms, following immediately the emotion aroused by [Cataldo's] taunts. There was a great, sudden heat in the head and a flash before the eyes and then a darkness; further on [Maria] denies every recollection.
>
> The deed was extremely abrupt, without the slightest warning to anyone, and it was brutal, particularly so, the slayer being a woman. Immediately before the deed a witness saw [Maria's] face turn deathly pale and her eyes roll. A second or two after the infliction of the wound there was a fall to the ground. A spontaneous rise soon after; no attempt to escape; pale features; some gesticulation on the sidewalk and some words. Then [Maria] says she noticed blood on her hands and, thinking she had injured her hands in some way, she examined them, and then washed them on the street in a pail of water from a grocery store. She was seen to act according to this description.[386]

Dr. Hrdlicka did not get off of the stand unscathed. McIntyre treated him rather roughly and at one point made him look rather foolish. He handed Dr. Hrdlicka sheets of paper bearing the outlines of human heads, getting the doctor to opine on the normality of the subjects.

The first outline, which suggested abnormality according to Dr. Hrdlicka, turned out to be that of the head of William Vanderbilt, the son of the railroad tycoon. Another that was "not quite normal" was that of a United States senator. The third, which was "normal" but "a little too big," was that of the trial judge.[387] In his memoir Dr. Hamilton takes credit for having set up Dr. Hrdlicka for this little trap.[388] At Dr. Hamilton's death the exploit was celebrated in an article in *The New York Times*.[389] The author of the article went so far as to credit Dr. Hamilton with the exposure of an "audacious imposter." One assumes that it was a moment of some embarrassment for Dr. Hrdlicka, but in the end it does not seem to have made any difference.

One can imagine many lawyers and law students in attendance as Judge Henry A. Gildersleeve delivered his charge to the jury.[390] The judge singled out the testimony of Dr. Hamilton, who had testified that Maria was in possession of her faculties at the time of the murder. In his discussion of the conflicting expert testimony, the judge described Dr. Hamilton as the one expert "who is practically not attacked by either side."[391] One might have thought that this would have been a road sign pointing to a conviction. The judge was also careful to instruct the jury that Cataldo's bad character was not to be considered as a justification for the attack.

For its part, the defense had certainly made every effort to inject the theme that Cataldo had deserved what he got.[392] House had declared in his closing argument that "[t]he only truth here is that Maria Barbella suffers from epilepsy. Distressed at Domenico's insults and unaware of her own illness, she killed a man whom, at any rate, the city will certainly not miss." This drew an "ovation" from the crowd and a rebuke from Judge Gildersleeve.[393]

This time the jury was out for only forty minutes, which might have suggested that another guilty verdict was coming. The verdict was "not guilty!" One suspects that the expert testimony, which took up so much time, may have made little difference in the end. Perhaps the lady from Cape Cod was onto something when she referred to the

Brown case in Kentucky. The jurors would not be moved by "science" but by sympathy for Maria or perhaps even more so by revulsion for the victim—if you will, the unwritten law that some people deserve to be killed.

Hamilton was critical of the likes of Cesare Lombroso, the Italian criminologist, and popular excuses for crime like psychic epilepsy;[394] and he was not exactly trusting of lawyers. This is what he had to say of the *Barbieri* case,[395] looking back on it:

> In 1881 [*sic*] Maria Barbieri was tried for the murder of her paramour and convicted by a hard-hearted jury who regarded the brutal killing as one calling for a first degree verdict. It was found possible to upset this on appeal, and a second trial was ordered. In the meantime an American woman of philanthropic inclination, who had married an Italian nobleman, became interested in the prisoner and secured for her a bright, energetic Jewish attorney. The defence now was to be insanity, or rather "psychic epilepsy" and Maria was to present that form of loss of memory or epileptic amnesia which had for a time been a fashionable defence. This called for a carefully prepared arrangement of the pawns on the board. Hereditary insanity was to be established, and as most of her family lived in the Italian province of Naples, the field was to be visited and a hunt made for defectives. I am told that some one went from town to town asking for information regarding apocryphal invalids and sowing the seeds of suggestion. A month or two later a second seeker for truth would traverse the same field and there then really seemed to be some knowledge that epileptic or insane persons who were connected by blood with the woman to be put on trial had really lived and died in the particular community. When the trial took place the court room was filled with bullet-headed Italians from the East Side of New York who according to the learned experts for the defence were brachycephalic or short-headed, "and therefore clearly degenerates." The medical testimony was certainly the most extraordinary I have ever known, and it had its effect,

for she was acquitted. The prisoner herself went on the stand and for an hour pretended she could not remember a single incident of the murder, although on the previous trial a year before she minutely detailed not only the successive steps of the killing, but her motives and alleged justification. Maria subsequently married a man who must have been quite devoid of the emotion of fear.[396]

Legitimate critique or sour grapes?[397] What the doctor was told is interesting but not evidence. On the other hand, after reviewing Hrdlicka's file, my own medical friends at the University of Kentucky question the diagnosis of epilepsy,[398] while speculating that Maria may have had issues relevant in a sentencing context, maybe even fetal alcohol effects; but, surprisingly, they credit the defense lawyers for their ingenuity. Hrdlicka's contemporaries were not even that generous. Dr. Ira Van Gieson, the director of the Pathological Institute of the New York State Hospitals for the Insane, and Boris Sidis, associate in psychology at the same institute, published Hrdlicka's study of Barbella, with the caveat that "The Institute does not hold itself responsible for anything advanced in this paper except the anthropological measurements." The two were critical of the concept of psychic epilepsy:

> So elastic is the term "psychic epilepsy" that it has been made to shelter cases where distinct consciousness and clear recollection of the acts committed are present. Such instances where the patient could give a detailed description of the acts, knew their nature and consequence, knew right from wrong, have been placed under "psychic epilepsy" simply because the patient declared that during the commission of the act he had not the will or power to refrain from violent, indecent or untoward acts, or because he really was under the dominance of an irresistible impelling power.[399] ...No theory can be applied to "psychic epilepsy," for "psychic epilepsy" is not at all a scientific concept.[400] ...Granted even that "psychic epilepsy" means something

definite, what it may possibly mean is a sudden onset of blind destructive fury. But if this be the case, shall we set down any one who commits a crime or an assault in an accession of rage as an epileptic?[401] The nature of epilepsy is such that its visitations permit of no premeditation or design in committing crime nor does it give time and thought for revengeful "epileptics" to get razors out of trunks wherewith to hack a man's throat open to the back-bone, particularly after previously announcing intention to revenge.[402] ...It often occurs in criminal cases that forgetfulness, "oblivion" or amnesia of the criminal act is taken to strengthen the plea of irresponsibility, the reason being that lawyers and "experts" frequently confuse amnesia with unconsciousness. From the fact of amnesia, unconsciousness is inferred, because the two are thought to be identical.[403] ...[A]mnesia in no wise implies unconsciousness. The two are not the same. ... The fact that one can not remember what has happened to him does not in the least imply that the past state was an unconscious one.[404] "[P]sychic epilepsy" must not be given any serious considerations on the witness stand. And we sincerely hope that the time is not far off when the encyclopedic "experts" with their fondling "Psychic Epilepsy" will be barred out from our courts of justice.[405]

Of the evidence presented in the *Barbella* case, they had this to say:

In the efforts made to vindicate the woman a whole, unsuspected, highly complicated and well-rounded life history of the culprit, suddenly sprang up—a history that read as smoothly as a novel and which strongly appealed to the emotions of the jury and community. This life history, entirely incompatible with, and contradictory to, the whole course of examination of the first trial, seemed as if suddenly to have arisen in the second trial—to offer a plea for the presence of "psychic epilepsy" during the commission of the crime.[406] ... The compilations and investigations from legal sources in the paper following this [that is the Hrdlicka study] show evidence of neuropathic manifestation in the family history of Maria Barbella, and in so far as the sources of the testimony which furnished the anamnestic data [These are taken in substance from the hypothetical question in the second trial.] in that article are to be considered trustworthy there is presumptive evidence of attacks of some kind resembling epilepsy at rare intervals in Maria's past history. [However] [t]he subsequent paper does not offer any sort of proof that the crime was committed in the midst of an epileptic visitation, nor does it confront the incompatibility of the testimony in the first trial (dead perhaps to subsequent court procedure, but not to science) with the whole story of the epileptic visitations in the commission of the crime.[407]

Maria's case would not be the last in which psychic epilepsy was offered as a defense. It was used successfully to secure the acquittal of Dr. Elmore E. Elliot, a prominent[408] physician who was charged with an inexplicable assault on a Mrs. Catherine Walsh, her husband, and a police officer, on Lexington Avenue at Sixty-fourth Street in 1907.[409] Dr. Elliot testified that he had suffered from attacks of psychic epilepsy since childhood and that he had no memory of the activities he was charged with. "Lawyers who heard the defense and members of the District Attorney's staff... agreed that [the scope of the defense] was practically limitless, and asserted that psychic epilepsy would undoubtedly prove a successful defense, even for murder."[410] Strangely, no mention was made of the Barbella case.[411] A few days later, several medical men commented on the case. Among them, Dr. Hamilton warned of the possibility of "impostors" or fakers, known as "dummy chuckers."[412]

My own opinion is that the defense was completely bogus, if well intentioned.[413] Still, there will always be curious defenses and unlikely outcomes. The Calgary Sun recently reported that a Canadian judge has accepted the proposition that a man was not responsible for beating an "escort" with a baseball bat and raping her—because he was sleepwalking at the time.[414] There was also the infamous "Twinkie Defense."[415]

Debate over the role of experts is not new and continues to this day. Dr. Hamilton, prosecutor McIntyre, and defense lawyer Abraham Levy were all able to discuss the subject intelligently.[416] I will leave you with the words of a skeptic, published in *The New York Times*:

> The "eminence" of the experts, upon whom the public search-light is now being thrown, is due principally to their pull and to reportorial boosting. Much more than mere reading and self-assurance are needed to qualify a physician for expert work in such a difficult field as that of forensic psychiatry. In ultimate analysis, however, it is our legal and political system which is responsible for this deplorable state of affairs.
>
> Medicus
> New York, July 13, 1906 [417]

To be fair to Dr. Hrdlicka, he played an important role in securing justice in another case. In 1915 in Blount County, Alabama, Bill Wilson was convicted for the supposed murder of his ex-wife, Jenny Wade Wilson, and her nineteen-month-old child. The couple had been divorced in 1908. Shortly afterward, Jenny and her child disappeared. In 1912 bones were found sticking out of a bluff in Warrior River. It was speculated that the bones might be those of Jenny and the child. With the aid of a jailhouse snitch, the prosecution secured a conviction in the face of medical evidence that the bones were those of an elderly person and a child who had second teeth. After the conviction, Dr. Hrdlicka (now curator of physical anthropology at the Smithsonian) determined that the bones were old remains of as many as four persons. While a plea for clemency was pending, Wilson's lawyers found Jenny and her child quite alive, living in Indiana.[418]

The press had one more go at Maria. It seems that a reporter tried to get Mrs. Julia Sage, the wife of the Warden of Sing Sing, to cooperate in persuading Maria to participate in a mock execution.

The proposal was rejected.[419] Nothing has much changed with the media since then—anything for a story.

In the Southern ballad tradition, when anything really bad happens, somebody writes a song about it. But that is not exclusively a Southern tradition. Here are the words of a street ballad sold at the time of Maria's second trial:

> 'Tis not for me to speak aloud
> On lofty themes. I tell
> As one among the lowly crowd
> How Young Maria fell.
> Swift as a flash a glittering blade
> Across his throat she drew,
> "By you," she shrieked, "I've been betrayed:
> This vengeance is my due!"
>
> Behold her now, a wounded dove:
> A native of a clime
> Where hearts are melted soon with love
> And maddened soon to crime.[420]

Chapter Seven

Mr. Howe's Last Case:
The Best Show in Town

"I had the prettiest case, and here is all my work shattered—
all my roses frosted in a night."[421]

R ichard Rovere's amusing summary of Nack-Thorn-Guldensuppe,
what he calls "the last of ['Big Bill's'] many celebrated cases when
he was sixty-nine,"[422] fills a scant six pages[423] in *Howe & Hummel:
Their True and Scandalous History*. After tracking down the contemporary newspaper accounts to get the true facts, I discovered Rovere's
account was wildly inaccurate in several important respects. Just as
Hollywood invariably tampers with history, coming up with stories
much less interesting than the truth, Rovere mangled and severely
abbreviated a really good story. Still, Rovere's version is catching, and
I will try to summarize it.

Augusta Nack, the unlikely *femme fatale* of a love triangle, a
midwife by profession, is described by Rovere as "a woman of operatic
contours [as in the fat lady who sings last?], handsome features, and
volcanic emotions."[424] The original Mr. Herman Nack, her husband,
had been the proprietor of a "bologna shop" when he succumbed to
excessive drink and lost his business. Without bothering to secure
a divorce, Augusta hooked up with Willie Guldensuppe, a good
looking "rubber" at a midtown Turkish bath. Then along came barber
Martin Thorn. When Guldensuppe did not appreciate being replaced
by Thorn, he beat Thorn up. But the controlling Augusta convinced
Thorn to help her dispose of Willie.

The *locus in quo* was a cottage in Woodside (in Queens County, New York). Augusta lured Willie to the cottage, where Thorn (well-equipped with a revolver, a bottle of acid, a hammer, a poisoned dagger, a rope, and a knife)[425] lay in wait. The victim was apparently shot, stabbed, decapitated, and then cut up. Rovere asserts (the truth is less certain) that Augusta used her midwife skills to dismember the body in a bathtub, with the thought that running water would get rid of the blood while the two conspirators took a ride on the ferry, at which time they committed Willie's plaster-of-Paris–coated head to the sanctity of the East River.[426] Alas, the best-laid plans "oft gang agley." The cottage drains had burst, and water and blood mingled in a small pond where a duck discovered it—only after much of the water had evaporated. The owners of the duck were alarmed by the blood adhering to the little creature's feathers, and they reported the anomaly to the police. So, at least according to Rovere, the mysterious disappearance of Willie was "solved by a duck."[427]

Thorn hired Howe to represent him, and Augusta retained separate counsel. Again, according to Rovere, this was done to avoid the appearance of an alliance,[428] although Howe expected to control the case. After all, information control is the name of the game for the criminal defense lawyer, sometimes even in the face of obvious conflict of interest. Because the pair had done such a thorough job of dismembering Willie and scattering his parts (the head was never found, nor was a telltale fruits and flowers tattoo, which had been sliced off of his chest.)[429] Howe stuck to the theory that the dismembered body found by the authorities was not Willie. Assuming that he ever existed, Willie could still be alive. Rovere continues:

> In the view of most correspondents at the trial, Howe was unquestionably on his way to winning an acquittal *for both* [Martin] *Thorn and* [Augusta] *Nack* when Mrs. Nack confessed. Her confession was the by-product of a conversion. The confession, of course, took care of Thorn; he got life, and Augusta got nine years. It was scarcely less calamitous for

Howe. *The trial was nearing its end when it came*, and he was already at work on a summation that would probably have been his crowning glory.[430]

In fact, Augusta Nack had her own lawyer who was his own man, the confession came shortly after jury selection in the first of two trials, and in the end, Thorn paid with his life for his part in the murder.

My narrative is based on the wonderful, illustrated coverage of the proceedings which appeared in *The New York Herald* from November 7, 1897, through August 2, 1898. As I read *The New York Herald*'s daily record, I was taken by a number of things. First, the quality of newspaper reporting of court proceedings was, in my opinion, far superior to today's newspaper and television coverage. Crime reporting was something of a minor art form. Admittedly, the journalistic ethics of the day were somewhat wanting. The reporters certainly heaped a lot of praise on Howe, and one assumes that he paid for some of it. The unnamed reporters in *The New York Herald* often wrote in the first person and, at times, seemed to have had a participatory role. Still, whether journalistic ethics have improved any since the turn of the century is probably debatable. Who would deny that all forms of today's media have their own share of shills and claqueurs?

This quaint case may be a distant mirror in other respects. As in the high-profile cases of today, the flamboyant defense counsel would take center stage from the start. He was the celebrity, and his client's fortunes would ebb and flow depending on points scored with the rustic jurors. Moreover, all through the coverage of the case, the journalists stalked the jurors and caricatured them. Since time immemorial, juries and judges have provided useful scapegoats.[431] There would also be planted stories, at least one alleged to have been fraudulent,[432] juror interviews, and other familiar trappings of today's trial by media.

Howe came on with his usual theatrics. During jury selection in the first trial, "His enormous shoulders were covered with a grey business suit, a flaring Medusa's head of jewels sparkled upon his vivid necktie and his fingers scintillated with gems."[433] Not only did he glitter in his magnificent finery, but he also had his own counsel table brought into the little courtroom in Long Island City.[434] The trial was the best show in town. The corridor adjoining the courtroom was wired for telegraph service so that the New York papers could follow the trial blow by blow. It was also reported that several new saloons were opened to "gather a harvest during the famous trial."[435]

The prosecution's theory of the case was set out in the November 8, 1897, issue of *The New York Herald*, an opening statement for all to see, alluding to evidence, confessions, and the like:

> [The murder] was supposedly committed on Friday, June 25 [1897] in a cottage rented for the purpose in Woodside, Long Island. William Guldensuppe, a Turkish bath attendant, was killed by Martin Thorn, a barber, and his rival in the affections of Mrs. Augusta Nack, while the latter nonchalantly waited in the yard below until the deed had been done.

> Then the body was dismembered in a rather crude way and the headless and legless trunk, wrapped in oilcloth and other coverings, was thrown into the east river, where it was found by two boys, floating near the foot of East Eleventh street. This within twenty four hours after the supposed commission of the crime.

> Scarcely has the police decided that a murder had been committed when, on the morning of June 27, another part of the mutilated body was found in Ogden Woods, near Washington Bridge. This grim bundle was wrapped as the other had been, in oilcloth, brown wrapping paper and cheese cloth. That oilcloth will prove one of the strongest links in the chain of evidence that the State is attempting to wind about Martin Thorn and Mrs. Nack, for it was afterward learned that the woman had bought oilcloth of a similar pattern.

In spite of the fact that the head was never found, the mutilated remains were identified by several as those of Guldensuppe. Later the missing legs were found near the Brooklyn Navy Yard. They, too, were in oilcloth and wrappings similar to those employed on the other parts of the body. By these, on account of certain physical peculiarities, it is claimed, the identification was made positive.

Finally came the arrest of Mrs. Nack, then of Thorn, the latter being found through a confession that he made to John Gotha, a barber, employed in the shop in which the supposed murderer had worked.

According to this confession, Mrs. Nack enticed Guldensuppe into the Woodside cottage, while Thorn waited for him in a closet above. As the bath rubber passed the closet, it is alleged, Thorn shot him, and then dragged the body to the bathtub, where he dismembered it. He afterward, according to Gotha's story, wrapped the parts of the body up and threw them into the river; the head he coated with plaster of Paris before it went into the water. Since he has been under arrest Thorn is alleged to have made another confession to the Long Island City authorities, and also to have been found with a letter making damaging admissions, which letter he attempted to swallow when discovered with it.[436]

In spite of this preview of the district attorney's case, Howe was supremely confident as the first trial opened. Although Martin Thorn and Augusta Nack were to be tried separately, he assumed that the unity of the defense would not break, and he was equally certain that the prosecutor would not be able to prove that the dismembered remains were those of Guldensuppe. He reportedly had a lineup of "analytical and anatomical experts" prepared to controvert the prosecution's forensic evidence.[437] Certain "distinctive marks" shared by the remains and by Guldensuppe—the great toe of the right foot protruding over the second toe, and a scar on the left forefinger caused

by the removal of a felon (in this case, another word for an abscess)—
were said by Howe to be "comparatively common."[438] Furthermore,
few bloodstains were found in the cottage in Woodside, which Howe
argued would have been "deluged in blood."[439] He felt strongly that his
defense could not be upset unless the missing head were found and
were proved to be Guldensuppe's.

At first even Augusta seemed to exude confidence. She
presented her lawyer, Emanuel "Manny" Friend, with a "huge
bundle of lace" which she had produced during her confinement.[440]
Friend, too, was upbeat. Not only was he in attendance to view
the evidence which might later be presented against his client, but
also he had his own fans in the audience, including a former client,
Maria Barberi.[441] Maria sat in the gallery with her new husband,
basking in the sunshine of her own celebrity status.[442] In those days
it was not uncommon for defense counsel to place "bullet ads" in
the daily papers, working the public at large if not potential jurors.
Friend placed ads—"No Direct Proof of Guilt"—stressing the fact
that the case was one of circumstantial evidence only and that the
defendant could not be convicted unless all theories of innocence
could be excluded.[443]

At first Howe and Friend expressed concern that it would be
difficult to find jurors who had not been affected by pretrial publicity,
and suggested that it might take as many as ten days to complete
jury selection. It came as a surprise, then, that a jury was selected
in a single day.[444] Although most of those selected had read news
accounts of the case and had held conversations about the case with
their friends, all counsel seemed well pleased with those selected.
Howe even expressed satisfaction with Juror Bumstead, who was a
friend and neighbor of the district attorney![445] Many of the jurors
were "the familiar country types," and "rawhide boots outnumbered
by far the patent leathers."[446] The names and faces of each juror—and
many personal particulars about them—were splashed across the
pages of the newspaper.

It was not long before *The New York Herald* would begin to caricature these "guileless farmers." In a story titled "Jurors Live Like Kings," a reporter told of an extravagant dinner served up to the jurors at the county's expense. Here was the menu:

> Oysters, Half Shell
> Mulligatawny, Crout au Pot
> Consomme, en l'asse
> Olives, Radishes, Lettuce
> Boiled Halibut, Egg Sauce
> Cucumbers, Potatoes, Natural
> Corned Beef and Cabbage
> Chicken Fricassee, with Peas
> Scallops en Case Paulette
> Sweet Corn Fritters, Brandy Sauce
> Ribs of Beef
> Roast Duckling, Apple Sauce
> Stewed Parsnips, New Beets, Spinach
> Mashed and Boiled Potatoes
> Fried Sweet Potatoes
> Cottage Pudding, Peach Pie
> Jelly Turnovers
> Assorted Cakes, Vanilla Ice Cream
> Fruits, Crackers, Cheese, Nuts and Raisins
> Coffee

Overheard conversations between these "rubes," accurate or invented, about their good fortune in being selected to partake of this cornucopia were printed with the sarcastic comment that "the county pays the freight."[447]

Opening statements would begin on Wednesday, November 10, 1897. But before Martin Thorn's trial proper could even begin, Augusta did a terrible, unspeakable thing (I am speaking as a lawyer, of course)—she confessed! A *New York Herald* reporter had confirmed the fact of Augusta's epiphany the night before, when he

ambushed Emanuel Friend outside the Harlem Opera House. The
excited Friend admitted that:

> Mrs. Nack has confessed. That is all I can say. She has
> confessed and will go on the stand tomorrow for the State
> against Thorn. Even Mr. Howe does not know. I shall go
> home, disconnect my telephone, and refuse to see any one or
> answer any questions. She has made a full confession, that's
> all I can say.[448]

Friend did call Howe before retiring, and Howe was furious. Talking
to *The New York Herald* reporter, Howe exclaimed in frustration:

> This is atrocious. I had the most perfect defence ever presented
> in a court, and only this evening I wrote to Mr. Hummel, "Abe,
> I was never so happy. I can demonstrate first that they can't
> identify that body as that of Guldensuppe, and further that it
> was not cut up in the Woodside cottage."
>
> I had the prettiest case, and here is all my work shattered—
> all my roses frosted in a night.
>
> I am utterly at a loss to understand how any lawyer with the
> entire absence of evidence against her, could have sanctioned
> her making a so-called confession.
>
> I do not believe Thorn killed Guldensuppe, if the man was
> killed. That woman Nack may have done it, if there was any
> cutting up, but Thorn has denied to me from the first to last
> that he did any killing or that he did any cutting. And I say
> that all my surgeons and anatomists have agreed with me that
> only a person skilled in anatomy could have dismembered
> the body the way it was dismembered. Mrs. Nack has shown
> herself to be an expert anatomist, and if there has been any
> cutting up of anybody of the name of Guldensuppe, I say she
> did it, not Thorn.[449]

Augusta's confession seemingly derailed Howe's "misidentification" train; but the great bear had always been light on his legal feet, and he recovered quickly enough with a new theory—what lawyers nowadays would call "Plan B." Augusta had killed and dismembered Guldensuppe; Thorn had been but an accessory![450] Thorn would not give up. Let the trial begin! Howe made a gruesome promise. He told the reporter that he would subpoena Augusta's husband to testify about his wife's "disposal of infants' bodies"![451] (More about this later.)

Why did Augusta confess? It is possible that she did so on counselor Friend's advice. He certainly defended her decision—and his own conduct—against Howe's attacks.[452] For his part, the district attorney insisted that he had made no promises to her to induce the confession. There is also the possibility that her initial confession was not done on the advice of counsel at all or with the knowledge or participation of the prosecution. A story emerged that a Rev. Robert H. P. Miles, of the Ravenswood Presbyterian Church, and his little son had visited her in her cell and that the visits had worked on her conscience. On one visit, and reportedly at Augusta's request, Rev. Miles brought a rocking chair from her Ninth Avenue house—a chair that the unfortunate Guldensuppe had supposedly favored. Rev. Miles delivered a carefully worded plea that she unburden her mind and ease her conscience if she were indeed guilty. As the little boy sat on her lap, she reportedly broke down and confessed.[453] Rovere suggests that this morality play was the invention of William Randolph Hearst, whose paper, the *American*, was in hot competition with *The New York Herald*.[454] There is some evidence that Augusta had already confessed to others, and that her jailhouse conversion to the truth had been the brainchild of Hearst and had been sold to Augusta and then the district attorney, who presumably would have wanted to cast her betrayal of Thorn in the best light possible. In any event, Augusta ultimately made a full confession to the district attorney, and she agreed to testify at trial.

Howe would respond with further attacks on Friend and a bullet ad of his own, describing his client as the "Chivalric Thorn" and Augusta as "Delilah Nack."

> Mrs. Nack's late in the day concoction has already been so thoroughly dissected that the entire community looks upon her with abhorrence. Borgia in her palmiest days was a white winged angel in comparison with this destroying, as well as creative, creature."[455]

His was not the only negative assessment of Augusta Nack. Not long after her arrest, *The New York Herald* published a remarkable psychological analysis of Mrs. Nack, provided by Dr. E. C. Spitzka, whom we met in our discussion of the murder of Carrie Brown. On the opening day of the first trial, *The New York Herald* triumphantly republished Dr. Spitzka's opinions and speculations about "her life of dark intrigue," including a prediction that she would confess to her part in the murder.[456] According to *The New York Herald* writer, "Dr. Spitzka said…that if guilty she was looking for an accomplice whom she could betray if cornered." Like the lawyers and other "expert commentators" on modern television court shows, Dr. Spitzka was not shy about reading all kinds of things into "body language."

> [Dr. Spitzka] "I noticed a frequent moistening of the lips with the tongue and an occasional nervous glancing over her shoulders."
>
> [Reporter] "What do you infer from this?"
>
> [Dr. Spitzka] "That if she is guilty and the accomplice is caught she will turn State's evidence against him. She is not of the type that would sacrifice herself for another or refuse any avenue of escape because it compromises another.
>
> "If, as is said, she was not registered as a midwife and never reported a birth to the Board of Health that fact would throw ghastly suspicions upon her and lead to the inference

that she might have been in the habit of disposing of the bodies of children stillborn or prematurely born in exactly the way she disposed of Guldensuppe's body. If, in addition, the report be true that she was contemplating baby farming on a large scale, you can easily imagine how callous she might have become to cutting up human bodies for the purpose of concealing a doubtful occupation."[457]

Howe could not have asked for a better talking head. This reportage set things up for Howe's expected cross-examination of the confessed murderess and State's star witness, if and when she were to repeat her confession in court. One wonders if Howe or one of his minions had reached some prior understanding with the helpful Dr. Spitzka.

Meanwhile, the prosecution used the first day of trial to present the testimony of sixteen witnesses,[458] who together accounted for the finding and identification of Guldensuppe's body parts, as well as the red and gold oilcloth purchased by Augusta to wrap them in. The oilcloth made for a particularly loathsome and odoriferous exhibit, and the court attendants who had to handle it wore black rubber gloves for the occasion. Despite the obvious difficulties presented, the prosecution proceeded methodically and laid the proper foundation for the admission of the physical evidence, in spite of the "grinding" of Howe's "objection mill." Howe demanded that no photographs be admitted, insisting that all actual body parts be presented. Needless to say, these objections were summarily overruled.

The most important witness of the day was the "morgue keeper" and prosecution forensic expert, the aptly named Isaac Newton. Newton was a knowledgeable and cautious witness who consulted his notes and memoranda carefully before answering questions. He had examined more than five thousand bodies during his career, and he had been called by the prosecution to identify and assemble the parts and come up with a Guldensuppe. Howe cross-examined him vigorously and professionally. He wanted to establish that the body could have been that of a missing Virginia photographer by the name of Edwards, who had supposedly been identified by certain visitors to the morgue. Newton was able to dodge this bullet, but Howe seemed to be scoring some points as he looked at each of five so-called identifying peculiarities one at a time. Defense lawyers always stress that each individual piece of evidence, or circumstance, means little on its own.

Nothing plus nothing is nothing. He got Newton to admit that Newton himself bore a scar on the same finger as the victim, also the result of the removal of a felon. Newton also admitted that he had seen an overlapping great toe on a number of victims. There was a mole under the right arm, but moles are common too. The scar from another minor surgical operation was a bit more of a problem, but Howe was obviously very pleased with himself. District Attorney William Young rose to the occasion:

> "You have seen other bodies with such strange features as twisted toes, or moles in certain spots, or scars in other spots, or possessing one of the five peculiarities mentioned. But did you, [very solemnly], did you ever before see a body *bearing all five marks?*" [emphasis added]

"No," said Newton promptly.[459]

Howe responded with the suggestion that Newton had recently made a false identification of a young murder victim. The question seemed to shock and surprise the prosecutor, but Newton did not overreact and he steadfastly denied any such thing. Howe must have been reaching, because he accepted the denial and let the witness go. Overall, the prosecutor had had a good day, but Howe was still in the game. Indeed, the judge wrapped up the first day with a mild rebuke of the prosecution for running out of witnesses. The prosecutor indicated that the next day he would call the coroner, Dr. Philip O'Hanlon, to testify that the cause of death was a stab wound through the heart. He would also present barber Gotha's testimony regarding Thorn's confession to him, testimony corroborating Gotha from a jailbird by the name of Frank Clark, and, of course, Mrs. Nack. The stage was set for the great confrontation between Big Bill and Augusta. Would he prove himself, once more, to be the irresistible force; or would she prove to be an immovable object?

On the second day of the trial, Thursday, November 11, 1897, Augusta took the stand to recite her self-serving version of the crime, which more or less jibed with Gotha's repetition of Thorn's confession to him. She insisted that her role in the murder was to rent the Woodside cottage and lure the victim there and to hire a surrey to transport the parcels containing the body parts. At the close of the direct, she wept when asked by the prosecutor why she was now confessing. She answered between sobs that she was testifying "for the people, for the world, and for God."[460]

Howe then cross-examined Mrs. Nack in a manner that was "comparatively brief" but ruthless and relentless. He soon drew her anger. Howe mocked her tears and her claim that she had been controlled by her "frightful love" and then suddenly changed track: "How many children did you kill?"—"Is it not true that you shot Guldensuppe?"—"Is it not true that you cut his body to pieces?"— "What did Mr. Friend tell you to do?" Howe brought out that, although the pistol used had belonged to Thorn, it had been taken away from him by Guldensuppe after their earlier fight and had been put in Mrs. Nack's charge. She, not Thorn, had the knowledge of anatomy to cut up the body. When she was arrested, she had $200 sewed into her corset. "Did you not intend to go to Europe?" "Well, er, yes," (Mrs. Nack taken aback). All this was the prelude to Thorn taking the stand to insist that she had committed the murder alone. When the cross-examination had been completed, the prosecution called a series of witnesses who knew Guldensuppe well, to testify that the remains they had seen at the morgue—and the photographic evidence representing the body—were Guldensuppe. Howe did not ask a single question of any of them.

Then the sixth juror, Magnus Larsen, became very ill with appendicitis. Howe was much distressed by this development because he was convinced that as things stood he could win. He liked this jury, he thought he had bested Mrs. Nack, and he was ready to put on a show. He had even brought an elaborate manikin to court in a big box to use in demonstrations. Now Larsen was "under the knife," and his doctors predicted that, if he were to recover, he would not return for at least three weeks.[461] A desperate Howe suggested that the eleven other jurors be re-empaneled, that a new juror be added to replace Larsen, and that all the testimony be re-read to all; but Judge Wilmot Smith decided to declare a mistrial. Howe became angry and excited, confronted Manny Friend in the courthouse corridor, and violently denounced him.[462] Meanwhile, the eleven jurors had been enjoying their day off and, when they were discharged, they "mourned the loss of a good thing."[463] They were ridiculed in an elaborate cartoon.[464]

Jury selection in the second trial began on Tuesday, November 23, 1897. There would be a new judge too. Judge Samuel Maddox took the place of Judge Smith, who had become ill and had retired from the case. This time Howe was committed to the new defense—that the remains were indeed those of Guldensuppe but that Augusta—not Thorn—had killed him. Jury selection proceeded apace, and it is worth noting that Howe used a technique in *voir dire* familiar to one used by modern lawyers. He asked elaborate hypothetical questions in an effort to indoctrinate the jurors. It is hard to tell how effective he was. Again it is fair to say that Howe was a pioneer in the use of modern techniques; but you have to have something to work with. The jurors seemed to be more baffled than indoctrinated.[465]

Howe's new technique during jury selection was not the only new forensic twist. District Attorney Young was about to snooker his old adversary after all. In his opening statement Young laid things out much as before, but he did not mention Mrs. Augusta Nack as a witness![466] Howe was taken by surprise. He still believed that, if she had not broken down, he could have won the case based on reasonable doubt about the identity of the remains. He still had hope that he could successfully attack her on the stand and deploy his army of forensic experts to prove that the murder—and dismemberment in the bathtub—could not have occurred as she said it had. After all, several of the jurors from the first trial had told reporters that they had not believed Mrs. Nack. The prosecution was not going to call her as a witness? With the benefit of one trial run under his belt, District Attorney Young had apparently concluded that the case could be made, and made stronger, without her. In any event, there was no need to make a final commitment one way or the other. Augusta Nack could be held back in reserve as a rebuttal witness.

Howe was surprised, but he recovered to the extent that he formulated a plan to bring her former testimony back in and to make her the issue by reading sections of her testimony back to Thorn and asking him if he remembered hearing it in the first trial. Still, it is obvious that he was taken aback and worried,[467] and there were other disturbing features to the new trial. The disgusting oilcloths in which the dismembered Guldensuppe had been wrapped had not been disinfected. The Long Island City courthouse was "deficient in ventilation"[468] and reeked of death. In spite of this, Howe again contemplated demanding that the actual body parts be produced at trial. When his associate Joseph Moss went to the morgue to check the condition of the disassembled Guldensuppe, he "was overcome." Reporters could not resist adding (a nice journalistic touch) that Augusta went too and viewed the remains without emotion, picked up a shriveled hand to look for the scar associated with the removal of the felon, and then ate a hearty meal afterward.[469]

The trial proceeded with the witnesses called at the former trial before Augusta Nack had testified. That is, the jury heard from the boys and men who had found the body parts, the policemen, the morgue keeper, and Guldensuppe's fellow employees at the Turkish bath who identified the reconstructed victim. It was anticipated that the next day's testimony would include that of John Gotha, to whom Thorn had allegedly confessed. But there were two other surprises.

First, there was a sensational and inexplicable development when police Captain Stephen O'Brien, who had been in charge of the investigation, was called as a witness. O'Brien had examined the defendant after his arrest, but he had kept the results to himself. There had been rumors of the third degree. Thorn had originally denied any role in the murder and had named alibi witnesses, but the witnesses had "flatly contradicted him."[470] During Howe's cross-examination of the captain, the witness refused to tell all that had passed between him and Thorn. "There was something else said, but I passed my word of honor not to reveal it, and I won't." O'Brien would not reveal it to the prosecutor either, on redirect, and surprisingly, the judge sustained an objection by Howe!

The suspicion was that Thorn had told O'Brien that he would admit his part in the crime if he were spared death in the electric chair. There seemed to be a difference of opinion as to whether Thorn was trying to shield Mrs. Nack in the process or whether he was willing to give her up.[471] A *New York Herald* reporter claimed that at that point Thorn was willing to admit that he had shot Guldensuppe to death, dragged his body into the bathroom, and cut him up in the tub.[472] Legal experts joined in the fray, opining for the benefit of *The New York Herald*'s readers that O'Brien had no basis for refusing to testify and might be stonewalling to cover up his own misconduct in the course of obtaining a coerced confession.[473]

Also surprising was a new line of testimony from the coroner that Guldensuppe's death was caused by a stab wound to the heart.[474] This was inconsistent with the shooting theory, but it could still be reconciled with Gotha's anticipated testimony that Thorn told him that Guldensuppe was still alive when he was thrown into the tub for the dismemberment. The first "cut" could have been a fatal wound to the heart. Other notable testimony included that of more witnesses who would place Thorn at the scene of the crime and would identify him as the person who paid the rent for the Woodside cottage.

Less sensational—but in some ways more interesting—was the duck evidence alluded to by Rovere, of which I promised the reader confirmation. Again, after the ruling on O'Brien's testimony, the prosecution called witnesses to trace the movements of the players at the Woodside cottage on the day of the murder. Among them he called a Mr. Walley to the stand. Walley testified that he saw a man in a blue suit, whom he identified as Thorn, enter the cottage at half past eleven. He saw the same man leave a half hour later and then return. He then described a ditch at the roadside.

Q: "Did you see anything in that ditch on June 26?"

A: "Yes. I saw blood."

Walley would explain how his ducks, by coming home blood-stained, had led to a search of this ditch, into which the drain of the cottage emptied. Howe could not shake his testimony that the blood came from the cottage drain.

Q: "Are you the man that saw the ducks?"

A: "I own the ducks."

Q: "Was the drain dry?"

A: "It might have been slimy."

Q: "And that which you call blood was mixed with the slime?"

A: "Yes."

Q: "Are you sure it was blood?"

A: "It looked like blood."

Q: "How do you know that drain came from the cottage we speak of?"

A: "I saw the plumber put it in."[475]

Walley said that he saw a woman, whom he identified as Mrs. Nack, go into the cottage at noon and leave between three and four o'clock in the afternoon. Walley's wife confirmed his testimony.

She had seen a man and a woman enter the cottage at about eleven in the morning. She identified Guldensuppe as the man and Mrs. Nack as the woman. She never saw Guldensuppe come out. She saw another man enter the cottage around noon and come to the door of the cottage several times during the afternoon.

Thanksgiving meant a day off for the jury. Some jurors attended services at the Garden City Cathedral, while others treated themselves to a round of the "newfangled" game of golf. Then there was lunch and, afterwards, billiards. Some found their day monotonous, but a sumptuous dinner put them all back into the proper humor and fortified them for the next day's work.

DINNER

··

··

Thanksgiving Day
Garden City, November 25, 1897

··

··

Oysters, Half Shell
Soup
Mock Turtle au Champagne
Consomme in Cup
Olives, Radishes, Celery
Broiled Bluefish
Cucumbers, Potatoes
Small Fillet of Beef
Sweetbreads, Brains-en-Caise, Doulcase
Mutton, Caper Sauce
Peignets Souflees a l'Orange
Ribs of Beef
Spring Turkey, Cranberry Sauce
Turnips, Boiled Rice, French Peas

Mashed and Baked Potatoes

Sweetbreads

Mallard, Duck

Fried Hominy, Lettuce Salad

Indian Pudding, Brandy Sauce,

Apple Meringue Pie

Cakes, Nuts, Sherry Jelly

Crackers, Cheese

Coffee[476]

The prosecution would rest its case on the testimony of John Gotha. For his part, Howe planned to put Thorn on the stand—not to deny that he spoke with Gotha but rather to deny that he had told Gotha the details of the crime. Thorn would stand fast with his story that he was still trying to shield Augusta Nack at that point. Howe still assumed that the prosecution would be forced to call her in rebuttal.[477]

Gotha's testimony tracked earlier accounts of what he had told police the day after Thorn's arrest. He told the jury how Thorn had threatened to kill Guldensuppe for the beating he gave Thorn at Mrs. Nack's place. He had shown Gotha the pistol and knife he was going to use. He also added some interesting details to Thorn's confession to him—that Thorn had said that Mrs. Nack had "made a botch out of the job" by buying the oilcloth in Astoria and that he, Thorn, had also made a fatal mistake by not investigating the connection of the Woodside cottage plumbing to the open ditch outside. *The New York Herald* reporter noted with interest that Gotha had obviously been following the reports of the investigation printed in *The New York Herald*. Howe would later plead in the paper that the "confessions" attributed to Thorn by Gotha were nothing more than elaborations of these earlier news accounts.[478]

In any event Gotha's testimony was quite gruesome. Thorn said that he had shot Guldensuppe in the back of the head and, after reporting the same to Augusta, he then dragged Guldensuppe and put him into the bathtub. Next he cut off Guldensuppe's head with a razor while the victim was still "snoring."[479] Then he cut up the body into four parts—cutting off the telltale tattoos, as well—and wrapped the parts in oilcloth bundles. The two wrapped the head in cheese-cloth and plaster of Paris. The body parts and the head were dumped in the river and somewhere near Kingsbridge. Although Howe was able to "hammer" an admission by Gotha that he had received money from the district attorney's office for subsistence,[480] he was unable to break the witness.

A few more prosecution witnesses followed, tying up some lose ends relating to various items of physical evidence. Some of this tended to corroborate the details that had been related by Gotha. Then, after a recess, District Attorney Young announced to the surprise of the crowd, "May it please the Court, the People rest their case."[481]

Howe opened his case on Monday. He spent much of his opening statement painting a portrait of Augusta Nack as "the Lady Macbeth of modern days." She was the killer, and Gotha was an "inebriate" and "a paid and perjured witness." Thorn was "merely a poor, infatuated idiot."[482]

Thorn took the stand to tell his story. He had not killed Willie Guldensuppe. Instead he had gone to meet Augusta Nack at the Woodside cottage where she had gone the previous evening. When he got there, she had already shot Guldensuppe. She wanted him to help her dispose of the body. He helped her undress the body and get it into the tub. He held back the head as she cut through the flesh of the neck and then sawed through the bone. He then went to a nearby grocery for plaster of Paris and, after encasing the head, he went to the Ninety-second Street ferry and dropped the head into the river. The two of them got rid of the rest of the body the next day. Thorn apparently held up well under cross-examination, and one headline said that he "Evaded the Prosecution's Dangerous Question so Skilfully [sic] as to Cause Mr. Howe to Chuckle."[483]

Coverage of the rest of the defense case is limited. Perhaps, as in modern high-profile cases, much more was promised by the defense in the media warmup than could actually be delivered at trial.[484] Three barbers who worked with Thorn were called to give him a good character. Furthermore, Howe requested a jury view of the crime scene, and *The New York Herald's* Wednesday edition includes among "Characters in and Incidents of the Last Day of the Thorn Trial Illustrated" a drawing of the jurors inspecting the bathtub. What Howe had in mind is not clear. Presumably the view would provide grist for his closing argument. Howe accompanied the jurors and said that Thorn was waiving any right to be present. Later he would assert that a defendant cannot waive any such right and that he would appeal on that ground in the event of a conviction.

It was reported that Howe was in bad health, but he was credited with "one of the ablest [summations] he ever made"; District Attorney Young was also credited for an "Eloquent Appeal."[485] The jury was instructed by Judge Maddox and, after a few hours, the crowd scattered for lunch.

At half past four Judge Maddox returned to the bench. More time passed, and then something happened. The jury had reached a verdict. It was 5:34 p.m. when they announced, "We find the defendant guilty." A voice "almost pleading in its softness was raised."[486] It was Howe. He was asking that the jury be polled. Later it was reported that a guilty verdict would have been returned after five minutes, had not one juror spoken up and suggested that they should take more time lest they be accused of "unseemly haste"; and seven ballots were taken, if only for appearance's sake.

On Friday, December 3, 1897, Thorn was sentenced to death. It was said that he took the sentence coolly and "did not move a muscle." An illustration of the proceedings shows Howe slumped in his chair, spent, chastened, and dejected. Still, he clung to his hope that he could get the case reversed, apparently on the basis of his odd theory that Thorn could not legally waive his right to be present at the jury view. Thorn was taken to Sing Sing. On the way, someone stole his hat as a souvenir.[487] The remains of Willie Guldensuppe were placed in the possession of "the association of bath rubbers" for burial.[488]

Whatever the grounds of appeal, Howe was unable to save his client.[489] Martin Thorn went to his death on Monday, August 1, 1898. Even after he had received a telegram from Governor Frank Black that there would be no commutation of his sentence, he seemed to maintain his nerve.[490] Much was made in print of the fact that he was resigned to his fate and that he had confessed to his guilt before God, but as he made his final walk to death he lost his nerve and was a "pitiable sight."[491]

The *New York Herald* reporter observed that the setting of the electric chair was "like a little wayside chapel" and quipped that "[t]he electric chair suggested its appropriateness to the man who had spent his life over a similar chair as a barber."[492] He spared the reader nothing in his description of Thorn's last moments:

> The priests were chanting the "De Profundis" in a heart breaking cadence, and when the solemnity and terror of it all was at its height, there came a jerk and a blow, a shock as if a cable car at [sic] struck the chair, which could not move because it was bolted to the floor. Thorn's chin and jaw shot upward only an inch or two, as if from a blow. Thorn was dead as if struck by lightning. Not a word was said. Every man was immovable except the electrician, who threw his lever over again, gave Thorn another shock, which a little later was again repeated. This time we looked around to see what was burning. A barely perceptible odor like that of an overhot flatiron on a handkerchief pervaded the chamber, but there were no blue flames playing about the exposed calf of the leg, nor any of those horrors said to have taken place at executions in years gone by.[493]

Thorn's body was claimed the next day by his brother-in-law,[494] and his body was buried in Calvary Cemetery in Queens County, New York. It was reported that:

> A conspicuous feature of the funeral [was] a massive floral wreath of blue, mauve and green, containing a floral cross of white. It [reportedly cost] $45, and the name of its donor [was] a closely guarded secret. When asked if it was from Mrs. Nack the undertaker smiled and said: "I will neither deny nor affirm your question." Then he smiled again.[495]

What happened to Augusta Nack? The question of her punishment was the source of much journalistic excitement. Again the talking heads emerged. A variety of lawyer-experts, mostly former prosecutors, shared their views as to the proper and expected punishment in the papers.[496] In the end she made a plea deal and was sentenced to fifteen years.[497] Further comment would be superfluous.

Strangely enough, Guldensuppe would make another appearance. According to an article in *The New York Times* dated December 1, 1900, Peter Piernot, who was living with a family occupying the house in the Woodside where Guldensuppe was murdered, saw Guldensuppe's ghost. The apparition can be explained by Piernot's consumption of turkey and rich puddings, washed down by French wines and American whiskey, all while engaging in an extended discussion of the murder. The inevitable nightmare followed, and a screaming Piernot, wrapped in a blanket, fled to the train station, where he was collected by a Detective Sheridan.

I must give Richard Rovere the last word:

> [Howe] tried a few cases after that, but not many, and none that were famous. In 1900, he lapsed into chronic invalidism. He had several heart attacks, and then, on September 2, 1902 he died in his sleep at his home on Boston Road in the Bronx.[498]

Chapter Eight

Emanuel Friend:
"The Best Lawyer in the City"

A. [Witness Dr. Newton Whitehead stated that Sergeant Frink]…insisted that I should take a lawyer—Friend.

Q. Is that Emanuel Friend?

A. Emanuel Friend.

Q. Is that gentleman in court here?

A. If he stands up; I cannot see him.

Q. You can see Mr. Friend without that?

A. Oh, yes; the gentleman over there; I wanted Howe & Hummel, but [Sergeant] Frink said that Howe & Hummel was played out now and was no good, and that Lawyer Friend was the best lawyer in the city; he was mistaken about that.

Q. Never mind doctor?

A. And that Friend was in with the people at the courts and at headquarters.

[The thrust of the witness's testimony was that Friend took money from clients and shared it with the police and others to get cases dismissed.]

From *Report and Proceedings of the [New York] Senate Committee Appointed to Investigate the Police Department of the City of New York [The Lexow Committee, Clarence Lexow Chairman, John W. Goff Chief Counsel, William Travers Jerome Associate Counsel]*, Vol. IV at 4229 (1895).

Despite this suggestion, after the Nack-Thorn-Guldensuppe affair Emanuel Friend would have other cases worthy of note. The Scharn murder stands out because it remains to this day one of New York City's most frequently cited unsolved murders.[499]

On the morning of August 19, 1900, Young Kathryn Scharn was found murdered in her apartment on the third floor of 674 Second Avenue. The victim had been struck with a hammer several times, but none of the blows would have been fatal. According to the coroner, the cause of death was strangulation, and it was suspected, at first, that the ineffectual hammer blows pointed to a jealous woman as the murderer. This did not pan out and, in their search for a plausible suspect, the police tried to build a case against her brother, Frederick Scharn, who had found the body.[500] Inexpensive rings had been ripped from the victim's fingers and were found in a pawnshop. Frederick had an alibi, but the police seized on the fact that he had apparently stolen a watch from a neighbor and pawned it.[501]

Emanuel Friend entered the scene as Frederick's counsel and made sure that his client did not talk to the police.[502] The shoes and underwear of Frederick Scharn were examined but offered no clues, and the police were still baffled after a week's investigation.[503] Friend defended his client with zeal. "Do you intend this to be another 'Frenchy' case?" shouted Friend to a Coroner Bausch.[504] He insisted that this was a case of a police conspiracy—an attempt to "railroad" his client.[505] Frederick Scharn was saved when Friend produced a surprise witness at the coroner's inquest. Young Ella Conroy, the cashier at a grocery store, testified that she remembered Kathryn Scharn purchasing pears at the store around six thirty on the night of the murder, which corroborated the testimony of Frederick's other alibi witnesses—witnesses whom the police had marginalized throughout the investigation.[506]

There had been other suspects but, for reasons known only to the police, they had been disregarded. There was druggist Doc Tyler, who was Kathryn's landlord. Four years earlier, Mamie Cunningham had been murdered over on East Thirty-fourth Street. Tyler had owned that house too, and Mamie had been beaten with a hammer and then strangled. A man named Francis Farrell had been charged, but there was a hung jury. He was discharged.[507] Then there was a mysterious "man in gray" who, witnesses said, had been shopping with Kathryn. That lead was also ignored by a Police Inspector Harley, the man in charge, who apparently dismissed any evidence that did not fit into his theory of the case. It did seem like this was the Frenchy case all over again. Crime writer Lawrence Treat (Lawrence Arthur Goldstone) made the following observation:

> For some reason, Harley took a dislike of Fred Scharn. The inspector used all the power and trickery at his disposal to pin the murder on him. The inspector disregarded the trial of the man in gray and sought to twist evidence to his own uses. He was stopped cold by [the alibi witnesses] a grocer boy, a timid cashier and a girl of sixteen. Often enough, the little people get stepped on. But, though there was tragedy enough in the case of Kathryn Scharn, the little people emerged on top. Sometimes they do.[508]

Then there was the infamous *Kennedy* case. Friend and his partner Frederick House unsuccessfully defended Dr. Samuel J. Kennedy, a dentist, in his first trial. He was charged with the murder of Emeline "Dolly" Reynolds. The unfortunate Dr. Kennedy would be tried three times before finally being released. Here again there were suggestions of police incompetence or corruption. The case ended up on the shelf—one more famous, unsolved New York City murder.[509]

In his study of the case, written as a discussion between fictional characters Inspector Larry Davis and the brilliant, blind detective Captain Duncan Maclain, crime novelist Baynard Kendrick has the two crime fighters taking a hypothetical look back at the case fifty years after the fact. At the outset Inspector Davis makes the spot-on observation that "[t]he popular pastime of every witness connected with the case, including the police department, was changing his or her mind from day to day."[510] In the end Maclain came up with a solution to the mystery of the Dolly Reynolds murder which is probably correct—a burglar did it—but took some rather speculative reaches to account for some of the unexplained facts in the case, as well as the conduct of some of the players. I have based the following account on articles in *The New York Times*, as well as on the detailed statement of facts in the opinion of the court of appeals, reversing the judgment of conviction after the first trial.[511]

On the morning of August 16, 1898, a chambermaid opened the door of fourth-floor room 84 of the Grand Hotel and found the body of Miss Emeline Reynolds, also known as Dolly. Her head had been battered with a bludgeon, which was found in the room, but the coroner determined that the cause of death was a broken neck caused by one of the blows. The bludgeon was made out of a lead pipe, which was about seventeen inches long. An iron rod had been inserted in the pipe, and the whole instrument was wound at one end with tape. It was the sort of weapon that street thugs and burglars of the day might have carried. The rings had been stripped from the victim's fingers and her earrings from her ears. A satchel she was known to carry was found near her body—opened. What was odd was the fact that a check for $13,000, made out to "Emma Reynolds," was found underneath her corset when the body was undressed during the autopsy. The check was drawn on the Garfield National Bank, where Kennedy had an account. It was signed by "Dudley Gideon" and endorsed on the back by "S. J. Kennedy." Gideon did not exist, and the check was worthless. Some torn pieces of paper were also found. When the pieces were assembled, they proved to be a physician's prescription blank made out to "E. Maxwell and wife, Brooklyn." The prescription form was decorated with the words "Phillips Milk of Magnesia, 12 oz." Similar prescription blanks would later be found at Dr. Kennedy's office, but one assumes that others had access to similar prescription blanks. When the police confronted Dr. Kennedy with the check, he denied having seen it before, denied that the endorsement was his signature, and denied having been at the Grand Hotel in the company of the victim. He was arrested.[512]

The police investigation revealed that the victim had come to the Grand Hotel alone and had registered in the name of "E. Maxwell and Wife." She had dinner and then left the hotel, returning between five or six o'clock in the evening, accompanied by a man described as being about thirty years old with a dark mustache, wearing a blue suit and sporting a straw hat. The couple ordered a bottle of champagne. They left at seven o'clock and returned about midnight. The night elevator boy, Patrick Lenahan, claimed to have seen the same man sneaking down the stairs at two thirty in the morning.

Dolly had been living in a place paid for by a broker named Maurice Mendham. He visited from time to time, and a servant at the place thought they were man and wife. Her parents did not appear to know of these arrangements and believed that she was making her way selling books, while attempting to prepare herself for the stage (a familiar story, even today). The only apparent connection with Dr. Kennedy is that she had sought his services. However, her mother reported to the police that Dolly had told her that Dr. Kennedy advised her that if she gave him $500 to place on a horse, she could make $4,000. Assuming that Dolly had told her mother such a story, there was no way to verify it or to determine whether Dolly had some motive for making such a thing up.

Dr. Kennedy practiced with his father, and he had a wife and child. He denied having any connection with the victim other than a professional one.[513] He said that he did not own a straw hat, but he did wear clothing similar to the mysterious "man with a straw hat." His mustache was light, not dark like "the man in the straw hat." There was no apparent motive for Dr. Kennedy to have done the deed, and it seemed unlikely that a man of his education and station would have killed with a bludgeon of the type used by thugs and burglars. Still, he was "positively identified" by five hotel employees: chambermaid Mary Higgins, headwaiter Charles McCurry, waiter Stephen Burns, bellboy J. A. Davis (who had delivered the champagne), and elevator boy Patrick Lenahan.[514] Armed with this eyewitness identification (which we now know is famously unreliable), the police continued to focus on Dr. Kennedy, without regard to other possible suspects. They came up with a theory that Dr. Kennedy killed the victim when he was trying to recover the $13,000 check, which they theorized he had forged. That is, they thought the murder resulted from his attempt to cover up a crime. However, the check was dated August 15, 1898, the day that the "man with the straw hat" and Dolly Reynolds met at the hotel. Why would he give her a forged check and then kill her to try to get it back? Kennedy had some difficulty accounting for his whereabouts on the night in question and said that his memory was foggy because he was a user of chloral—meaning chloral hydrate, which was used as a sedative in pediatric dentistry. He said that he had spilled some on his clothing and that his memory might have been affected by it.[515] The detectives seized clothing from his home, and a pair of pants had a stain which might have been caused by his carrying a lead bar used in the construction of the bludgeon. Kennedy suggested that the mark could have come from a key chain he carried. The detectives also tried to establish that he had not returned to his home in New Dorp, on Staten Island, by way of train or streetcar at the time he had claimed.[516] The case took a turn for the worse for Kennedy when a store clerk at an establishment right across from the Grand Hotel identified the dentist as a man who bought a straw hat from him the very day of the murder.[517] How likely does it seem to the reader that a man planning a murder at a nearby hotel would, for the occasion, pick up an item of garb he was not known to wear? Kennedy's father hired the firm of Friend, House & Grossman,[518] and the "wrangling" over production of the prosecution's evidence began. It must be remembered that these were the days before evidence had to be provided to the defense in a timely manner.[519] Needless to say, Kennedy was indicted, and the police boasted that they had an "ideal case."[520]

Kennedy's first trial began on March 3, 1899, Justice Pardon C. Williams presiding. The prosecution laid out its glittering array of incriminating facts, emphasizing the eyewitness identifications. There were a few bumps in the road. Friend's cross-examination drew out some hedging from Lenahan regarding the certainty of his identification. An Officer Craven, who was the first cop on the scene, was forced to admit that he had not marked the bludgeon. He could only say that he was pretty sure it was the same one found in room 84. Friend also established that there was a fire escape at the windows of the room. Dolly's maid testified that she had never seen Kennedy visit.[521] Friend was planning on calling a Mrs. W. S. Logan to testify that she had occupied room 52, immediately below room 84, that she had heard what sounded like a body falling to the floor above, at about one o'clock in the morning, and that she later heard what sounded like someone climbing down the fire escape.[522] However, when she appeared, it was at the call of the prosecution, and she was uncertain as to when she heard the fall and would only say that later she heard a "rumbling sound" outside the Grand Hotel. Had the prosecutor gotten to the witness? Frustrated, Friend was unable to get what he wanted on cross-examination. The clincher came when Detective Arthur Carey testified as to the incriminating mark on the defendant's clothing and identified an iron bar (Exhibit 45) that he had found at the defendant's home, which he said corresponded in size to the iron bar found in the bludgeon. He also produced a two-inch piece of lead pipe (Exhibit 46) the "exact size" of the bludgeon. He went on to say that he found a vice in the cellar that had serrations corresponding to marks on the bludgeon.[523] Dr. Ernest J. Lederle, chief chemist of the Health Department, took apart the bludgeon and showed that its component parts were "identical" to the materials found at Kennedy's home. Then the prosecution over-egged the pudding with testimony from a Detective Sergeant Valley, who told the unlikely story that Kennedy had admitted to him "that while his mind was blank he might have gone to the hotel and killed the woman without knowing it."[524] Finally the prosecution called several handwriting experts to tie the written materials to the defendant.[525]

It was now time for the defense to respond. The defense produced the usual evidence of good character from a minister, along with the testimony of Kennedy's father that, at the relevant time, the defendant said he was going to the theater, that he was not wearing a straw hat, and that not one of the handwriting exemplars was his son's. Then there were alibi witnesses. Of particular importance was the testimony of Edward Ufer that on August 15, the evening of the murder, at about 6:45 p.m., he met Kennedy walking on the west side of Sixth Avenue. He was wearing a dark serge suit and a brown hat.[526] Mrs. Julia Sleyton testified that she saw the defendant at the South Ferry just before 12:20 a.m. and saw him, not long after, sitting in the ferryboat asleep. She remembered this because she had been looking for her son, who had disappeared from the army and was thought to be in New York. She was followed by the defendant's mother, who testified that she saw her son the night of August 15 about 2:45 a.m. He was asleep in bed. In his summation, lawyer House stressed the rather obvious point that the check alleged to be forged by Kennedy had been made out on August 15, the day of the murder. "Why should the defendant make a deadly bludgeon and lay plans to kill a woman to procure that which he had not given her?"[527] The judge gave an unfavorable charge to the jury. The jury returned in less than three hours to declare Dr. Kennedy guilty.[528] He was sentenced to death, although he declared his innocence and blamed his conviction on police perjurers.[529]

On appeal Dr. Kennedy was represented by William W. Cantwell and Robert M. Moore. There were a number of issues. In the press the defense stressed the absence of motive, as well as the illogic of the prosecution theory that Kennedy had prepared the bludgeon in New Dorp in preparation for murder but killed Dolly to get a check back that he had just given her.[530] The defense also came up with an affidavit made by Daniel S. Melville, a plumber on Staten Island, to the effect that he had been visited by a Staten Island policeman and an unidentified detective—who turned out to be Detective Carey[531]—who asked him about the effects from cutting lead pipe with a knife and with a saw. Melville claimed that after the visit he could not find the piece of lead he had used in his illustration to them. Was this the piece of lead that Carey swore at the trial was the piece of lead pipe he found in Dr. Kennedy's cellar? The affidavit went to the court of appeals, along with all of the original exhibits in the case.[532] This was an unusual procedure.

Rev. John Munro, the Tombs chaplain, visited Kennedy at Sing Sing after his conviction and before the court of appeals issued its opinion:

> I had a few words with Dr. Kennedy. I could see that he was in a state of great nervous excitement bordering on collapse, and no wonder, for his case was that day before the court of appeals. It was in the balance. The judges were then considering the circumference of the lead pipe which was the one thing in his case that lead to a new trial. A sixteenth part of an inch decided his fate! I looked at Kennedy again and again; he was a study! His eyes were like balls of fire, his hair stood upright, his hands held onto the steel bars of his cage and braced him while he spoke to his wife. The strain was telling on him! His face was pallid and he looked as if he had not slept in a month. Not only did he look dejected and worried on account of the ordeal through which he was then passing, but he looked like a man almost beside himself.[533]

The court of appeals reversed the conviction on a point of evidence which had not been raised by defense counsel by way of an objection.[534] Then, as today, counsel must make a contemporaneous objection to preserve an issue for appeal, but there had always been a safety valve, which today we call plain error. At trial, bellboy J. A. Davis had given his testimony identifying Dr. Kennedy as the man in the hotel room with Dolly when he served them. He had been subject to cross-examination. However, a Captain Price, who conducted the initial lineups, not only referred to the prior identification by the bellboy but also gave elaborate testimony of his instructions to the bellboy regarding the importance of the identification and of his duty to testify at trial, which tended to bolster the credibility of the identification. Davis also testified as to the identification made by waiter Stephen Burns, who did not testify at trial. He also alluded to an identification by the captain of the dining room. In other words, prejudicial hearsay[535] on the issue of identification, the critical issue in the case, had been admitted. The prosecution tried to argue that, because all of these pretrial goings-on took place in the presence of the defendant, the out-of-court statements were not barred by the hearsay rule and could come in as the defendant's adoptive admissions. The court rejected this argument, and quite properly so, because Dr. Kennedy had not been free to speak at the time and had even been ordered not to speak by the captain.[536] There were those who criticized the opinion of the court of appeals,[537] but Kennedy now had a second chance. When Kennedy received word of his reversal of fortune, he was congratulated by inmate Roland Molineux, who was in the next cell. Molineux's words triggered "a chorus of congratulations" from the other six prisoners on death row.[538]

Now for round two.

Kennedy's second trial would take several odd turns. Cantwell and Moore, who had secured the reversal of Kennedy's conviction, would try the case. To the surprise of many, they were successful in moving to exclude the testimony of the prosecution's handwriting experts on a technical ground.[539] Justice Edgar L. Fursman's reasoning was not sound,[540] but it appeared to be a big win for the defense. However, there were problems. The hat salesman was dead. Still, the court would allow in his former testimony. Mrs. Sleyton, one of Kennedy's alibi witnesses, was dead too. Worst of all, Daniel Melville, the plumber who had suggested that something was amiss in the bludgeon evidence, had disappeared—almost certainly with the help of the police. His steamship ticket to Florida had been procured by someone representing himself as a police officer.[541] But the good news was that Dr. Lederle's concessions, secured on cross-examination by Moore, were sensational. Remember that the police theory that the pipe supposedly found at Kennedy's home was the same as that used in the construction of the murder weapon:

> "Are the diameters of the lead pipe in the bludgeon and that of the piece claimed to have been found by the police the same?" began Mr. Moore.
>
> "They do not seem to be the same," answered the chemist.
>
> "If a piece of iron bar is severed, the ends should preserve some degree of lustre, should they not?"
>
> "Yes, if kept under the same conditions."
>
> "The end of the bar at the hook end of the bludgeon has some lustre, hasn't it?"
>
> "Yes."
>
> "And there is no lustre at either end of the separate rod, is there?"
>
> "No."
>
> "If these rods have not been tampered with and have been kept under the same conditions they could not have been, in your opinion as an expert, cut from the same bar, could they?"
>
> "No."
>
> "Doesn't the separate rod appear to have been drawn under a hammer and the rod in the pipe through a mold?"
>
> "The rod in the pipe seems quite uniform. The other seems irregular."

Dr. Lederle then conceded "that there was more rust on the separate rod than on the piece in the bludgeon." The cross-examination continued:

"Are the walls of the exposed end of the rod at the crook in
the bludgeon of the same thickness as the piece of lead pipe?"

"The walls of the bludgeon pipe are in places of different
thickness from the walls of the separate piece of pipe."[542]

The examination continued with Dr. Lederle admitting that
the inside diameter of the pipe supposedly found in Kennedy's cellar
was "considerably less" than the middle diameter of the bludgeon
pipe or the diameter at the exposed ends. "The walls of the detached
pipe, he testified, were also thicker than the walls of the bludgeon
pipe."[543] This was followed by the testimony of a teller at the
Garfield National Bank that the endorsement on the back of the check
was not in Kennedy's handwriting.[544]

Despite all of this, the jury was out twenty-three hours. Another
mistrial, but the votes had been eleven to one for acquittal. The prosecution put out a false story that the vote had been seven to five for
conviction. Sources for *The New York Times* confirmed that there
was only one holdout for guilty and that that juror was a close friend
of one of the prosecutors. One of the jurors would be moved to con-
tribute a check "for a substantial amount" for the defense in the event
of a third trial.[545]

Now a new prosecutor, the zealous, indeed relentless, James W.
Osborne, who had secured the conviction of Roland Molineux,
would have his shot at Dr. Kennedy. Osborne had been critical of
Justice Furman's ruling on the handwriting evidence and had opined
that the result might have been different had the evidence been
admitted.[546] In fact, the new judge, Joseph E. Newburger, would do
just that. Would it make a difference?

The third time around saw the prosecution's case crumble. First,
there was an *A Tale of Two Cities* moment[547] when many in the
courtroom "commented on the striking resemblance between the
contours of the profiles of the accused man and the Foreman of
the jury, Joseph E. Aue. They look[ed] remarkably alike."[548] A city
surveyor named Towle showed, by way of a diagram, that no one

sitting at the cashier's desk could have seen anyone coming down the stairs or go out the Broadway exit of the Grand Hotel, which contradicted one of the prosecution witnesses. Finally the proprietor of the hotel admitted that a burglary had occurred on the same floor the night of the murder and that entrance to room 84 could have been gained from the fire escape or from doors connecting the rooms.[549] Then the headwaiter who had identified Kennedy in prior trials admitted that he saw Dolly and her escort only momentarily and that he had more of a side or back view of them. His assistant also balked and said that, after he first "identified" Kennedy at the station, he admitted to the brother of an assemblyman that "it was Kennedy and it wasn't" and had been told to "keep his mouth shut." The star witness bellboy admitted that, the first time he saw "Kennedy," the man had a newspaper over his face and that the second time he only saw "Kennedy for a moment." He also conceded that the man he saw had a dark mustache and sharp features—Dr. Kennedy had a light mustache and a round face. Lenahan, the elevator boy, would only say that the man whom he took to the fourth floor with Dolly only "looked something like" Kennedy.[550] To top it all off, the prosecution's handwriting expert admitted on cross-examination that there were some dissimilarities between handwriting exemplars written by Kennedy and the endorsement on the $13,000 check.[551] A defense expert would follow up with testimony that in his opinion Dr. Kennedy did not write the endorsement or the "E. Maxwell and Wife" memorandum on the check.[552] Finally, the defense proved that Dr. Kennedy's commutation ticket for August 16, 1898, had not been "taken up" but remained in its place in his ticket book and confirmed his story.[553] Still the jury could not agree on a verdict. Kennedy was released on bail and was not tried again.[554]

Chapter Nine

The Guilty Girl Who Beat the Case

Emanuel "Manny" Friend died at the young age of fifty-one on November 1, 1904, at the height of his powers. He had gone to his office in the Pulitzer Building to attend to a client, after which he remembered that a payment on his life insurance was due. He filled out a check for the payment and gave it to one of his clerks to attend to. The clerk suggested that it would be easy enough to mail it, and Manny joked, "No, you'd better take it now, as I might drop dead this afternoon." Around noon he felt ill and went home. He went to bed, drifted into unconsciousness, and died before the family physician arrived.

The reporters who commented on his famous cases did a poor job. He was properly credited with securing a relatively light sentence for Augusta Nack in the Nack-Thorn-Guldensuppe case;[555] and it was correctly noted that he had represented the Algerian Ameer Ben Ali (or "Frenchy"), a.k.a. George Frank, in the so-called Jack the Ripper murder case of Carrie Brown. This was one of Friend's first cases (his actual contribution to the case was lackluster), in which he was aided by Abraham Levy and Fredrick House, as we discussed in chapters three and four. Indeed, it was suggested incorrectly that he later established Frenchy's innocence and secured his release from Sing Sing, which as far as I can tell is wrong on two counts. Frenchy was released from Matteawan, and I have found no evidence that Friend was involved in the pardon process. Governor Odell pardoned Ben Ali largely due to the efforts of social reformer Jacob Riis. Friend was certainly not the moving force.[556] Also mentioned was his successful defense of Maria Barberi (Barbella) who *The New York Times* noted had "shot" Domenico Cataldo (with a razor, you will recall).[557]

The obituary did not mention the infamous Patrick case, which will be discussed in chapter ten. Nor did it mention the Scharn murder or the sad ordeal of Dr. Samuel J. Kennedy.

By the time of Dr. Kennedy's first trial, Abraham Levy had set up shop with Henry W. Unger, a former district attorney who was something of a bookish genius on the intricacies of the criminal law. The year Manny died, Levy was forty-three and at his peak. Arthur Train, the creator of the fictional lawyer Ephraim Tutt, reportedly "compounded him [Tutt] out of three characters—Abe Levy, Abraham Lincoln, and Jesus Christ."[558] It was no surprise, then, that Abe would be selected to defend Nan Patterson, a "Florodora Girl"[559] accused of killing Thomas "Caesar" Young, a well-known gambler and "man about New York." In a way this case takes us full circle back to Ella Nelson's case—a man, a woman, and a pistol. Who brought the gun? Who was holding it when it went off? This is an old, old story but one that still draws court watchers to this day. According to Levy's son, Newman Levy, the trial of Nan Patterson inspired Bayard Veillier to write a popular play, *The Trial of Mary Dugan*—first performed in 1927.[560]

Let us set up the scene of the crime. Caesar Young was married when he met Nan Patterson. He was open about his relationship with Nan, and he more or less juggled his two relationships. Nan was not satisfied and pressed him to divorce his wife. This was not going to happen. Possibly in an attempt to break off the relationship, Young booked passage to Europe for him and his wife. On June 3, 1904, the night before their departure, Young spent the evening with Patterson. The two argued openly, trading recriminations in a Manhattan restaurant. At about seven o'clock the next morning, making excuses regarding last-minute preparations, he left the hotel where he and his wife were staying. He promised to meet his wife at the dock, before the nine thirty departure time. He met up with Nan in a tavern near Columbus Circle. After sharing an alcohol-laced breakfast, they got into a hansom cab for a ride to the pier. The style of the cab was such that the driver sat up above and behind the enclosed cab, so he would not have had a view of what was going on. At some point on West Broadway near Franklin Street, there was a gunshot. The driver and curious passers-by realized that Caesar had been seriously wounded, and the cab made off to the Hudson Street Hospital, where he was pronounced dead. Curiously, the smoking gun was found in Caesar's right pocket. He had been shot just below the left shoulder. In spite of this, Nan claimed that a despondent Caesar had shot himself in the chest! At one point she told the police that she had handled the gun, taking it out of Caesar's pocket and then putting it back in. The police also found several threatening letters which they tied to her.[561] One was a letter to Young from Julia Smith, Nan's sister, which suggested that Nan might do something to Young or to herself if Young left her.[562] This would come to be known as the "Julia letter." Nan was charged and would be put on trial for murder. She would be prosecuted by District Attorney William Travers Jerome, who had been elected on Seth Low's fusion ticket forged between the Citizens Union folks and the Republicans. The theme was reform and opposition to Tammany Hall. The assistant district attorney who would present the case against Nan was William Rand. The aggressive Rand has been described as having "a rather toplofty manner which did not always sit well with commoners on the jury."[563] Still, the forensic evidence looked good for the prosecution. The track that the bullet had taken and the powder burns made a suicide defense implausible.

To prove that Nan murdered Caesar Young with malice and with premeditation, the prosecution would try to prove that the gun was Nan's. The theory was that Nan's sister and brother-in-law had pawned jewelry to pawnbroker Hyman Stern, who then sold them the pistol. With considerable difficulty, the Smiths, who had made themselves scarce, were finally found.[564] In the meantime a number of unlikely witnesses would have their moments of fame in the newspapers.[565]

The first trial of Nan Patterson opened in November 1904, Justice Vernon M. Davis presiding. By the standards of the day, it promised to be dramatic. Both sides promised to use skeletons during their presentations to show the path of the bullet and to prove murder or suicide.[566] Levy even promised to bring the hansom cab into court and have Nan sit in it, although he did not say whether Nan would testify. During jury selection Rand surprised those present by announcing that there would be no eyewitnesses to the shooting and that his case would be entirely circumstantial. Still, the possibility of new eyewitnesses was brought up by the defense. Indeed, one of the talesmen reported the existence of a witness.[567] There were some dark clouds on the horizon. Julia's husband, J. Morgan Smith, had been subpoenaed, but this stockbroker who might identify the purchaser was reportedly incapacitated.[568]

Rand delivered his opening statement, laying out his case against Nan,[569] while Levy worked up an alibi for Smith, claiming that he and his wife returned from the track too late to reach the pawnshop.[570] Some new evidence came to light. Cabmen testified that they had seen a drunken Young strike Nan and force her into a cab in the early morning of June 4. A newsboy said that he had seen the two quarreling at about eight thirty the night before the shooting and that Young had struck Nan and pushed her into a cab.[571] All would come to a halt with a juror's illness.[572] There would be a mistrial.[573]

Nan's case would start anew on December 5, 1904. At this point, the prosecution was still stymied by the unavailability of the Smiths. Jerome, the so-called "Reformer," assumed that the defense had procured their unavailability and decided to employ a trick of his own by leaking to the press the notion that the Smiths had hightailed it because pawnbroker Stern could identify them as the persons who purchased the pistol that had been found in the victim's pocket. One assumes that he was trying to influence prospective jurors through the newspaper reporting.[574] In fact, when jury selection had been completed and Rand delivered his opening statement, he told the jury, "I will show you why Smith ran away, where he ran to, and who helped him run."[575] Rand followed up by calling, as a witness, defense lawyer Daniel J. O'Reilly. It is unusual for an opposing lawyer to be called as a witness and, in some instances, it can disqualify the lawyer-witness from continuing to serve as trial counsel. As far as I can tell, there were no arguments about such niceties in this case, but Rand's move must have caused a sensation. O'Reilly admitted that he knew the missing witnesses.[576] He would then spin this into a surprise attack on the defense, accusing the Smiths of being part of a conspiracy to harm Young and suggesting that unnamed members of the defense team were involved in improper conduct. He carefully excepted Levy from any such plot. Then things got interesting.

First, Dr. Ernest J. Lederle, former health commissioner, testified that he was unable to say whether black stains on the victim's finger were caused by gunpowder. Then Police Surgeon Charles Phelps testified that the bullet that killed Young had traveled from left to right and that the muzzle of the pistol was from four to five inches from the body when the shot was fired. Pawnbroker Hyman Stern was less helpful. He could remember that a man and a woman had purchased the pistol on June 3, but he could not describe them. He could not identify Nan as the woman.[577] Other highlights included the testimony of Young's widow. Nan was unable to look at the witness. Then there was a fight over the admissibility of the "Julia letter." It had been written by Julia Smith and had been intercepted by Mrs. Young. It could be taken as a threat by Nan against Young. It said:

> You know how my sister Nan loves you. She loves you better than your wife, and cannot be happy without you. I will not be responsible for what she will do to yourself if you continue to keep away from her.[578]

Levy and Unger argued, correctly, that it should not be admitted. Nan had not written it, and there was no evidence that she had known about it. To Levy's distress, Judge Davis changed his mind and admitted the letter. This was considered a serious blow to the defense. Mrs. Young provided additional testimony. Rand was ending with a strong and sympathetic witness, who would top off the prosecution case by testifying that Caesar did not own a gun.[579]

Levy's motion for dismissal was denied. What kind of defense would be presented? Would Nan testify?[580] In fact she did, perhaps over Levy's objection.

As Nan took the stand, she removed her large ostrich-plumed hat. Sitting on the bench with Justice Davis was the Earl of Suffolk. It must have been quite a scene. Levy took her through the story of how she met Young. She denied knowing anything about the "Julia letter" and denied ever having been in Stern's pawnshop. She explained that Caesar's wife had "trapped him into promising to go to Europe," denied that she and Caesar had quarreled that night, and said that Caesar had not struck her. She said that Young asked her to follow him to Europe and that she told him she did not want to go.

> As the witness reached this point in her story the spectators leaned forward and breathlessly waited for her description of the tragedy.
>
> "Do you really mean that Nan?" he asked me. "I've lost a lot of money, and now I'm going to lose my girl."
>
> "I answered that I did mean it, and he grabbed me and pressed me to him with such force that it hurt me badly. I struggled free. As I did so I heard a muffled report, and he fell forward on my lap. I saw no pistol. He half rose again, and I began to scold him, not realizing what had happened. Then he fell forward again, and I couldn't attract his attention. It seemed ages before I could get anybody to help me. Finally a policeman got on the front of the cab, and I was so glad that I cannot express it."
>
> "Nan," said Mr. Levy, "look at me. Did you shoot Caesar Young?"
>
> Miss Patterson returned his gaze steadily. "I did not," she replied. "I swear I did not. God knows if I could bring him back to life, I would."
>
> "That is all." said Mr. Levy...[581]

Rand had overnight to study a transcript of Nan's testimony that had been ordered up—what lawyers of my generation today call the "daily record."[582] The best description of the cross-examination is in Newman Levy's book.[583] It was hard on Nan but she held up well.[584]

Her testimony was followed by the testimony of Milton W. Hazelton, an elderly and somewhat eccentric businessman and inventor.[585] He had surfaced early on in the investigation. He had met a Masonic brother (whose name he could not recall) on the street at around eight o'clock the morning of the shooting. The place was West Broadway.

> I saw the defendant in a cab, which was coming in my direction. She was seated on the left side of a man. First I saw their hands making rapid motions in the air. Then the man had both his hands raised above his left shoulder, and I saw the flash and heard the report of the pistol. The man's head fell into the woman's lap, and she placed her hands upon it. His hands were not up at the time the shot was fired.[586]

He was not shaken by cross-examination.[587]

He had not wanted to get involved but had gone to the district attorney, who did not seem very interested.[588] Surprisingly, Hazelton said that earlier on he had been brushed off by the defense too.

Rand's closing argument was savage and was praised by many. In it he attacked opposing counsel, again without naming names:

> "I say," declared Mr. Rand, "that all this evidence of hers was prepared. I don't want to make any charges about my brothers in the profession, but I will say that there are those among her defense who are capable of manufacturing testimony which they know to be false. I name no names, but I stand ready to prove my statement."[589]

The jury deliberated for fourteen hours before reporting deadlock. A mistrial was declared.[590] The final vote had been six for conviction and six for acquittal.[591] Several letters to the editor of *The New York Times* argued that the press had been biased toward Nan and that there should be a retrial.[592] On the other hand, the popular feeling was that there would never be a conviction.[593]

Nan's second trial, if we don't count the mistrial, opened in the spring of 1905. By this time the Smiths had been run to ground and were firmly in hand.[594] The year 1905 was a very big one indeed. The Russo-Japanese War brought newspaper readers descriptions of huge land battles, ending in Russian defeat and the Russian Revolution of 1905. Einstein published his theory of special relativity and gave us $E=mc^2$. The Wright Brothers made the first flight that lasted more than thirty minutes. These were shades of things to come. But the big news story in the sensational press was Nan Patterson.

The fearsome Recorder John W. Goff, whom we met in the Maria Barbella case, would preside. Ordinarily, this would not bode well for the defense but, unknown to court watchers, by this time Goff and Jerome, who had been allies in the past, were at odds for some reason. Furthermore, Goff was not a fan of Rand.[595] No doubt there were some betting on the prosecution, on the assumption that pawnbroker Stern would identify the Smiths. However, as Richard O'Connor, a Jerome biographer, notes:

> The Prosecution's confidence in Stern as its key witness should have been diminished...by three factors: he was extremely nearsighted, he had sold the gun almost a year ago to a couple he had no reason to suspect of any criminal motives, and he was an almost painfully conscientious man.[596]

The jury ended up being packed with married men.[597] How would that play out? Sadly, no transcript of the trial is available, so I am somewhat dependent on Newman Levy's account. The prosecution laid out the same case against Nan, but there were some dramatic moments worthy of note.

To begin with, Rand opened boldly with a promise to prove that Smith bought the pistol from Stern. This apparently "crushed" Nan, and Recorder Goff adjourned court and had the windows opened to allow Nan to recover her composure.[598] At the risk of spoiling the surprise, the reader should know that it is never a good idea to promise in the opening statement what one is not sure can be delivered.

A police officer testified that, when he looked in the cab, Nan's gloves had been neatly folded. Dr. O'Hanlon would testify that there was no evidence of powder on Nan's hands, but the gloves were now missing. Odd?[599] Levy jousted with the experts. Then came the big moment, with pawnbroker Stern on the stand:

> "Is that the man [pointing to Smith] who purchased the pistol?" asked Mr. Rand.
>
> The crowd in the courtroom looked on with intense interest while Stern glanced at Nan Patterson's brother-in-law.
>
> "I cannot say that he is," was the reply. A sigh, as of relief, went up and the defendant leaned back in her chair with a smile.
>
> "I think that is a point in my favor," she whispered to Mr. Levy.[600]

Still, Rand pressed on with his case. Dr. Charles Phelps, an authority on gunshot wounds and the like, delivered his opinion that the bullet had gone from left to right and that the muzzle had been "not less than three and not more than five inches from [Young's coat.]"[601] Since Young was right-handed, suicide seemed unlikely, though perhaps not impossible. The defense would suggest that Young could have held the gun in such a way as to push the trigger with his thumb, but that seems a bit convoluted.

At the risk of digressing, Newman Levy's account of the trial leaves out any mention of two admittedly minor characters. Both were involved in the authentication of letters which did Nan no good. The first was Ada Patterson (no relation) who was a famous sob sister and who became known as the "Nellie Bly of the West."[602] Ada had made a name for herself when she moved from San Francisco to St. Louis to work for the *St. Louis Republican*.[603] Filling in for a drunken co-worker, she covered the sensational trial of Arthur Duestrow. Duestrow was the son of a wealthy man who had made millions in mining stock. He lived a life of leisure on his inheritance. He attended Missouri Medical College but did not graduate. Duestrow was an alcoholic and was considered a "cigarette fiend." He openly consorted with a prostitute named Clara Howard, who ran a "house of assignation." He abused his wife, beating her on several occasions prior to her murder. On the day of the crime, he had spent the morning with Clara and returned home with a sleigh to take his wife on a promised ride in the icy streets. Drunk and in bad humor, he assaulted his wife and the maid, Katie Hahn. Before it was all over, he shot his wife and then he shot and killed his child. Soon afterward, his wife died of her wounds. Duestrow immediately turned himself in, telling the police that the shooting was "an accident," which was completely implausible.[604] He was defended on a theory of insanity—the expert testimony was to the effect that his condition could be traced to the excessive use of alcohol by his mother during her pregnancy and by his excessive use of alcohol as early as in his childhood.[605] The press made much of his smoking, noting that he smoked at least forty cigarettes a day during his incarceration, which led to a calculation that he smoked a total of 43,000 cigarettes before his execution.[606]

Duestrow did not take the stand, and the defense offered no facts surrounding the shootings. The judge and jury did not buy the insanity defense. Neither did the famous Dr. Edward Charles Spitzka (yes, our old friend), who could not resist opining on the subject.[607] It was reported that Duestrow sat coolly smoking a cigarette as the verdict was returned.[608] His conviction was affirmed,[609] and he was hanged.[610] Ada interviewed him before the hanging, and he claimed to be "Count Von Brandenburg." However, shortly before his execution, he admitted the crime.[611] There was quite a lot of press coverage, and it is reported that someone came up with a popular ditty: "Cigarettes drove Duestrow crazy—killed his wife and little baby."[612] That was not the only indignity. When it was reported that his sister would have been entitled to the family fortune but had chosen to become a nun, a news writer gratuitously added that she "is not handsome... she weighs about 200 pounds."[613]

Ada's work on the Duestrow case got the attention of the editor of the *New York American*, who assigned her to cover the Nan Patterson case. She interviewed Nan in jail and always believed that Young had shot himself.[614] Unfortunately this interview would force Ada onto the stand in Nan's final trial. She had come to Nan by Nan's handwritten invitation, and she was called to identify Nan's handwriting.[615] She was not permitted to testify as to their discussions, but this letter provided a handwriting exemplar,[616] which allowed a prosecution expert witness, handwriting expert David Carvalho, to connect her to the letters. Carvalho was also an interesting character. He testified for the defense in the first and second Molineux trials and achieved some fame as a defense expert in both of the famous Dreyfus trials.[617]

Another stunning blow to the prosecution came when Mrs. Young was on the stand. Rand would try to put the "Julia letter" in through her. As we noted, she had intercepted it. Recorder Goff excluded the "Julia letter," although it had been admitted in the previous trial. Unexpected as the ruling was, it was certainly correct.[618] Levy wisely chose not to cross-examine Mrs. Young, getting her off the stand as soon as possible.

Rand was able to get in a different letter in Nan's handwriting. The letter was written to another man, Leslie Coggins. From its contents Rand would argue that Nan had a relationship with this other man, and that established mercenary motives in her dealings with Young. Of course, he also wanted to generally blacken her name.[619]

Finally, in an effort to patch up the damage done by pawnbroker Stern's inability to identify Smith as the purchaser of the fateful weapon, Rand pulled a dirty trick. When Julia Smith was on the stand, he asked a series of questions relating to the pawning of some of her jewelry by her husband. As he did so, he held in his hand several pawn tickets. He had had them marked for identification, but he played a game of keeping them from defense counsel. He intimated that the tickets were dated June 3, 1904. They were not. He was bluffing. Levy called his bluff. They were dated in October. Rand doubled down and suggested that they were renewal tickets for items pawned June 3, 1904. He was caught, but he tried to save face by putting the tickets into evidence himself. They were dated October 7, 1904.[620] It is not clear that the press fully understood what was going on.[621]

The lawyers summed up, and the case went to the jury.[622] After thirteen hours the jury deadlocked, eight to four for manslaughter.[623] A third trial seemed unlikely.[624] Prosecutor Rand received considerable criticism from the public.[625] Here is a sample:

> To the Editor of *The New York Times*:
>
> I rejoice to know that the slow people of these "fast times" are just accompanying Spring in awakening to the fact that Mr. Rand, our eloquent Assistant District Attorney, has been ignorant of the fact that the girl whose name has occurred so much in print, Nan Patterson, is as innocent, and is entitled to this treatment of such, as the best person living, until she is properly convicted of that appalling crime of which she has been accused.
>
> By such treatment as she has received since she has been tried for this crime, Assistant District Attorney Rand has ignored the forces which tend to improve civilization in this country. It is a broad statement to make, but I feel that I have a better and a more intelligent idea of the betterment of our laws than he, for I blushed to acknowledge to an alien who conversed with me on this topic that such language as has been used in this trial would not be tolerated in the European courts.
>
> E. P., New York, May 15, 1905[626]

The press did not escape unscathed either, for many felt that the news commentary had not only sensationalized the case but also had tilted the outcome in favor of Nan. Consider this curious letter to the editor from "A Juror":

> To the Editor of *The New York Times*: Our legislature should pass a law entirely prohibiting, under severe penalties, all editorial discussion of capital cases until the accused person has been either finally convicted or acquitted. If that law had been in force Nan Patterson would now be on her way to the electric chair.
>
> A JUROR. Brooklyn, May 15, 1905 [627]

This was certainly District Attorney Jerome's view,[628] although *The New York Times* turned back his complaints with a biting editorial:

> [W]e must remind Mr. Jerome that the methods and behavior of a prosecuting officer in a murder trial are things open to public criticism, and within the sphere of proper newspaper castigation. He stands by his assistant—that is all very well. But the community does not approve the methods that have been employed in this and other murder trials in this and recent years…. If the theory that it is the duty of the District Attorney and his assistants to pursue with ferocious hatred every person under indictment for murder, to employ every available method and device to secure conviction, and to piece out unconvincing evidence by inference, suggestion, innuendo, and declamatory art to be the true one, then the District Attorney would have been called, not the public prosecutor, but the public hyena.
>
> We hope it will not become our duty again to remind District Attorney Jerome that the people of the City and County of New York want no more murder trials conducted as he and his assistants saw fit to conduct the trial of the Patterson woman.[629]

However, the role of the press was not the only controversy. Several others arose from the second mistrial (hung jury), which many viewed as a "virtual acquittal."

Justice Vernon M. Davis, who had presided over Nan's first two trials (the mistrial and the first full trial, in which Nan testified) was invited to preside over a dinner at the Phi Delta Phi Club, a club of city lawyers, where he spoke in defense of Prosecutor Rand. He went on in his speech to state that most people believed that Nan held the gun that killed Caesar Young, that it was discharged by her, and that it had been bought by J. Morgan Smith. He said that he thought that there had been an argument, that Young had taken hold of the gun, and that, in the struggle, it went off.[630] He suggested that if Nan had taken the stand in the second case and had told the truth, she would have been acquitted.[631] Davis said that he thought she had lied when she took the stand at the second trial (first full trial) and told a story of suicide. Many felt that the judge's comments were inappropriate and unprofessional.[632] Nor did Abraham Levy escape criticism. A contributor to *The Bar*, the journal of the West Virginia Bar Association,[633] opined:

> The only credible thing which this lawyer for the defense did in the conduct of the trial was that he did not put this woman on the witness stand to perjure herself. Those who followed the case know that she was defended on the theory of suicide of the victim in the tragedy; yet there is only one conclusion to be drawn from the evidence, which was the conclusion drawn by the able judge who presided, by the intelligent public, and by those who had inside information from those nearest the defendant—and that conclusion was that it was neither a suicide nor a murder.

The critic then quoted an extract from *The Sun*, which reported that a "reputable lawyer," C. A. Irwin, said that Levy had repeated to him Nan's story of the shooting:

"Mr. Levy told me," he said, "that Nan Patterson admitted that the revolver was in her hand when the fatal shot was fired." According to Levy's statement of Miss Patterson's story, both she and Young were considerably under the influence of liquor, and when in the cab began quarreling about the intended departure of Young.

"Nan Patterson finally drew a revolver, which she declared to Mr. Levy, was done for the purpose of a bluff. Young grabbed the gun, and in the struggle which followed, the trigger was pulled and Young was shot…

"Mr. Levy told me that if he put forward that defense, Nan Patterson would have been convicted without a doubt. Mr. Levy entertained great fears that such a story would not be believed by the jury. That is the reason why suicide was the theory of the defense."[634]

Our critic indignantly observed:

It is humiliating to believe that a man who is regarded as a representative lawyer, occupying a prominent position at his local bar, should go into Court to defend a client upon a "theory" which he, himself, had concocted and knew to be contrary to the facts, hoping to make it plausible enough to deceive the jury and secure the acquittal of the accused…

What right has a lawyer to concoct a theory for the benefit of a client!

Who doubts that with a conscientious and able lawyer, presenting the real facts of Nan Patterson's case before a jury she would have been acquitted—acquitted on the first trial instead of hanging three juries in the attempt to prove a lie.

"What right has a lawyer to concoct a theory for the benefit of a client?" This is actually an interesting question, but I suspect that the reality is that it's not the least bit uncommon. What is also interesting, and seems unlikely, is that Levy would break confidence to reveal such things to another person, even another lawyer. One also wonders why the lawyer recipient of Levy's information would make such a disclosure. Of course, stranger things have happened. Some people just can't keep their mouths shut, but one wonders if this lore is not legend.

I also ran across an interesting statement about the case made by Arthur Train, a prosecutor, contemporary, and author of the famous Ephraim Tutt stories, who was present throughout the trial:

> There will always be some persons who think that every defendant should be convicted and feel aggrieved if he is turned out by the jury. Yet they entirely forget, in their displeasure at the acquittal of a man whom they instinctively "know" to be guilty, that the jury probably had exactly the same impression, but were obliged under their oaths to acquit because of an insufficiency of evidence.
>
> An excellent illustration of such a case is that of Nan Patterson. She is commonly supposed to have attended, upon the night of her acquittal, a banquet at which one of her lawyers toasted her as "the guilty girl who beat the case." Whether she was guilty or not, there is a general impression that she murdered Caesar Young. Yet the writer, who was present throughout the trial, felt at the conclusion of the case that there was a fairly reasonable doubt of her guilt. Even so, the jury disagreed [the jury "hung"], although the case is usually referred to as an acquittal and a monument to the sentimentality of juries.[635]

Although Nan had declared that if she were acquitted she would devote her attention to "good works,"[636] she quickly changed her mind and tried to return to the stage. She pled poverty and suggested, among other things, that she needed money from the theater to pay her defense lawyer. This offended Attorney Levy.[637]

For a while Nan enjoyed her celebrity. She made a splash at the famous forty-two-round fight between Joe Gans and Battling Nelson (Oscar Mathaeus Nielsen) in Goldfield, Nevada,[638] in 1906:[639]

> By fight day everybody in America knew about Goldfield, the fabulous mining camp where $7 million had been taken from a dozen mines in less than three years. Celebrities flocked into the town for the fight, including Nan Patterson, just out of jail for shooting Caesar Young. Dressed, in the words of one news writer "beyond appreciation in the best finery in the land," she strolled the dusty mining-camp streets, her face shaded by a hat of ostrich plumes.[640]

However, her return to a career in vaudeville was not successful.[641] A letter to the editor of *The New York Times* suggests the mood of many:

> To the Editor of *The New York Times*:
>
> The story of Nan Patterson, her relations with Caesar Young, and her possible responsibility for his death is getting to be a nuisance. She was not proved guilty of murder; she is not of mental calibre sufficient to make her an interesting subject for editorial or even repertorial [sic] comment. Let us drop the subject.
>
> CHARLES E. PENY[642]

Nan remarried an early husband[643] and continued to turn up in the press from time to time; but her popularity as a tragic heroine faded as a new "It Girl"—Evelyn Nesbit—appeared on the scene. I will have more to say of Evelyn in chapter ten.

Abraham Levy went on to appear in many famous criminal trials.[644] One involved William A. E. Moore and his wife Fayne Moore. The couple was accused of working the "badger game" on New York hotel owner and millionaire Martin Mahon.[645] In the badger game a woman lures a mark into a compromising position so that her partner can burst in on the scene and obtain evidence for blackmail. Perhaps the most famous practitioner of the art was "Chicago May," who wrote her own memoir[646] and who is the subject of several books.[647] William Howe's partner, Abe Hummel, actually specialized in working out discreet deals in aid of similar extortion schemes, using the rubric of breach of promise [to marry].

For her part, Fayne was apparently a dazzling beauty with "hypnotic eyes."[648]

Levy represented both Fayne and her husband William. William was convicted and given a nineteen-year sentence, which was affirmed on appeal.[649] Fayne was tried separately before Recorder Goff and, in her first trial, Levy was assisted by "Special Counsel" Benjamin Hill, a Southerner who was brought in by Fayne's family.[650] Hill's oratory was highly praised,[651] and the jury split seven for conviction and five for acquittal.[652] This prompted Assistant District Attorney John F. McIntyre to accuse the jurors of being "fixed." This angered the jurors and angered Levy. Levy accused the prosecution of engaging in unprofessional conduct throughout the trial. At one point defense counsel had recommended that Fayne testify against her husband, but she supposedly refused because she would not commit perjury.[653] That was the story anyway. For his part, Levy reportedly made the complaining witness, Mahon, so uncomfortable during cross-examination that at one point Mahon said that "he wanted to be rid of the whole matter."[654] After the jury had been selected for Fayne's second trial, Mahon could not be found, the case was repeatedly continued, and Mahon was found in contempt.[655]

Finally, Fayne Moore was set free.[656] During her husband's first months in prison, Fayne repeatedly expressed loyalty to her husband—but that did not last. She divorced her husband[657] and went to London to appear as a "Gaiety Girl," a member of the chorus at the Gaiety Theatre's production of *The Messenger Boy*. Gaiety Girls were courted by "Stage Door Johnnies," wealthy "sports" who would hang out at the back of the theater. Sometimes one of the girls would get a hook (if you will excuse the expression) into a wealthy admirer—or even into a member of the nobility—for a husband. Fayne managed to snag Henry D. Lewis, who had interests in the Kimberley and DeBeers diamond mines.[658] This was quite a catch indeed.

Abe Levy would also represent the unfortunate Daniel O'Reilly, a former prosecutor who had assisted the defense in the Nan Patterson case. As an assistant district attorney, O'Reilly had prosecuted Fayne Moore and he had also been on the prosecution team in the murder trials of Dr. Samuel Kennedy. Later he would assist the defense in both of the famous Thaw trials. O'Reilly had gotten himself involved in the "Bancroft Bond Theft" and was convicted and imprisoned, despite Levy's efforts and the testimony of a number of character witnesses.[659]

Another of Levy's cases involved lawyer-actor Lorlys Elton Rogers and Ida Sniffen Walters, his second wife. There was already another Mrs. Rogers living in Chicago, but Lorlys had failed to inform Ida. When he decided to go back to his real wife, Ida despaired and ended up attempting a murder-suicide using a poison of bichloride of mercury on herself and her little ones. The children died, but Ida did not. She was tried for murder,[660] but the jury found that she was insane at the time of the acts in question.[661] Lorlys was indicted for "white slavery,"[662] which was a stretch, but it does not appear that the case got very far.

In 1917 Mrs. Elsie Lee Hilair was garroted in the Hotel Martinique. Unknown to her husband was her fascination with tango parlors. Her body had been stripped of $2,500 in jewelry. A salesman named Benjamin Sternberg was indicted for the murder, but again Levy got the indictment dismissed for lack of evidence. The identity of the murderer apparently remained a mystery. It was suspected that a gang of "tango thieves" was involved.[663]

Abraham Levy's last big case involved the defense of Charles E. Chapin, the city editor of *The Evening World*, who had shot his ailing wife of more than thirty years in what appeared to be a planned murder-suicide.[664] After Chapin was indicted, Levy applied for a commission to determine Chapin's sanity. The commission determined that Chapin was legally sane.[665] The district attorney wanted a first degree murder conviction but finally accepted a guilty plea to second degree murder.[666] Chapin was sentenced to a minimum of twenty years in Sing Sing.[667] While he was imprisoned, he wrote an autobiography, and his dedication to a rose garden he started in the prison earned him the nickname "The Rose Man of Sing Sing."[668] He died in prison December 13, 1930. He was supposedly mean to his colleagues, and one has been quoted as saying, "They had known he would be involved in a murder someday, but had always assumed that he would be the victim."[669]

Abraham Levy died in December 1920. *The New York Times* alluded to some of his famous cases, including his first big criminal case, in which he defended "Frenchy the Algerian" who had killed "Mother Shakespeare" (also known as "Old Shakespeare") and his defense of Nan Patterson. It was reported that he died of "a combination of ailments that became serious in September. An operation for gall stones was followed by another for a gathering in the throat."[670]

Chapter Ten

The "Reformer"

William Travers Jerome, the prosecutor known as the "Reformer," went on to other things. It was said that "[s]ince William Travers Jerome became District Attorney, he has sent more than a score of lawyers to prison for various acts of dishonesty, and some of them were men of prominence in the profession."[671] Arthur Train wrote, "As they say down-town, if Jerome had never done anything else, he would have 'made good' by locking up Abe Hummel."[672]

The story of how Jerome finally put an end to Abe Hummel's nefarious career has been told by others.[673] Hummel was convicted of suborning perjury in the notorious Dodge-Morse case after jury deliberations of eighteen minutes. After all of the effort expended to sink Hummel's ship, Jerome had actually cut the charges down to a single count of conspiracy and had recommended leniency. Hummel's conviction was affirmed, the story preserved in a published opinion.[674] Hummel served a short sentence on Blackwell's Island and repaired to Paris and London.[675] Why the leniency? This takes us to the murder of architect Stanford White by wealthy and troubled Harry Thaw.

I have alluded to the Thaw case numerous times. Surely it is the most written up of American murder cases.[676] Fans of The History Channel and such probably know of it because of the story of *The Girl in the Red Velvet Swing*.[677]

In 1906 Thaw shot and killed White in front of loads of witnesses at the rooftop garden and restaurant at Madison Square Garden. Thaw considered it a sort of honor killing—revenge for White's seduction of the young celebrity "It Girl" and member of the "Florodora Sextette" (along with Nan Patterson), Evelyn Nesbit, whom Thaw had later married. Thaw was obviously insane. Our favorite expert, the noted Dr. Allan McLane Hamilton, agreed,[678] and Jerome planned to prove that up and ship Thaw off to Matteawan. Thaw would not willingly agree to such a disposition, fired his lawyer, and defended on a theory of temporary insanity—the "brainstorm defense."[679] At this point Jerome shifted to the theory that the case was a straightforward murder caused by jealousy. The new defense counsel, Delphin Delmas, would not simply rely on the brainstorm defense but would also try to demonize the victim and hope for a defense verdict based on the unwritten law.

Jerome's cross-examination of Evelyn Nesbit was brutal. In one of the most bizarre moments in the trial, Jerome produced a copy of an old affidavit in Evelyn's name that had been prepared by Abe Hummel at Stanford White's request. The affidavit told a horror story of Thaw's insanely abusive treatment of her while the two were on a European tour, before their marriage. Evelyn thought that the affidavit had been destroyed by Hummel.[680]

Jerome had gotten the copy of the affidavit from Hummel. Jerome's biographer hints that Hummel's cooperation "may have explained the rather light sentence he received in the Dodge-Morse case."[681] How odd to put a man in jail for subornation of perjury but, to prove a point, to use an affidavit by that very man who is known for using perjured affidavits to shake down wealthy marks. Evelyn tried to repudiate the affidavit, and the defense claimed that it was a forgery,[682] but Hummel was actually called to testify as to the truth of its contents![683]

Sensing that things were not going his way, Jerome would shift gears once again and try to prove that Thaw was not only insane at the time the crime was committed but also insane now, at trial. Justice Fitzgerald, who was presiding, appointed an insanity board to consider the matter. To Jerome's dismay, the board found Thaw sane and the trial continued.[684] In his autobiography, Dr. Hamilton expressed disgust "that [t]he lavish use of money enabled the defendant...to employ a perfect cloud of so-called experts..."[685] In the end the jurors could not reach a verdict. The vote was supposedly seven for conviction and five for acquittal.[686]

There would be a second trial. In the hope of avoiding an execution in the electric chair this time, the defense plead insanity. Harry Thaw apparently thought he was free, but he went off to Matteawan after all. He was freed in 1915 only to return to the asylum in 1917. He was again released in 1924.

The reporter who covered the Thaw case for *The New York Herald* was none other than Roland Molineux, who had been twice prosecuted by Osborne for the poisoning of Katherine Adams![687] The Molineux case[688] was a landmark in the law of evidence, as it made it clear that evidence of other crimes or wrongs done by the defendant, proved by conviction or unproved, could not be admitted against the accused except in exceptional instances—to prove intent, identity, *modus operandi*, absence of mistake or accident or to prove a common scheme or plan. Otherwise, the defendant might be convicted because of the influence of prior bad acts not having anything to do with the charge at issue.[689] Today, New York lawyers still move for a "Molineux Hearing" to keep such evidence out,[690] and the Molineux rule is reflected in Federal Rule of Evidence 404(b).

Goff, the presiding judge in the Molineux case, exhibited bias throughout the trial, and this was an issue on appeal. The court of appeals said only this:

> The claims of defendant's counsel that "error was committed in the opening and summing up of the District Attorney," and that "the defendant did not receive that fair and impartial trial to which he is entitled under the law," have been so urgently presented that we should be inclined to these heads, were it not impossible to do so, fairly and impartially, without a full and critical review of the twelve thousand folios of this record for that sole purpose. Such a review would extend this opinion beyond all reasonable and useful limits, and in view of the result reached we deem it unnecessary to discuss or decide

the questions raised as to the conduct of the recorder and the
district attorney upon the trial.[691]

Molineux was a roommate on death row with Dr. Kennedy, and
there was considerable camaraderie between the two condemned
men.[692] Rev. Munro, the chaplain of the Tombs, spoke well of both
after visiting them in Sing Sing.[693] Jerome was the district attorney
when Molineux was tried a second time. Osborne was to have a
second crack.[694] The jury was out but a few minutes before returning
a verdict of not guilty.[695] Rev. Munro had this to say:

> I knew that in time Mr. Molineux would secure another trial
> and it came, thank God, and I was one of the first to con-
> gratulate him after the jury had filed into Court and said,
> "Not Guilty."[696]

While in prison, Molineux wrote a book called *The Room
with the Little Door*,[697] about his experiences in the Tombs and in
Sing Sing, and he would later write a play, *The Man Inside* (1913).
Sadly, he would go insane and die in 1917, supposedly from the effects
of syphilis.[698]

Jerome presided over most of the work in another controversial
case, the trial of Albert T. Patrick for the murder of William M. Rice
(as in Rice University, where Rice's money ended up).[699] Again the
trial work was done by Assistant District Attorney James Osborne.
It was charged that Rice was done in with chloroform by his valet,
Charles F. Jones, whose services had been procured by one of Rice's
lawyers, Albert T. Patrick. The prosecution theory was that Patrick
wanted to take over the Rice fortune, by way of a forged "new will,"
leaving the boodle to Patrick. The scheme was foiled by Rice's longtime personal lawyer, James A. Baker.[700] Patrick was tried before
Judge Goff and defended himself with the assistance of Frederick B.
House and Emanuel Friend,[701] who had been on Ameer Ben Ali's
("Frenchy's") defense team. Patrick was sentenced to death, and his
conviction was affirmed;[702] but with the backing of the Medico-Legal

Society, he fought on. Indeed, he was aided on the medical evidence
by none other than Dr. Austin Flint, one of the experts who had
testified against Ben Ali. Governor Frank W. Higgins commuted
Patrick's death sentence to life imprisonment in late 1906, based on
the sharp division in the court of appeals.[703] The dissenting opinion by
Justice Denis O'Brien was particularly noteworthy. Some might think
it involved a question of "impossibility," but it would be more correct
to say that he was arguing that there was not sufficient proof of the
corpus delicti (proof of a crime).[704] That is, even if the valet wanted to
kill Rice, the prosecution failed to show to Justice O'Brien's satisfaction that Rice was not already dead. If the principal were not proved
guilty of murder, how could his co-conspirator be guilty of murder?
Moreover, the chief witnesses against the defendant "were testifying
at the trial for great prizes and great rewards. ... The self-confessed
murderer [valet Jones] was released [the jury did not know he had
been given complete immunity], the doctors had their money, but the
jury did not know that each of these three most important witnesses
was testifying against the defendant with a strong inducement to help
make a case out against him."[705] If District Attorney Jerome had felt
uneasy about the deal that had been cut with Jones, he wouldn't admit
it. After Patrick's conviction he told the newspapers that any promises
made were made by Assistant District Attorney Osborne, before he,
Jerome, had assumed office.[706] In the end, Patrick was pardoned by
Governor John Alden Dix. Among the signatories to his petition for
a pardon were Grover Cleveland, Mark Twain, and the omnipresent
Dr. Allan McLane Hamilton.[707] You might say that it was something
like Old Home Week. Many felt that the pardon was outrageous, but
there was nothing to be done about it.

A case I find particularly amusing involved Jerome's encounter
with Florence Burns in 1902. This was not an important case, and
Jerome left the heavy lifting to one of his assistants. Still, the case
remains unsolved, and the record tells us much about the social
mores of the times, in addition to the court procedures and the
police methods of the day. The evidence was presented to a judge

who seems to have been wonderfully fair and quite modern in his legal sensibilities.

Florence was accused of murdering Walter S. Brooks, a young merchant, shooting him in the head in a room at the Glen Island Hotel. It is obvious that the two had had an intimate relationship, but the details were murky. Florence was a beautiful blond and had a younger sister who looked very much like her. The sister would figure into the case as a potential alibi witness. Life in the Burns family may have been less than ideal.[708] Florence left or was put out of her house because of her infatuation with young Brooks. At one point he put her up in rooms, but this proved beyond Walter's means and she moved into the Brooks household.[709] It would seem that she was pressing the issue of marriage on Brooks, and he was not being sufficiently responsive. Neither family seemed to like the other and, although the Brooks family did not favor the marriage, the Burns family made it clear that they would not take Florence back into the family unless she and Walter were married.[710] Mrs. Brooks would tell the lawyers and would later testify that, while Florence was living in the Brooks house, she had threatened to kill Walter and commit suicide if Walter did not marry her. A messenger boy at Walter's place of business related how excited Florence had gotten when she came looking for Walter at his place of business on the Friday before the shooting and was told that another woman had called for him at the office.[711] It also seems that Walter had a fiancée, one Ruth Dunn of Brooklyn,[712] and that the district attorney possessed a letter from Brooks to Dunn expressing his intention of breaking up with Florence on the night of the killing.[713]

When Walter was found in the Glen Island Hotel with a bullet in his head, the unlighted gas lights turned up, suspicion fell on Florence. A "colored" bellboy, George Washington, identified her as being the woman present with Brooks at the *locus in quo*.[714] His story seemed to be corroborated by that of John Earl, the night clerk. Florence's lawyer, former Assistant District Attorney Foster L. Backus, claimed that she had an ironclad alibi. Her sister would testify that she could not have been at the hotel at the time of the murder because she had come to the Burns home early in the evening. On the other hand, this was contradicted by A. Weibles, the conductor of the Brighton Beach Branch of the Kings County Elevated Road, who would testify that she was in the area and on his train right after the killing.[715]

Almost from the start, the newspapers remarked on Florence's cool, calm, and almost disinterested demeanor, noting that the notorious poisoners "Albert T. Patrick and R. B. Molineux [were] more nervous than she."[716] Tombs officials would describe her as an "enigma."[717] The "well-to-do" toured the Tombs in the hope of getting a glimpse of her.[718]

Jerome could see that it would be difficult to get a jury to convict. The identification of the woman who had been with Brooks rested almost entirely on the testimony of the bellboy, George Washington. Also complicating the case was the fact that there had been plenty of time for any guilty party to escape. Jerome was cautious from the start and made an uncharacteristic pledge to be "fair" and to do as much to prove Florence's innocence as to prove her guilt.[719] Rather than taking the case to the grand jury, Jerome opted to present it to Justice Julius M. Mayer, who was sitting as a magistrate at a preliminary examination of the court of special sessions. Perhaps he was hoping that the eminently fair Justice Mayer would screen out a bad case. A grand jury would surely indict, leaving him with a full trial before a jury, and a not guilty verdict that might embarrass him.

Florence was taken under the wing of Rebecca Foster,[720] the "Tombs Angel"[721] who had championed Maria Barbella. Mrs. Foster deserves a book of her own[722] and at least some mention here, especially in the context of the Burns case.

John Munro, the former chaplain of the Tombs, wrote that Mrs. Foster "stood by [Florence] as her best friend, when all others had apparently forsaken her."[723] Sadly, as the hearing proceeded, the Tombs Angel died in a fire at the Park Avenue Hotel.[724] Florence was said to be greatly depressed when she heard of her death.

From the start, things did not go well for the prosecution. George Washington testified that the woman he saw was very dark,[725] but Florence was light complected and had natural blond hair. Still, he claimed that the defendant was the woman he saw:

> When Washington was told to look at her and describe her nose and said it was long and thin, [Florence] laughed heartily. When Justice Mayer asked Washington whether he thought Miss Burns light or dark, he said he thought she was dark. This also amused her. He was asked by the judge how long he had looked at the girl in the room of the hotel [whom he had identified as the defendant]. He replied three minutes. The Justice took out his watch and held it for some time and asked Washington if it was as long as he had held the watch. The witness replied that it was not as long. Justice Mayor [sic] said that he had held the watch but a minute.[726]

John Earl, the night clerk, also proved to be a weak reed, saying that he took no particular notice of Brooks's companion. She had not come into the light, and two other couples registered at the same time.[727] Train Conductor Weibles would be contradicted by Peter Beilman, an interpreter in the surrogate's court of Brooklyn. He would testify that he knew Florence by sight, that he was on the train in question, and that she was not a passenger.[728] Meanwhile, Florence's canny defense lawyer refused to "produce" Florence's parents and sister, which provoked a fight between him and Jerome. Jerome accused him of secreting them away[729] and announced that he had made a mistake in being "fair." Jerome protested petulantly and perhaps too much:

> I have desired in this case, as well as in all cases to get at the truth. I see that the District Attorney's office has made a mistake. I have erred in trying to be fair, and can be criticized justly by the people for being negligent in handling their case.

> Never again as long as I hold office of District Attorney will
> I offer the resources of my office to clear a defendant. [730]

Jerome ran into other problems. Backus was an aggressive cross-examiner, and he secured from Dr. Sweeney, who had been called to attend Brooks, the fact that when he first saw the body it was completely nude. This contradicted the testimony of Washington and Earl that Brooks was attired in his underclothing. Witnesses also contradicted each other as to the position of the body. Backus's suggestion was that "the dead man after being taken sick was murdered by some unknown person, and that afterward the pistol with which he was shot was stolen, and that he was stripped of his underclothing." Dr. Sweeney was also unable to identify a comb found at the scene of the crime which the prosecution wanted to tie to Florence. The failure of any witness to tie this comb to Florence, at least to the satisfaction of Justice Mayer, would pop up on more than one occasion during the proceedings. A reporter noted that the comb had scratched upon it the letters "W. C." These happened to be the initials of the detective in the case, William Colby. [731]

After Sweeney's testimony, Justice Mayer launched an attack on the police for conducting what we would today call an overly suggestive lineup to secure an identification from Washington. He would later go so far as to brand the identification made at the station house "worthless." The court "would not consider it." [732] If that were not a good enough day for the defense, the coroner's physician who had performed the autopsy approached Backus and told him that the characteristics of the wound pointed to suicide. [733] He would contradict Dr. Sweeney on several points and would explain that the wound was a "contact wound" most likely self-inflicted. [734]

The prosecution attempted to shore up its case with the testimony of a Detective Reardon. He reported several statements of the defendant which he gained in an interview with her and which he deemed damaging admissions (e.g., "She asked me if there had been a pistol found. ... She asked me if there was a woman seen leaving the hotel."). However, the admissions had been extracted after Florence had refused to speak without her counsel being present, and lawyer Backus offered some evidence that he had been prevented from seeing his client. Backus also established that bellboy Washington had been exposed to Florence at the station house before the hasty and questionable lineup had been constructed, so he would have been sure to pick out Florence. This prompted the following from Justice Mayer:

> I want to inform you, Mr. Backus, and the District Attorney also, that I consider this testimony as to the identification worthless and the court will not consider it. I do not want to criticize the police, as they are obliged to act hastily. But this lining up of persons beside an accused utterly dissimilar in physical appearance I regard as an absurd, ridiculous, and worthless proceeding. It is but a remnant of obsolete methods, and the sooner it is stopped the better it will be for justice.[735]

Mrs. Brooks, Walter's mother, took the stand to testify about Florence's threats and to make an unconvincing effort to identify the comb found at the murder scene as Florence's. She added a bit of drama by fainting on the witness stand.[736] Mr. Brooks, Walter's father, would make a similar attempt to identify the comb and to relate conversations in his presence between Florence and Walter about her unwillingness to work to support herself—and his inability to shelter her any longer.[737] Then there was a friend of Walter's, William Eyre, who testified that, before the killing, he had gone to a theater with Florence and Walter. He related that the couple had "wrangled" all evening. In the play, one actress had a line, "If you desert me I will kill you." Eyre claimed that Florence told Walter, "If you desert me I will do the same to you."[738] It turned out later that he did not actually hear that, and he explained that he was repeating what Walter Brooks had told him. The poor boy had no appreciation of the rule against hearsay.[739]

Judge John William Goff, as he appears in
Notable New Yorkers of 1896–1899 (Moses King, 1899) (33)

William Travers Jerome, as he appears in
Notable New Yorkers of 1896–1899 (Moses King, 1899) (34)

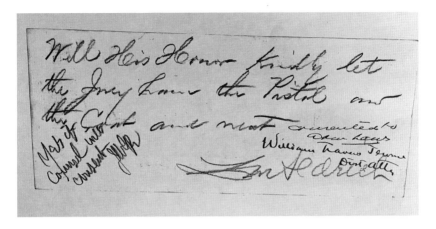

A note from the jurors in the Nan Patterson case requesting permission
from the judge for the jury to view the pistol and other evidence
from the trial, circa 1905 (35)

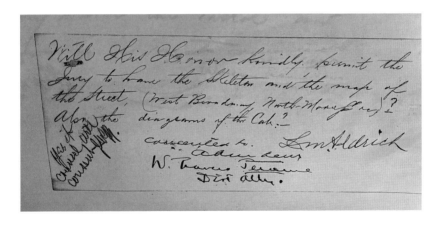

A note from the jurors in the Nan Patterson case requesting permission
from the judge for the jury to view the skeleton and the map
of the street, circa 1905 (36)

Bain News Service, publisher, Nan Patterson, 1900 (37)

District Attorney's Office.
County of New York

Wm Travers Jerome,
DISTRICT ATTORNEY.

May 11th, 1905.

The People
vs.
Nan Patterson. } Murder 1st Degree.

The defendant has been tried twice upon the indictment in this action. At each trial the jury disagreed. All the evidence available to the People was submitted to the jury at each trial. There is no other or further evidence obtainable by the People. I do not think that at this time, in this county another trial would have any other termination than a disagreement. I recommend that the defendant be discharged upon her own recognizance.

Wm Travers Jerome,
District Attorney.

A handwritten note dated May 11, 1905, signed by
District Attorney Jerome, throwing in the towel in the Nan Patterson case (38)

Photo of Dr. Allan McLane Hamilton, the grandson
of Alexander Hamilton, circa 1916 (39)

Jacob August Riis (1849–1914), photographer,
"The Tombs: Murderers Row," circa 1890 (40)

Photo of the memorial to Rebecca Salome Foster,
the "Tombs Angel," inscribed, "On her lips was the law of Kindness,"
dedicated on January 1, 1904, at the City Club for installation in the
Court of General Sessions, New York City (41)

At this point the most important testimony had come from the detectives and the bellboy. As to the detectives, Justice Mayer felt that Florence's admissions had been secured before they had informed her of the actual charges against her.[740] He had already discounted the bellboy's testimony. He threw out the evidence, and he found that the comb had never been identified to his satisfaction. He discharged the defendant. The crowd was eager to congratulate her, but she showed little emotion and no expression of joy.[741] Technically she could still be charged. Jerome went to the press to complain that she was guilty and that there had been a miscarriage of justice.[742] He pledged to get more evidence. Jerome took the matter back to the coroner for an inquest. It appears that he had little to add in the way of evidence. A new witness with whom Florence had once boarded was willing to identify the comb.[743] Another witness who knew Florence, William Fink, testified that she carried a revolver in her muff for self-defense—but he did so reluctantly. It appears that he was sympathetic to her. Joseph Wilson testified that he had met Florence at a dance hall and that she had told him that she loved Walter and was very jealous. Both Fink and Wilson were denizens of the Elmira Reformatory, which no doubt raised a question of their credibility. In response, lawyer Backus presented a theory of suicide, explaining that Walter had been in court five times on charges by the health department for selling bad milk and that his business was ruined.[744] The case went nowhere.

Now free, Florence Burns latched onto a husband, Charles W. Wildrick, the son of a distinguished army officer and grandson of a contemporary of Henry Clay in the United States Congress. It was reported that Wildrick had been a rival of Brooks, but Florence had been infatuated with Brooks and had not been interested in Wildrick's advances. Wildrick was not so distinguished as his ancestors. He had served time in prison for passing a bad check.[745] The next we hear of Florence, she had turned to the stage, "appearing...at the head of a mediocre vaudeville aggregation" touring the Hudson Valley. She was billed as "The most persecuted and most beautiful young woman in America." She was not well-received by the public.[746]

Well, everyone has career changes. In 1910 Florence was busted playing the "badger game." Curious as it seems, her partner in crime was a man named Edward H. Brooks, who was no relation to the late Walter Brooks. He told reporters that he planned to marry Florence once she obtained a divorce from Wildrick.[747] The complaining witness was a lawyer named Charles W. Hurlburt. Hurlburt claimed that Florence had lured him to a house on West Twenty-fifth Street, where Brooks and another man forced him to give up cash and sign a note for $500.[748] Florence and Edward were convicted on his testimony and got seven years. Lawyer Hurlburt was later found drowned in the Hudson River.[749]

We last hear of Florence Burns in 1922, when she was arrested in a police raid on a tenement on East Thirty-first Street. She had gotten rid of Edward Brooks and had married Alonzo Frederick Rutledge, who soon left her. On her arrest, she gave her name as Rutledge, but the police recognized her. She was charged and convicted of threatening a police officer with a .32 Smith & Wesson and violating the Sullivan Act, New York's first gun control measure.[750] When his men arrested her, a Captain Ward asked her, "Did you shoot Brooks?" She replied, "That's what Jerome would like to know."[751] The Tombs Angel might have wept.

An Afterthought

The reader will note that I have not favored the prosecution in the cases I have discussed. However, I am not the least bit ideological about all this. In William Howe's heyday, "On the [P]eople's side…the ethical tone was scarcely more elevated. Assistant district attorneys dressed like gentlemen with tall silk hats, frock coats, and high stiff collars. They smoked big black cigars, got their jobs through political sponsors, and kicked back ten per cent of their salary to Tammany."[752]

William Jerome may have been an anti-Tammany reformer, but he played rough. We have already noted that he was not above trying cases in the newspapers.[753] Jerome's successor, Charles S. Whitman, was even more driven by politics and the press. Whitman obtained the conviction of New York City Police Lieutenant Charles Becker for the murder of a gambling house owner named Herman Rosenthal. Becker may have been innocent but railroaded[754] by Whitman, whose victory propelled him to the New York governorship. No doubt evidence of Becker's grafting influenced the jury. When Whitman became governor, Becker's pregnant wife put a silver plate, engraved with the words "Charles Becker Murdered July 13, 1915, by Governor Whitman," on her husband's coffin. Justice Felix Frankfurter once said that "Whitman was getting in indictments because Hearst's *American* was shouting blue murder."[755] It is also reported that Frankfurter once wrote that Whitman "was a politically minded district attorney, one of the great curses of America."[756]

Acknowledgments

I am grateful for the librarians at the John Jay College of Criminal Justice who managed to preserve a bit of the history through the preservation of trial transcripts. Also, my thanks to *The New York Times* archives, for readily available "daily record" of many of these cases. Thanks also to the assistant commissioner and staff of the New York City Department of Records and Information, the reference services staff of the New York State Library and the New York State Archives, and the research librarians at the University of Kentucky College of Law, who managed to procure less readily available copies of The Sun and the wonderfully illustrated *The New York Herald*. I am also indebted to Dr. Greg Davis for his Foreword. He has also helped me teach law students a thing or two about forensic evidence. We are to that extent "partners in crime."

Notes

Preface

1. Herbert K. Russell, Edgar Lee Masters: A Biography 60 (2001).

2. Eric Homberger, The Historical Atlas of New York City 105 (2005).

3. *Id.* at 102.

4. *Id.* at 107.

5. *Id.* at 116.

6. *See* Kenneth Whyte, The Uncrowned King: The Sensational Rise of William Randolph Hearst (2009).

7. Robert Miraldi, The Pen Is Mightier: the Muckraking Life of Charles Edward Russell (2003).

8. *See* John Mortimer, "Rumpole and the Younger Generation," *in* The First Rumpole Omnibus (1983).

9. Gene Fowler, The Great Mouthpiece (1931).

10. Alfred Cohn & Joe Chisholm, "Take the Witness!" (1934); Adela Rogers St. John, Final Verdict (1962); Michael Trope, Once Upon a Time in Los Angeles: The Trials of Earl Rogers (2001).

11. Richard O. Boyer, Max Steuer: magician of the law (1932); Aron Steuer, Max D. Steuer, Trial Lawyer (1950).

12. Richard H. Rovere, Howe & Hummel: Their True and Scandalous History (1947).

13. *Profiles: 89 Centre Street, Part I—Can Lawyers Be Honest?* 36 New Yorker, Nov. 23, 1946, and *Part II—The Weeper,* 44 New Yorker, Nov. 30, 1946.

14. *See* Sam Zolotow, *Howe & Hummel Due Next Season— Teichmann Play About Law Team to Get Simultaneous Presentation in London,* N.Y. Times, May 15, 1953; Val Adams, *2 Signed to Star As Lawyers on TV; Dennis King and Skulnik in 'Howe & Hummel' Series,* N.Y. Times, Nov. 12, 1957; Sam Zolotow, *Seven Arts Adds 2 Stage*

Projects; To Back 'Howe & Hummel…,' N.Y. Times, Nov. 21, 1962.
It is also noted that Harold Rome, *Pins and Needles* (1936), *Destry Rides Again* (1959), and *I Can Get It for You Wholesale* (1962) (which introduced the world to newcomer Barbra Streisand), took a crack at a musical version of *Howe & Hummel* in the period 1962 to 1965, although I don't believe that his collection of tunes and lyrics ever went into production. *See The Harold Rome Papers,* Irving S. Gilmore Music Library, Yale University.

15. Oddly enough, Howe and Hummel and Inspector Byrnes turn up as characters in Michael Blaine's historical novel, The Midnight Band of Mercy (2004).

16. After finishing my study of Howe, chapter one of Gaslight Lawyers, and long after my 2007 study of the Nack-Thorn-Guldensuppe case, which appears in law journal format in Richard H. Underwood, *Mr. Howe's Last Case,* 31 Legal Stud. F. 801 (2007), and with new material in chapter seven of Gaslight Lawyers, I discovered the then-newly released Scoundrels in Law: The Trials of Howe & Hummel (2010) by Cait Murphy. Unlike Murphy, I was only interested in Howe's criminal cases, and I only briefly touch on the work of Abe Hummel and the history of the firm of Howe & Hummel.

17. *See Mark Twain Hauled Up—A Suit Over "The Prince and the Pauper." E. H. House Says He Was Authorized by Twain to Prepare the Play and That His Ideas Were Stolen,* N.Y. Times, Jan. 27, 1890.

18. For an account from House's perspective *see* James L. Huffman, A Yankee in Meiji Japan: The Crusading Journalist Edward H. House 215–220 (2003). *See also* Paul Fatout, *Mark Twain, Litigant,* 31 American Literature 30–45 (Mar. 1959).

19. For a more recent work that includes a discussion of Mandelbaum, *see* Timothy J. Gilfoyle, A Pickpocket's Tale: The Underworld of Nineteenth-Century New York (2006).

20. Frances Wellman gives him a bit of grudging praise in his book The Art of Cross-Examination (4th ed., 1936).

21. Rovere, *supra* note 12, at 38.

22. *Id.* at 19. Quibble's motto was "No fact is too patent to be denied."

23. *See* Underwood, *supra* note 16. This article deals with the celebrated Nack-Thorn-Guldensuppe murder trial of 1897. This case provided the subject matter for a furious battle for circulation between William Randolph Hearst (Journal) and Joseph Pulitzer (World). *See* Kenneth Whyte, *supra* note 6 at 214–218; John Winkler, William Randolph Hearst: A New Appraisal 110–111 (1955); Joseph Campbell, The Year That Defined American Journalism: 1897 and the Clash of Paradigms 83–85 (2006). For a short but colorful take on the case *see* Richard Zacks, An Underground Education 61–65 (1997). The case was revisited by A. J. Liebling, *Annals of Crime: The Case of the Scattered Dutchman*, New Yorker, Sept. 24, 1955.

24. Rovere reported that Howe did not practice civil cases, but that is not entirely correct. One of Howe's clients was Chu Fong, a Chinese merchant and criminal who is remembered for his Chinese Theater on Doyers Street (possibly the inspiration for the Chinese theater in the movie Gangs of New York (Miramax Films 2002); no such theater existed during the time period covered by the movie). *See* David Freeland, Automats, Taxi Dances, and Vaudeville 31 (2009). Chu Fong so admired Howe that he copied Howe's style of dress. Howe represented him unsuccessfully in a civil suit brought by another Chinese merchant named Foo Long. Foo Long had given Chu Fong $3,200 to purchase smuggled opium. Chu Fong kept the money, but didn't deliver on the opium. There was no war on drugs at this time, and Foo Long was able to sue and get a plaintiff's verdict. *See Chu Fong's Syndicate—Some Peculiarities of the Heathen Chinese*, N.Y. Times, June 22, 1888; *Foo Long Versus Chu Fong— The Defendant Giving His Side of the Transaction*, N.Y. Times, June 23, 1888; *Foo Long Smiling Blandly*, N.Y. Times, June 24, 1888. Chu Fong later received the distinction of being the first Chinese convicted of forgery in New York City. *See Chu Fong Was His Dupe—How a Wicked 'Melican Man' Fooled Poor John Chinaman*, N.Y. Times, Feb. 16, 1890; *Chu Fong Convicted—Jurymen Decide that He Is Guilty of Forgery*, N.Y. Times, Jan. 27, 1892. Chu Fong was represented in the case by Joseph Moss. Also, as discussed in the text of the preface of this book, Howe and Hummel were also involved in a famous case brought by Edward House against Mark Twain to enjoin the theatrical production of The Prince and the Pauper by Mark Twain.

25. One of my favorite works along these lines is Richard F. Hamilton, The Social Misconstruction of Reality: Validity and Verification in the Scholarly Community (1996), which pokes holes in such myths as Mozart's poverty, unattended death, and pauper's funeral.

26. The Nack-Thorn-Guldensuppe case provides a good example. Rovere provides more detail (six pages) about this case than others. However, he notes that Thorn got life and his accomplice Mrs. Augusta Nack got nine years after she confessed during the trial. *See* Rovere, *supra* note 12, at 130. There were two trials (the first ending in a mistrial when a juror was stricken by appendicitis). Thorn received the death penalty (one would think this an important detail) and Nack got fifteen years after pleading guilty. *See* Underwood, *supra* note 16, at 804.

27. *Queens to Destroy Noted Crimes Files.* "Memories of some of Queens County's most notorious crimes, including the Guldensuppe... murde[r], will flare briefly today when several tons of legal papers are pushed into the furnace of the seventy-seven-year-old County Court House in Long Island City." N.Y. Times, Dec. 7, 1949.

28. The preserved transcripts can be found in the Lloyd Sealy Library collection at John Jay College of Criminal Justice, The City University of New York [hereinafter "John Jay collection"].

29. *See* Herald, Nov. 9, 1897. Maria's last name is spelled in a variety of ways, even in the court records.

30. A transcript of Maria's first trial is in the John Jay collection, styled "Crime in New York 1850–1950," Trial #53. I also rely on Vols. I and II Contributions from the Pathological Institute of the New York State Hospitals (1896–1897), which contains the articles *Epilepsy and Expert Testimony*, by Ira Van Gieson, MD, & Boris Sidis, MA, PHD, and Ales Hrdlicka, *The Medico-Legal Aspects of the Case of Maria Barbella*, Contributions from the Pathological Institute of the New York State Hospitals (1896–1897), Surgical Bulletin (1898). I have also collected as much material as I could find in the archives of the N.Y. Times. It is possible that Pucci relied on articles from the Herald, Journal, and other contemporary papers. In those days newspaper crime reporting was something of an art, and coverage can amount to a daily record transcript.

31. Levy tried a number of celebrated cases, including the Nan Patterson case. *See* NEWMAN LEVY, THE NAN PATTERSON CASE (1959). Levy's exploits in the Nan Patterson case are also documented and discussed in chapter nine of GASLIGHT LAWYERS.

32. *See* Alan Bellows, "The Rise and Fall of William J. Sidis," https://www.damninteresting.com/the-rise-and-fall-of-william-j-sidis/ (last visited Jan. 23, 2017); AMY WALLACE, THE PRODIGY: A BIOGRAPHY OF WILLIAM JAMES SIDIS, AMERICA'S GREATEST CHILD PRODIGY (1986). The case of *Sidis v. F-R Publishing Corp.*, 113 F.2d 806 (1940) arose from the publication of an article titled "Where Are They Now? April Fool," in the NEW YORKER, Aug. 14, 1937, at 22–26, written by James Thurber under the pseudonym of Jared Manley. The article was neither false nor malicious, but the claim in the *Sidis* case was for violation of Sidis's right to privacy. The court severely restricted the rights of those who had become public figures.

33. Dr. Allan McLane Hamilton, a noted alienist of the day, left us with a lengthy, published memoir, RECOLLECTIONS OF AN ALIENIST—PERSONAL AND PROFESSIONAL (1916) [hereinafter HAMILTON, RECOLLECTIONS OF AN ALIENIST]. Dr. Hamilton held forth on a great number of subjects, including the "Kentucky Meat Shower." On Mar. 3, 1876, some kind of meat fell from the sky in Bath County, Kentucky. Some stalwart Kentuckians tasted it and were of the opinion that it was mutton or venison. *See Flesh Descending in a Shower—An Astounding Phenomenon in Kentucky—Fresh Meat Like Mutton or Venison Falling from a Clear Sky*, N.Y. TIMES, Mar. 10, 1876. Dr. Hamilton's connection to an investigation of the event is noted in SCIENTIFIC AMERICAN, Supplement No. 30, July 22, 1876. *See also,* Bec Crew, *Great Kentucky Meat Shower mystery unwound by projectile vulture vomit* (Dec. 1, 2014) at https://blogs.scientificamerican.com (last visited Feb. 11, 2017) (This blog post includes a photo captioned "One of the preserved meat specimens from the Arthur Byrd Cabinet at Transylvania University."); Troy Taylor, *Mysterious Falls from the Sky* (2002) at www.prairieghosts.com/falls_sky.html (last visited Jan. 23, 2017); The Royal Microscopical Society of Great Britain reports in XIV THE MONTHLY MICROSCOPICAL JOURNAL (July–Dec. 1876) that the consensus was the source of this manna from heaven was most probably vomit from a flock of buzzards. Apparently, when one

buzzard vomits, the others tend to follow suit—buzzard see, buzzard do. I did not know that, and I bet you didn't either. No comment from our Kentucky stalwarts regarding this scientific consensus is recorded.

34. Pecoraro also wrote a play about Jack the Ripper. *See* Hutchins Hapgood, *The Foreign Stage in New York: III The Italian Theater*, 11 BOOKMAN, Aug. 1900, 545–553. This article has a wonderful description of the puppet battles between Knights and Saracens, which may have inspired a scene in *Godfather II* (Paramount Pictures 1974).

35. IDANNA PUCCI, THE TRIALS OF MARIA BARBELLA 274 (1997).

36. *See* illustrations in this book.

Chapter One
The Search for William F. Howe: Tall Tales Retold

37. "Marm" Mandelbaum ran her operation out of a dry-goods store at 79 Clinton Street in the heart of a German residential section in New York City known as Kleine Deutschland. It is said that she amassed a fortune of over $1 million and that she kept the firm of Howe & Hummel at the ready with a yearly retainer of $5,000. *See* EDWARD VAN EMERY, SINS OF NEW YORK: AS "EXPOSED" BY THE POLICE GAZETTE (1930); LARDNER & REPPETTO, NYPD: A CITY AND ITS POLICE 96 (2000). When Mandelbaum was finally cornered by District Attorney Peter B. Olney, she fled to Toronto. *See Mrs. Mandelbaum Missing; The Notorious Receiver Flies from the City*, N.Y. TIMES, Dec. 5, 1884. She lived in Toronto until her death, unmolested due to the ministrations of Abe Hummel. *See Old 'Mother' Mandelbaum Is Dead—She Was a Famous 'Fence' Well Known to the Police of this City*, N.Y. TIMES, Feb. 27, 1894.

38. *Bulldozing the Court*, N.Y. TIMES, July 31, 1884. Howe's attempts to delay the prosecution with dilatory motions is recounted in *The Case of Mrs. Mandelbaum*, N.Y. TIMES, Dec. 3, 1884.

39. J.S. Ogilve & Co., Chicago, 1888 [hereinafter HOWE & HUMMEL, IN DANGER].

40. The New York press of the time was known for its sensationalism. *See* JOHN STEVENS, SENSATIONALISM AND THE NEW YORK PRESS (1991). One gets the impression from the press that horrific murders were quite common at the turn of the nineteenth century. The facts do not seem

to bear this out. *See* Eric Monkkonen, Murder in New York City 20–21 (2001).

41. Rovere, *supra* note 12.

42. *See* chapter two of Gaslight Lawyers.

43. "Defense lawyer miraculously secures acquittal of alleged murderess who shot her husband/lover" is a popular storyline. *See, e.g.,* Elmer Rice, Counselor-at-Law (1931). Rice was a New York lawyer before turning playwright. He was best known for Street Scene (1929), which won a Pulitzer Prize.

44. *Ella Nelson's Acquittal,* N.Y. Times, June 21, 1891.

45. My version is gleaned from the actual trial transcript and not from secondhand accounts. Unless otherwise noted, my summary, including all quoted text, is from the trial transcript.

46. *Decadence of New York's Criminal Bar; Death of Mr. Howe, the Last of a Long Line of Distinguished Criminal Lawyers, Calls Attention to Recent Changes in Legal Profession… Dramatic Scenes in Court in Which 'the Father of the Criminal Law' Figured,* N.Y. Times, Sept. 7, 1902. This was apparently Howe's recollection of how he had used the letter in his summation. Some view the result in the Nelson case as one more example of jurors going soft on female defendants. *See* Carolyn B. Ramsey, MD, JD, *Public Responses to Intimate Violence: a Glance at the Past,* 121(4) Public Health Rep., 460–463 (Jul.–Aug. 2006). But this may also have been an example of the lex non scripta—"some people need killin'." *Compare* Richard H. Underwood, *'Arch and Gordon': The Crime Behind the Ballad,* 31 Legal Stud. F. 825 (2007).

47. Francis Wellman, Gentlemen of the Jury 105 (1924). Wellman repeated the story in his book Success in Court 65–67 (1941). In the later account, he says Howe dug his nails into her neck, but again he said he did not actually see this as his back was turned. It seems odd to me that Wellman would have his back turned to Howe and the defendant during closing argument. According to the New York Herald [hereinafter cited as Herald], Wellman followed Howe with an able, "forceful" summation, so he could not have been too rattled. Herald, June 20, 1891.

48. Herald, June 20, 1891.

49. *More Than She Hoped For—Ella Nelson Found Guiltless of the Murder of Samuel L. M. Post*, N.Y. TIMES, June 20, 1891.

50. Transcript courtesy of John Jay, Trial #15 (244 pp.).

51. N.Y. TIMES, Sept. 7, 1902, *supra* note 46; *William F. Howe, Dean of Criminal Bar, Dead*, N.Y. TIMES, Sept. 3, 1902.

52. *Ella Nelson's Acquittal —The District Attorney Might Have Accepted a Plea of Manslaughter*, N.Y. TIMES, June 21, 1891.

53. WELLMAN, GENTLEMAN OF THE JURY, *supra* note 47 at 106. Of course, an offer to plead is not admissible in court.

54. *A Mystery Soon Solved—August Bolst [sic] The Man Cut Up and Put in a Trunk*, N.Y. TIMES, Jan. 28, 1887; *Capt. Unger's Victim—More Details of the Crime Brought to Light—A Vain Search for Bohle's Missing Head—How the Two Men Became Acquainted*, N.Y. TIMES, Jan. 29, 1887; Inquest in Bohle's Case, N.Y. Times, Feb. 2, 1887. Unger had a checkered history. He had run a grocery store on Mott Street and then worked on and off as a saloon keeper. At one time he kept a place at Number 315 Rivington Street which served as a hangout for the "Short Tail" gang. *See* N.Y. TIMES, Jan. 29, 1887.

55. *See Bohle's Butcher on Trial*, N.Y. TIMES, Feb. 15, 1887, which summarizes prosecutor Nicoll's opening statement.

56. *Examining Bohle's Body*, N.Y. TIMES, Jan. 30, 1887.

57. *Id.*

58. He employed this very tactic in his last big case, the Nack-Thorn-Guldensuppe case, which also involved a headless dismembered victim who was reassembled and identified by physical peculiarities. *See* Underwood, *supra* notes 16 and 23.

59. N.Y. TIMES, Feb. 2, 1887, *supra* note 54.

60. N.Y. TIMES, Feb. 12, 1887.

61. N.Y. TIMES, Feb. 15, 1887, *supra* note 55.

62. The complete confession is set out in *Unger's Crime Confessed… The Sights Which Unnerved the Prisoner and Led Him to Tell His Story of the Murder*, N.Y. TIMES, Jan. 31, 1887.

63. *Id.*

64. Later news accounts reported that he had been cashiered from the navy for a theft offense. *See* N.Y. TIMES, Feb. 19, 1887.

65. Unger had two sons and two daughters but only the younger son lived with him—his wife was in the insane asylum on Blackwell's Island. *See* N.Y. TIMES, Jan. 29, 1887, *supra* note 54.

66. *Capt. Unger on the Stand—He Tells the Story of a Horrible Night—How the Stolid Saloon Keeper Was Tortured by the Thoughts of His Crime and the Fear of Detection*, N.Y. TIMES, Feb. 18, 1887.

67. N.Y. TIMES, Feb. 19, 1887.

68. N.Y. TIMES, Sept. 3, 1902, *supra* note 51 and Sept. 7, 1902, *supra* note 46.

69. *Twenty Years for Unger—Guilty of Manslaughter in the First Degree*, N.Y. TIMES, Feb. 20, 1887.

70. *Id.*

71. The trial transcript can be found in the John Jay collection, *supra* note 30, at Trial #64 (180 pp.). Unless otherwise noted, my summary, including all quoted text, is from the trial transcript.

72. WELLMAN, GENTLEMAN OF THE JURY, *supra* note 47 at 103–104.

73. I suppose that nowadays, upon the failure of the prosecution to produce such evidence, the defense would move for a missing evidence instruction.

74. Popular accounts of the case can be found in N.Y. TIMES, Sept. 7, 1902, and in *Theron G. Strong on the Bar's Changes in 40 Years*, N.Y. TIMES, April 12, 1914.

75. I am reminded of the theatrical use of a similar prop by the prosecution in the Wallace case:

> "There was in the room there, and had been for some time, by the gas stove, an iron sort of poker thing, like that, amply sufficient to have done this deed."

> As [prosecuting counsel] Hemmerde said, "like that," he suddenly picked up the iron bar and flourished it menacingly above his head; then after adding "amply sufficient to have done this deed," he lowered the iron bar and let it fall with a resounding crash.

"The effect of prosecuting counsel's gesture was electric,"
says an observer.

Jonathan Goodman, The Killing of Julia Wallace
170 (1969).

76. Apparently there were such things. *See, e.g., Nailless Horseshoe—
An Important Invention Will Prove a Boon*, Weekly Argus News, Jan. 4,
1896. *See also* U.S. Patent 624650 (1899) and U.S. Patent 785006 (1905).

Chapter Two
The Search for William F. Howe Continues:
Stunning Victories That Were Not

77. *See, e.g.,* Freeland, *supra* note 24 at 19; Luc Sante, Low Life:
Lures and Snares of Old New York 212 (1991); and Blaine, *supra*
note 15, at 75.

78. Eddy Portnoy, *Jewish Abortion Technician*, Tablet Magazine,
Aug. 20, 2009, www.tabletmag.com/jewish-life-and-religion/13841/jewish-
abortion-technician (last visited January 23, 2017).

79. *See* Clifford Browder, The Wickedest Woman in
New York: Madame Restell, the Abortionist (1988); Allan Keller,
Scandalous Lady: The Life and Times of Madame Restell:
New York's Most Notorious Abortionist (1981).

80. Restell is frequently referred to as a client of Howe & Hummel.
But see the discussion of her below. Advertisements by Dr. Rosenzweig/
Ascher can be found in an editorial against the abortionists styled *The
Evil of the Age—Slaughter of the Innocents*, N.Y. Times, Aug. 23, 1871.

81. *The Evil of the Age—Satisfactory Progress in Developing the
Trunk Mystery—Discovery of the Truckman Through the Published
Accounts—Arrest of the Abortionist—Sketch of the Prisoner and His
Infamous Career*, N.Y. Times, Aug. 29, 1871.

82. *See The Evil of the Age—Later Developments in Regard to
the Trunk Tragedy—Important Admissions of Rosenzweig's Servant—
All Doubt of the Identity of the Victim Removed—Sketch of the Life of
Miss Alice Bowlby [sic]— Suicide at Paterson, N.J. of Her Supposed
Destroyer*, N.Y. Times, Sept. 1, 1891. *See also* Portnoy, *supra* note 78.

83. *Rosenzweig the Abortionist—His Fruitless Attempt to Get Out on Bail*, N.Y. TIMES, Sept. 8, 1891.

84. Bad pun intended. *Rosenzweig's Trial—Opening of the Case for the People—The District-Attorney Condemns the Law as Insufficient—Testimony for the Prosecution*, N.Y. TIMES, Oct. 27, 1891.

85. *Sentence of the Abortionist to Seven Years' Imprisonment*, N.Y. TIMES, Oct. 29, 1891.

86. *The Trunk Mystery... Rebutting Evidence Upsets Rosenzweig's Defense*, N.Y. TIMES, Oct. 28, 1891.

87. N.Y. TIMES, Oct. 29, 1891, *supra* note 85.

88. HOWE & HUMMEL, IN DANGER, *supra* note 39, at 159–160.

89. *The Rosenzweig Case—Important Decision of Judge Sutherland—The Notorious Criminal to Be Liberated*, N.Y. TIMES, Nov. 13, 1873.

90. *The Rosenzweig Case—The Notorious Criminal Let Loose on the Community*, N.Y. TIMES, Nov. 14, 1873.

91. The details can be found in N.Y. TIMES, Oct. 29, 30, and 31, 1888. Basically, Carlton and two others were assaulting one Julius Roesler, and Officer James Brennan was shot four times when he came to Roesler's assistance.

92. ROVERE, *supra* note 12, at 75.

93. *Henry Carlton Sentenced*, N.Y. TIMES, Dec. 22, 1888.

94. *Handsome Harry Must Die*, N.Y. TIMES, Oct. 18, 1889.

95. *Carlton Executed*, N.Y. TIMES, Dec. 6, 1889. Rovere says that "Handsome Harry swung in the Tombs courtyard a few days after Christmas." ROVERE, *supra* note 12 at 76. Christmas must have come early that year.

96. All quoted material from Rovere's account of the Annie Walden case is from ROVERE, *supra* note 12, at 80.

97. *Annie Walden in Court*, N.Y. TIMES, April 20, 1892.

98. *See Omen for Annie Walden—She Hears Wife-Killer Osmond Sentenced to Die*, N.Y. TIMES, April 21, 1892.

99. *James Walden Killed*, N.Y. TIMES, Oct. 31, 1891.

100. I am relying on *Mrs. Walden's Story Told—How and Why She Shot and Killed Her Husband—Frank Admission of the Kind of Life*

She Led—Cruelly Treated by Walden—No Recollection of the Actual Shooting, N.Y. Times, Apr. 22, 1892.

101. Wellman, Gentlemen of the Jury, *supra* note 47 at 107.

102. Wellman was, in effect, testifying to irrelevant facts not of record.

103. *Annie Walden Convicted—Declared Guilty of Murder in the Second Degree*, N.Y. Times, April 23, 1892.

104. *To the Island for Life… She Tells the Judge That She Was Not Fairly Tried*, N.Y. Times, April 29, 1892.

105. *Id.*

106. *Hints of Suicide—Murdress Walden Not Reconciled to Her Life Sentence*, N.Y. Times, April 24, 1892.

107. *Petition for Annie Walden's Pardon*, N.Y. Times, Nov. 20, 1893.

108. *Id. See also, Is Annie Walden Dying?* N.Y. Times, Nov. 23, 1893. Blackwell Island was renamed Roosevelt Island in 1971 after Franklin D. Roosevelt.

109. *Leniency for Brave Prisoners—Governor Told of Acts of Courage at Blackwell's Island Fire*, N.Y. Times, April 30, 1899.

110. *The Blackwell's Island Fire*, N.Y. Times, May 24, 1899.

111. North American, Almedia, Pa., Jan. 3 and 4, reported in *Annie Walden: The Tragic Story*, www.jowest.net/Genealogy/John /Farver/AnnieWalden.htm (last visited Jan. 23, 2017).

112. Dr. Allan McLane Hamilton notes in Recollections of an Alienist, *supra* note 33, at 330–331 that:

> Among these ["new and fictitious defenses of insanity"] was "psychic epilepsy," which for a time became a popular excuse for crime, and served more than once the purpose of some unscrupulous attorney.

The defense of "psychic epilepsy" was not wildly successful. *See Psychic Epilepsy in Law—Physician Cites a Case in Which It Failed to Excuse a Murderer*, N.Y. Times, June 28, 1907. But it did figure into the celebrated trials of Maria Barbella (there are a number of various spellings), of which I will have much to say in chapters five and six of Gaslight Lawyers. It was also used to secure the acquittal of

Dr. Elmore E. Elliot, who was charged with an unprovoked and motiveless assault. *See Psychic Epilepsy Excuses Assault—Doctor's Remarkable Defense Sets Criminal Lawyers Speculating; Psychic Epilepsy Defense Justified—Plea Which Won Dr. Elliot's Discharge in Assault Case Sustained by Experts—Disease Long Recognized—Patients Prone to Violence Without Consciousness of Their Acts—Warning Against Imposters*, N.Y. Times, June 28, 1907. *Edgar Allan Poe's Tragic Death Explained*, N.Y. Times, Jan. 20, 1907, alludes to the "discounted" theory that Edgar Allan Poe suffered from "psychic epilepsy." The author of this article quotes an "expert" who claims that Poe died of "mania-a-potu" or "water-on-the-brain." Others have suggested that Poe died at the hands of the brothers of Elmira Shelton, a widow to whom he was betrothed at the time of his death. *See* John Evangelist Walsh, Midnight Dreary— The Mysterious Death of Edgar Allen Poe (1998).

113. Much has been written on developments in late Victorian England during the same period. *See, e.g.*, Joel Peter Eigen, Unconscious Crime: Mental Absence and Criminal Responsibility in Victorian London (2003). For an interesting mental states case in Kentucky, where I teach, *see Fain v. Commonwealth*, 78 Ky. 183 (1879) (somnambulism as a defense to murder or manslaughter).

114. On June 25, 1906, Harry Thaw gunned down renowned architect Stanford White at a theater performance at the dining theater on the roof of Madison Square Garden. The motive was said to be revenge for White's past rape and abuse of Evelyn Nesbit, who was to become Thaw's wife. Nesbit became known as "The Girl in the Red Velvet Swing," because White had forced her to pose naked on a red velvet swing. Thaw was prosecuted by William Travers Jerome, but Thaw's attorney, California lawyer Delphin Delmas, convinced the jury that Thaw was not responsible for his acts. *See Thaw Lays Killing to a 'Brainstorm,'* N.Y. Times, July 30, 1909. Although it was ridiculed in the press, the "brainstorm" defense of temporary insanity was backed up by a number of defense experts—including five past or future presidents of the American Psychiatric Association and the American Neurological Association. *See* Emil Pinta, *Examining Harry Thaw's 'Brain-Storm' Defense: APA and ANA Presidents as Expert Witnesses in a 1907 Trial*, 79 Psychiatric Quarterly 83–89 (2008).

115. Rovere, *supra* note 12, at 92–93.

116. *See* HAMILTON, RECOLLECTIONS OF AN ALIENIST, *supra* note 33, at 328–329. Unless otherwise noted, the discussion of Dr. Hamilton's experience with such cases, including quoted text, is from this source.

117. For a somewhat different contemporary account of the unmasking of Rose's deception, suggesting that the "commission" was, at first, fooled, *see Value of 'Expert' Evidence—How Harry Rose Was Adjudged Insane but Finally Confessed to the Sham*, N.Y. TIMES, July 13, 1906.

118. *Shot Down in His Office—Lawyer Clinton G. Reynolds Fatally Wounded—Alphonse J. Stephani Assassinates His Mother's Legal Advisor—Mr. Reynolds Statement*, N.Y. TIMES, May 16, 1890; *Stephani Sent to the Tombs—Mr. Reynolds's Condition Is Critical, with Slight Hopes*, N.Y. TIMES, May 17, 1890; *Stephani Is Now a Murderer—His Victim, Lawyer Reynolds, Dies After a Five Days' Struggle*, N.Y. TIMES, May 21, 1890.

119. *The Trial of Young Stephani—For the Murder of Ex-Judge Reynolds—A Plea of Insanity*, N.Y. TIMES, Mar. 31, 1891. Nowadays a contingent fee in a criminal case is clearly unethical.

120. *Id.*

121. *Id.* Dr. Hamilton reported a similar history. *See* HAMILTON, RECOLLECTIONS OF AN ALIENIST, *supra* note 33, at 333.

122. *No Pardon for Stephani*, N.Y. TIMES, Oct. 20, 1899.

123. HAMILTON, RECOLLECTIONS OF AN ALIENIST, *supra* note 33, at 333.

124. It had been ruled that Stephani could make no disposition of his growing fortune and could make no use of it beyond that allowed by prison rules. *See Rich Slayer Seeks to Prove Sanity*, N.Y. TIMES, Aug. 4, 1914. *See also, Murderer Has $144,132*, N.Y. TIMES, Jan. 30, 1921.

125. *People ex rel. Stephani v. North, Medical Sup't, etc.*, 91 Misc. Rep. 616, 155 N.Y.S. 595 (1915).

126. *Rich Slayer Dies—Leaves Odd Will—A. J. Stephani in Prison 44 Years...*, N.Y. TIMES, Feb. 5, 1935.

127. *In re Stephani's Estate*, 159 Misc. 43, 288 N.Y.S. 486 (1936).

128. ROVERE, *supra* note 12, at 87.

129. Wellman, The Art of Cross-Examination, *supra* note 20, at 150–151.

130. Hamilton, Recollections of an Alienist *supra* note 33, at 280. As I have noted here and in other research, Howe was not so technically accomplished that he avoided common beginner's mistakes. *See* Underwood, *supra* note 16, at 817–818. (At a critical point in the Nack-Thorn-Guldensuppe case, Howe asked the proverbial one question too many and a question to which he did not know the answer.).

131. Asbury was the author of The Gangs of New York (1928).

132. There was considerable newspaper coverage of the case. *See The Dunn Homicide—The Coroner's Investigation of the Latest Eighth Ward Murder—A Verdict Against Sharkey*, N.Y. Times, Sept. 5, 1872; *The Trial of Sharkey in General Sessions—Ten Jurors Obtained*, N.Y. Times, June 17, 1873; *The Murder Record—The Dunn Murder—Trial of William J. Sharkey—The Case for the Prosecution*, N.Y. Times, June 20, 1873; *The Sharkey Trial—Testimony for the Defense—The Case to Be Given to the Jury To-day*, N.Y. Times, June 21, 1873; *Found Guilty—William J. Sharkey Convicted of Murder in the First Degree—The Recorder's Charge to the Jury*, N.Y. Times, June 22, 1873; *The Case of Sharkey—The Prisoner Not Yet Sentenced—A Postponement Granted*, N.Y. Times, June 24, 1873; *The Murderer Sharkey—Motion for a New Trial—Affidavits from Three of the Jurors—Decision Reserved*, N.Y. Times, June 29, 1873; *The Death Penalty—Sharkey's Case—A New Trial Denied—The Prisoner to Be Executed in August*, N.Y. Times, July 4, 1873; *The Sharkey Case—A Bill of Exceptions to Be Presented to Judge Pratt To-day*, N.Y. Times, July 25, 1873.

133. *See* Herbert Asbury, All Around the Town 155–156 (1934, new edition 2003).

134. *See 1873, Nov. 19* at http://home.eznet.net/~dminor/ NYNY1873.html (last visited January 23, 2017).

135. Asbury, supra note 133, at 158. *See also*, Herbert Asbury, *That Was New York—The Escape of William J. Sharkey*, New Yorker, Mar. 7, 1931, at 39.

136. *Sharkey's Escape—The Trial of Maggie Jourdan*, N.Y. Times, Dec. 30, 1873.

137. *Id. See also Sharkey's Escape—The Trial of Maggie Jourdan*, N.Y. Times, Dec. 31, 1873.

138. *Trial of Maggie Jourdan—Disagreement and Discharge of the Jury,* N.Y. Times, Jan 1, 1874.

139. *See A Murderer's Escape—Sharkey Walks Out of the Tombs at Midday,* N.Y. Times, Nov. 20, 1873. *See also Sharkey's Flight—A Reward of $2,000 Offered for His Body—His Prison Life—The Mode of His Escape—Another Prisoner Identifies Maggie Jourdan,* N.Y. Times, Nov. 21, 1873. In this later article, the paper reports that Abe Hummel initially appeared for both Allen and Jourdan in an effort to get them released on a writ of habeas corpus.

140. *Sharkey's Accomplices,* N.Y. Times, Jan. 28, 1874. Apparently one or more officials lost their jobs over the Sharkey escape, but they were exonerated by information wormed out of Sharkey by a Detective Davies, who had dealings with Sharkey in Cuba. *See Efforts to Secure Sharkey—Detective Davies on His Way to Cuba—His Plan of Operation—Sharkey Reported to Have Left Havana,* N.Y. Times, Mar. 20, 1875.

141. *The Murderer Sharkey,* N.Y. Times, Feb. 7, 1875. *See also Exiles from America: Wanted by the Police,* N.Y. Times, Aug. 20, 1905.

142. *Latest News by Cable—Sharkey—Rearrest at Santiago De Cuba with a False Passport—A Claim for British Protection Futile,* N.Y. Times, Mar. 23, 1875.

143. *The Middletown Bank Robbery,* N.Y. Times, Nov. 16, 1880.

144. *Freedom Got with Ease—John Jourdan, Maggie's Brother, Walks Out of Bellevue. Taken There from Jail Because of Illness—No Safeguards Against Escape—A Woman There, Possibly His Sister,* N.Y. Times, Apr. 16, 1881.

145. *A Noted Criminal—Maggie Jourdan's Brother Locked Up at Police Headquarters,* N.Y. Times, Aug. 9, 1884.

146. As in the case of Sharkey, who knows what corruption might have been involved. Lardner & Reppetto, *supra* note 37, at 96 notes that "[Howe & Hummel, for example] exemplified the maxim that it was better for a lawyer to know the judge than the law. In a three year period... Albert Cardozo [father of Benjamin Nathan Cardozo]... released two hundred of Howe & Hummel's clients in exchange for bribes."

147. *See,* for example, the *Wikipedia* entry for Carlyle Harris, as well as other online articles.

148. Jerome defended his client zealously. *See, e.g., Hot Words in Court, Lawyers in the Harris Case in a Wrangle—Mr. Wellman Calls Mr. Jerome a Liar...* N.Y. Times, Jan. 29, 1892. At one point, Jerome became so exhausted that he broke down in court. *See* Charles Boswell & Lewis Thompson, The Carlyle Harris Case 82–83 (1961). Jerome prosecuted the famous Thaw case, alluded to in *supra* note 114.

149. The pursuit of Abe Hummel is discussed in Rovere, *supra* note 12, and in Arthur Train, True Stories of Crime from the District Attorney's Office (1908).

150. I have found no less than fifty articles or entries in N.Y. Times alone.

151. The recorder or trial judge excluded such evidence on several occasions. *See Harris Has a Bad Record,* N.Y. Times, Jan. 23, 1892.

152. *See* the account of Charles Boswell & Lewis Thompson, *supra* note 148, at 92–93.

153. *Id.* at 56. Hamilton mentions his participation in his book, Recollections of an Alienist, *supra* note 33, at 276.

154. Boswell & Thompson, *supra* note 148, at 109–110.

155. *See* Rovere, *supra* note 12, at 85–86; Boswell & Thompson, *supra* note 148, at 90.

156. Wellman's account can be found in his book Gentlemen of the Jury, *supra* note 47, at 134–135. The transcript of the Carlyle Harris case can be found in the John Jay collection, *supra* note 30, at Trial #21, 1892/01/14, Reels 6–7. In this particular instance, the closing arguments of counsel were transcribed at some point. Wellman ends this way:

> "I ask you to go with me to that lonely church yard, and stand for a few moments with me by the grave of this unfortunate girl; and let us there, with bared heads say a few words in praise of her innocent life, she who had a right to live for years in this garden of God's beauty, suddenly taken from it and hurled into eternity. Let us write an epitaph on her grave. 'Murdered innocence.'"

157. Boswell & Thompson, *supra* note 148, at 115. *See also A Doubtful Story—What a Chicago Man Says Bearing on the Harris Case,* N.Y. Times, Feb. 13, 1892; *More Time for Carlyle Harris—Another*

Delay in His Case—Recorder Smyth Frees His Mind, N.Y. Times, Jan. 31, 1893; *Did Helen Potts Take Morphine?—Miss M'Kinstry Says She Did and Threatened to Kill Herself*, N.Y. Times, Feb. 1, 1893; *Harris's Forlorn Hope—Affidavits that Helen Potts Was a Morphine Eater Called 'Rank Perjuries' by District Attorney Nicoll*, N.Y. Times, Feb. 28, 1893.

158. *Id.* at 119. *See also* Francis Wellman, Success in Court, *supra* note 47, at 58.

159. Apparently "morphinism [was] far from being rare..." *See Women Victims of Morphine—Physicians Discuss the Danger in the Use of the Drug—Interesting Paper Read by Dr. M. J. Mattison Before a Section of the Academy of Medicine*, N.Y. Times, Oct. 25, 1895. One is reminded of a similar case in England where part of the successful defense was that the alleged victim of arsenic poisoning may have been an "arsenic eater." F. Tennyson Jesse, Trial of Madeline Smith 391 (1949 reprint from Notable British Trials Series).

160. *Harris's Appeal Denied—Recorder Smyth Refuses Him a New Trial... The Recorder Refuses to Accept the Statements That Helen Potts Used Morphine Habitually and Declares that They Are Offset by the Affidavits for the People*, N.Y. Times, Mar. 17, 1893.

161. *Carlyle W. Harris Is Dead—Executed at Sing Sing for the Murder of His Wife*, N.Y. Times, May 9, 1893.

162. *See, e.g.,* Lardner & Reppetto, supra note 37.

163. For a fascinating look at the reality of abortion before anti-abortion became an American policy see James C. Mohr, Abortion in America: The Origins and Evolution of National Policy (1978).

164. Keller, *supra* note 79, at 32.

165. *Id.* at 34.

166. *See also MME. Restell—Some Reminiscences of Her Career Twenty-Three Years Ago—Her Trial and Sentence in the Bodine Case*, N.Y. Times, Sept. 3, 1871.

167. *See* N.Y. Times, Feb. 14, 16, and 23, 1854, and Mar. 3 and 9, 1854.

168. *The Shackford and Restell Case—The Prisoners Discharged—Justice Stuart's Decision—Miss Grant Supposed to Be in Philadelphia,*

N.Y. Times, Mar. 23, 1854. The lawyer for Restell was reported to be a Mr. Jordan.

169. Throughout her career, certain elements of the press tried to link her to the celebrated case of Mary Rogers, "The Beautiful Cigar Girl," whose murder (almost certainly a death caused by a botched abortion) inspired EDGAR ALLAN POE's *Mystery of Marie Roget. See* DANIEL STASHOWER, THE BEAUTIFUL CIGAR GIRL: MARY ROGERS, EDGAR ALLAN POE, AND THE INVENTION OF MURDER (2006); AMY GILMAN SREBNICK, THE MYSTERIOUS DEATH OF MARY ROGERS (1995). The sensational Rogers case is alluded to in HOWE & HUMMEL, IN DANGER, *supra* note 39, in chapter IV, *Store Girls.* Inspector Thomas Byrnes also devotes several pages to her case in his 1886 book, PROFESSIONAL CRIMINALS OF AMERICA 344–347 (reprint 2000).

170. N.Y. TIMES indicated that her counsel was one Edward Mackinley. *See MME. Restell's Arrest—Efforts to Procure Her Release*, N.Y. TIMES, Feb. 14, 1878.

171. HOWE & HUMMEL, IN DANGER, *supra* note 39, in Chapter XVI, *Abortion and the Abortionists*, at 161–167.

Chapter Three
The Case of "Frenchy"—Part 1

172. *He Must Be a Lunatic and Dr. Hamilton Thinks He May Live in the Aristocratic West End*, HERALD, Oct. 3, 1888. Unless otherwise specifically referenced, the accounts and quotations attributed to all medical and legal figures are from this HERALD article.

173. The Honorable Frederick Smyth would end up being the trial judge in the "Frenchy" case, or more properly, the case of *The People v. George Frank.*

174. Dr. Allan McLane Hamilton was the author of several important works, including A MANUAL OF MEDICAL JURISPRUDENCE WITH SPECIAL REFERENCE TO DISEASES AND INJURIES OF THE NERVOUS SYSTEM (1890); TYPES OF INSANITY: AN ILLUSTRATED GUIDE IN THE PHYSICAL DIAGNOSIS OF MENTAL DISEASE (1883); and A SYSTEM OF LEGAL MEDICINE (1884). He also wrote a biographical tract on his grandfather,

Alexander Hamilton, as well as his own memoir, supra note 33, which will also be cited in other chapters of GASLIGHT LAWYERS.

175. Dr. Allan McLane Hamilton appears on stage in many cases in this book.

176. This theory is supported by Robert D. Keppel, PhD, of the University of New Haven. See Robert D. Keppel, Joseph G. Weis, Katherine M. Brown, and Kristen Welch, *The Jack the Ripper Murders: A Modus Operandi and Signature Analysis of the 1888–1891 Whitechapel Murders*, 2:1 J. OF INVESTIGATIVE PSYCHOL. AND OFFENDER PROFILING 1–21 (Jan. 2005).

177. Dr. Edward Charles Spitzka will play a bit part in chapter seven of GASLIGHT LAWYERS.

178. EDWARD CHARLES SPITZKA was the author of INSANITY, ITS CLASSIFICATION, DIAGNOSIS AND TREATMENT (1883).

179. *See Looking for 'The Face Within the Face' in Man*, N.Y. TIMES, Mar. 4, 1906. This article notes that Edward Anthony and others, including a Dr. Hrdlicka, who will star in chapters six and seven of GASLIGHT LAWYERS, served on a committee on brain bequests and preservation. Another interesting digression, one of their associates, the depressive and unfortunate Dr. Henry Cattell, was responsible for the accidental destruction of Walt Whitman's brain. *See* Brian Burrell, *The Strange Fate of Whitman's Brain*, 20 WALT WHITMAN Q. REV. 107 (2003); Sheldon Lee Gosline, *'I am a fool' Dr. Henry Cattell's Private Confession—14 October 1892* (Feb. 13. 2013) at the blog of the UCLA Center for The History of Medicine. For a long time, it was thought that an assistant had dropped the glass-jarred brain on the floor, and it has been speculated that this incident inspired the scene in the 1931 movie *Frankenstein* (Universal Pictures), where Dr. Frankenstein's assistant, Fritz, drops the jar with the good brain and covers up by substituting the bad brain of a convicted murderer. *See* Cynthia Haven, *Frankenstein and Walt Whitman's brain: 'This is a grewsome story!'* (June 2012) http://bookhaven.stanford.edu/2012/06/frankenstein-and-walt-whitmans-brain-this-is-a-grewsome-story/ (last visited Jan. 24, 2017).

180. There is a suggestion that Dr. Spitzka would later claim to have actually discussed treatment with a man he came to believe was Jack the

Ripper. *See Jack the Ripper,* Anaconda Standard, May 5, 1901. This is a rather fantastic claim.

181. This was published in The Journal of Nervous and Medical Disease (1888).

182. *See* J. P. Galloway, The Servant Girl Murders: Austin, Texas 1885 (2010) and Tim Huddleston, Annihilation in Austin: The Servant Girl Annihilator Murders of 1885 (2013).

183. *See* William Bryk, *Inspector Thomas F. Byrnes Inventor of the Third Degree,* (Sept. 4, 2001, 6:01 AM, updated Feb. 16, 2015), www.nypress.com/inspector-thomas-f-byrnes-inventor-of-the-third-degree/ (last visited Jan. 24, 2017).

184. Published in 1886.

185. *See, e.g.,* R. Michael Gordon, The American Murders of Jack the Ripper 29 (2003). This book has an extensive account of the Carrie Brown murder and makes an unconvincing case that the New York murder was in fact the work of Jack the Ripper. A recent biography of Byrnes also attributes such boasts to Byrnes. *See* J. North Conway, The Big Policeman: The Rise and Fall of America's First, Most Ruthless, and Greatest Detective (2010).

186. Wolf Vanderlinden, the author of *The New York Affair,* a series of articles appearing in Ripper Notes—The Am. J. for Ripper Studies, suggests that all of this has been derived from a newspaper article in London on October 4, 1888. Under the headline *An American Detective's Opinion,* Byrnes suggested ways in which the investigation of the Whitechapel murders might be undertaken. *See The New York Affair—Part 2* (from the January 2004 issue of Ripper Notes). The Byrnes biography, *supra* note 185, at 8, seems to conflate that article with an interview attributed to a N.Y. Times crime beat reporter. Vanderlinden's study of the Carrie Brown murder is, in my opinion, first rate. He relies on extensive newspaper sources for which he thanks one Robert McLaughlin. Both Gordon, *supra* note 185, and Vanderlinden are primarily interested in whether or not the murderer of Carrie Brown was (Gordon) or was not (Vanderlinden) the real Jack the Ripper. That is not my primary interest. I am looking at the Carrie Brown murder (the Frenchy case) from the viewpoint of an American lawyer, and I am interested in the performance of the prosecutors and defense lawyers. I have reviewed the

actual trial transcripts in the case, which I have had access to courtesy of the John Jay collection, *supra* note 30. I will cite the transcripts as "Tr. p. xx" In addition to the transcripts, I will cite newspaper copy from N.Y. Times archive and the Library of Congress, Chronicling America, Historic American Newspapers, both of which are readily available. Readers with great interest in contemporary newspaper clippings may wish to reference the New York County District Attorney newspaper clipping scrapbooks (1882–1940) available in the New York City Municipal Archives.

187. *See Choked, Then Mutilated—A Murder Like One of Jack the Ripper's Deeds*, N.Y. Times, Apr. 25, 1891. This article, being one of the first press accounts of the Carrie Brown murder in New York City, states in part:

> Inspector Byrnes apparently feels that the murderer must be arrested, for inspector Byrnes has said that it would be impossible for crimes such as "Jack the Ripper" committed in London to occur in New York and the murderer not be found. He has not forgotten his words on the subject.

Similarly, the evening edition of New York World, Apr. 25, 1891, includes a comprehensive story on the Carrie Brown murder, including accounts of the New York Police Department's response, which the story attributes, in part, to the statements of confidence previously made by Inspector Byrnes and Superintendent Murray "the day after the murder of the Ripper's ninth victim, November 9, 1888." After noting that he has been informed that no locality in New York "corresponds in misery and crime with [London's] Whitehall district," Superintendent Murray states:

> I am confident, though, that no such crimes could continue under the system of the New York police. The entire force would, if necessary, be sent out in citizens' dress to run down the assassin.

The New York World article further states, "Chief Inspector Byrnes was equally as confident that such a crime could not be committed in New York without the murderer being run down in forty-eight hours."

188. Julian Hawthorne, a writer and journalist [we will encounter him later, since he covered several trials discussed in this book for the

Hearst newspapers] and the son of Nathaniel Hawthorne, wrote a book of stories supposedly taken from the *Diary of Inspector Byrnes*.

189. Detractors included the influential Jacob A. Riis—who will figure into the Frenchy story—and muckraker Lincoln Steffens. *See* Bryk, *supra* note 183.

190. *Hunting the Murderer*, Sun, Apr. 27, 1891. Curiously, Carrie Brown was also known as "Old Jeff," after Jefferson Davis, because her husband had been a Southern sympathizer during the Civil War.

191. Sun, Apr. 25, 1891.

192. N.Y. Times, Apr. 25, 1891, *supra* note 187. *See also,* New York World, Apr. 25, 1891.

193. An exemplar in Sun actually looks like "Kniclo," and "Nicklo" and "Nicolo" appear in the trial transcript.

194. The N.Y. Times article says that Eddie Fitzgerald wrote "Kniclo" on the register.

195. *Id. See also Jack the Ripper's Mark*, Sun, Apr. 25, 1891.

196. *Hunting the Murderer*, Sun, Apr. 27, 1891.

197. Tr. p. 44.

198. Defense counsel would later stress this point during his summation to the jury. See chapter four of Gaslight Lawyers.

199. *It is Yet a Mystery—The Police Still at Sea in the East River Hotel Murder Case*, N.Y. Times, Apr. 27, 1891; *The Murderer Still at Large—No Light as Yet on the East River Hotel Mystery*, N.Y. Times, Apr. 28, 1891; *Byrnes Quite Mystified*, N.Y. Times, Apr. 29, 1891; *In the Dragnet. Many Blond Men with Mustaches Arrested on Suspicion Not Identified As the East River Hotel Ripper, and Set Free. Byrnes's Detectives Not Yet Sure of the Murderer's Identity*, New York World, Apr. 27, 1891.

200. Sun, Apr. 27, 1891.

201. *See We Know the Murderer*, The Sun, Apr. 26, 1891; *Byrnes Says He Has a Clue… There Are Two 'Frenchy's'; He Has One and Wants the Other*, N.Y. Times, Apr. 26, 1891.

202. He apparently had had an alibi. *Followed a Trail of Blood—Byrnes's Dramatic Recital of the Case Against Frenchy No. 1*, Sun, May 1, 1891.

203. *Id.* See also *Is He the Guilty Man—Facts Which Seem to Point to the Murderer of Carrie Brown*, N.Y. Times, May 1, 1891.

204. The transcript of the Coroner's Inquest is available on microfilm at John Jay.

205. Sun, May 1, 1891, *supra* note 202. *See also The East River Hotel Murder*, N.Y. Times, May 3, 1891 (Ben Ali told that the blood on his underwear—from his shirt—came from a fight he had had with a man. He would tell a different story at trial.)

206. See *'Frenchy' Was the Murderer—So Says the Coroner's Jury in the Carrie Brown Inquest*, New York Times, May 15,1891.

207. *'Frenchy No. 1' Indicted*, N.Y. Times, May 19,1891.

208. *City and Suburban News*, N.Y. Times, May 20, 1891.

209. Francis L. Wellman, Luck and opportunity: Recollections 78–79 (1938).

210. David P. Leonard, *In Defense of the Character Evidence Prohibition: Foundations of the Rule Against Trial by Character*, 73 Ind. L.J. 1161 (1998). This is usually referred to as propensity evidence— that the defendant has the propensity to commit a crime because of his character or past crimes. *See People v. Molineux*, 61 N.E. 286 (N.Y. 1901). To this day some New York practitioners refer to a pretrial hearing on a motion to exclude such evidence as a Molineux hearing. For a good read on the Molineux case see Harold Schechter, The Devil's Gentleman (2007).

211. 335 U.S. 469, 475–476 (1948).

212. *See also People v. Molineux*, 61 N.E. 286 (N.Y. 1901).

213. *See* Christopher B. Mueller & Laird C. Kirkpatrick, Evidence (5th ed., 2012) §4.12. For a classic explanation of the character evidence rules, see *People v. Zackowitz*, 254 N.Y. 192 (1930), opinion by Justice Cardozo.

214. *Id.*

215. Mueller & Kirkpatrick, *supra* note 213, at §4.12.

216. *Jury Ready for 'Frenchy No. 1'—The Algerian Talks About Himself and Protests Innocence*, N.Y. Times, June 27, 1891.

217. Tr. pp. 1–3.

218. Tr. p. 6.

219. *See* Sun, June 30, 1891.

220. Tr. pp. 6–9. *See also*, June 30, 1891.

221. *Invoking the Microscope—New Proofs Against Frenchy Promised at His Trial*, Sun, June 30, 1891; *Witnesses Against 'Frenchy'—The Prosecution Outlines Its Case Against the Algerian*, N.Y. Times, June 30, 1891.

222. Edwin M. Borchard, Convicting the Innocent 69 (1932).

223. Tr. pp. 1103–1105.

224. For the lawyers who may be reading this, there was an interesting objection regarding whether the defendant could make adoptive admissions if he could not speak English. Lawyer House cited *People v. Rafaele Izzo* for the proposition that he could not, but the judge brushed him off, saying that be believed the defendant knew some English.

225. An interesting "Sam Shine" postscript to the Frenchy trial appeared in *Sam Shine in Jail. 'Shakespeare's Murder Recalled by His Arrest for Excise Violation*, New York World, Aug. 15, 1891. The article reports that "[a]fter the character of the [East River Hotel] was disclosed," [referring to Frenchy's "Jack the Ripper" style murder of Carrie Brown], the Excise Commissioner revoked the hotel's liquor license, the hotel continued to sell liquor "clandestinely," and Sam Shine, the bartender, was "held in Tombs Court" for the violation.

226. Two photographs taken of the body are available on the Internet. I will spare the reader.

227. *See* Vanderlinden, *supra* note 186.

228. A good account of all the testimony, including this minor victory for the defense, can be found at *Yarns Frenchy Told… Lawyer House Gets a Very Big Exception [sic] to the Exhibition of a Knife of Frenchy's to the Jury…*, Sun, July 1, 1891; and *'Good Men Don't Hang Me'—Ameer Ben Ali Frantic on the Witness Stand*, Sun, July 3, 1891.

229. David Gilway, Tr. pp. 491–93; Edward Smith, Tr. pp. 502–03; Theodore Miller, Tr. pp. 513–15.

230. Constable Hiland, Tr. pp. 794–95; *see also*, New York World, July 2, 1891, stating that in the defense case in chief, House called Constable James R. Hiland to testify that he was in charge of the jail,

had arrested the defendant and searched the defendant thoroughly, and that the defendant did not have a knife. The article further reports that District Attorney Wellman's cross-examination of Hiland suggested that the constable volunteered to appear as a witness "to save himself from a charge of not performing [his] duty of searching [the] prisoner" and that he had not removed defendant's splints when he arrested him and "could not swear that the knife was not concealed in the splints." *See* Tr. pp. 799–802, 806–07.

231. Tr. p. 663.

232. Tr. pp. 660–772.

233. New York Med. J., July 26, 1902, at 514–518. This article was more or less a repeat of an earlier article, *Some Medico-Legal Points in the 'Frenchy' Murder Trial*, New York Med. J., July 19, 1891.

234. For a news account *see Experts Against 'Frenchy'—Three Physicians Testify About the East River Murder*, N.Y. Times, July 2, 1891.

235. Tr. p. 713. In Henry F. Formad, Comparative Studies of Mammalian Blood, with special reference to the Microscopical Diagnosis of Blood Stains in Criminal Cases 51 (IX:3) Journal of Comparative Medicine and Surgery (Philadelphia: A.L. Hummel, MD, 1888), Dr. Formad observed that similar statements made by Virchow and others were made as early as 1842 and 1857, and that he hoped that they had since changed their minds.

Chapter Four
The Case of "Frenchy"—Part 2

236. Tr. pp. 776–791.

237. Reports in the press detailed the description provided the police by Mary Miniter, the assistant housekeeper at the East River Hotel who saw Carrie Brown and her companion come in and go upstairs together on the night of the murder:

> [Miniter] says he was about 5 feet 8 inches in height and was lightly built. His features were sharp and his nose long and came down to a sharp point. His mustache was brown and heavy, and the ends, which were long, neither curled

nor drooped, but seemed to stand out perfectly straight, like the whiskers of a cat.

His clothing was dusty and well worn, and he wore a derby hat that was broken and dented at the top, which he pulled down over his eyes. His coat was of the cutaway pattern, and, like his trousers, was made of dark-colored cloth. He wore a cotton shirt and a collar that was much soiled.

Evening World, Apr. 25, 1891.

238. The modern court-watcher would be surprised by the fact that when the jury came in before the presentation of the defense, "Nearly all of them brought newspapers with them and commented on the pictures of themselves and of others connected with the trial that were published." Sun, July 3, 1891.

239. Sun, July 3, 1891.

240. Evening World, June 30, 1891.

241. Tr. p. 907.

242. Tr. p. 909.

243. Tr. p. 935.

244. Tr. pp. 941–942; Sun, July 3, 1891.

245. The reader is no doubt aware of the modern defense strategy of challenging forensic evidence based on "contamination." Of course, contamination usually does not lead to a "match."

246. He was not able to testify regarding other locations where tyrosine might be found, because he was relying on a text written by another expert. See Tr. p. 917. Such testimony would be allowed today under a "learned treatise" exception to the hearsay rule.

247. Tr. p. 918.

248. Tr. pp. 921, 924.

249. Tr. p. 931.

250. Tr. pp. 928–930.

251. Tr. p. 1023.

252. Tr. pp. 935–942, 963.

253. Tr. p. 944.

254. Tr. p. 932.

255. Sun, July 4, 1891.

256. Tr. p. 944.

257. Tr. pp. 949–950.

258. Tr. p. 951.

259. Tr. pp. 951–952.

260. Tr. pp. 959–960.

261. Tr. pp. 965–966.

262. Tr. pp. 994–995.

263. Some of the reporters felt, for whatever reason, that Ben Ali could understand English better than he was letting on, but one suspects that this was a case of armchair experts. *See Yarns That Frenchy Told—It Is Pretty Plain That He Talks and Understands English*, Sun, July 1, 1891.

264. Curiously, in his book, Luck and opportunity, *supra* note 209, Wellman repeatedly refers to Ben Ali's lawyer as "Charles Brook," and refers to Ben Ali as an Armenian (!) which is characteristic of his selective and creative memory.

265. Wellman, Luck and Opportunity, *supra* note 209, at 79–80 (1938). Ben Ali was agitated and frightened throughout, but the transcript does not suggest that this was apparent "after the first question."

266. See Vanderlinden, *supra* note 186, *citing* the Philadelphia Press, July 9, 1891.

267. To the same effect *see 'Frenchy's' Trial Nearly Over—It Is Expected that a Verdict Will Be Rendered To-day*, N.Y. Times, July 3, 1891.

268. *See, e.g.* Tr. p. 813.

269. *See, e.g.,* Tr. pp. 817 and 819, drawing a rebuke from the judge. Also, *see supra* note 264, regarding Wellman's repeated references to defendant's lawyer as "Charles Brook."

270. Tr. pp. 836.

271. *See* Tr. p 6.

272. Sun, July 3, 1891.

273. *'Frenchy's' Varied Stories*, N.Y. Times, July 1, 1891.

274. Wellman, Luck and Opportunity, *supra* note 209, at 80.

275. Wellman, Success in Court, *supra* note 47, at 75–76 (1941).

276. *Id.* at 75–76.

277. This contrasts with the views of some commentators that Wellman, the author of the now famous The Art of Cross-Examination, *supra* note 20, was something of a model of ethical practice. *See, e.g.,* J. Alexander Tanford, The Trial Process: Law, Tactics and Ethics (3d ed. 2002) at 289, *quoting* Wellman as having said "The purposes of cross-examination should be to catch truth, ever an elusive fugitive," *citing* the 4th edition of The Art of Cross-Examination, at 204–205. I have only the 1978 paperback edition, but it attributes those words to Emory B. Buckner, who wrote chapter twelve of the book. In any event, Wellman was a street fighter, and I do not necessarily condemn him for his art; but he was not exactly a truth catcher. Always self-promotive he revels in an incident during the Stephani case (see chapter two of Gaslight Lawyers) in which his nemesis, William Howe, was presenting the defense testimony of Dr. Allan McLane Hamilton. Howe apparently asked for an opinion from the famous alienist, without first laying out his credentials. It seems that Howe was hoping Wellman would fall for the bait and bring his illustrious history out during cross. Wellman said, "We have no questions." Wellman was sufficiently proud of this—he had cut off the testimony that Dr. Hamilton wanted to give—and he included it his book, The Art of Cross-Examination, as an example of "silent cross-examination." *See* the 1978 printing at 150. I agree that this was Howe's error, and today's lawyer would find no fault in Wellman's taking advantage of it. On the other hand, Dr. Hamilton (the naive doctor?) was not impressed and commented on Wellman's performance:

> Undoubtedly this was an inspiration, but can one conceive the attitude of a public prosecutor whose duty it is to present all the evidence against as well as in favor of the man in the dock? Speaking of this unfairness, there has always been too much disposition to proceed upon the lines that every defendant is guilty, and for many years this bias against the prisoner and his rights has been deplored by conservative members of the bar.

> Recollections of an Alienist, *supra* note 33, at 280.

278. Strangely, the reports in N.Y. TIMES and SUN did not appear to make much of this, although SUN's artist sketched a picture of Frenchy holding a knife. *See* SUN, July 3, 1891.

279. Wellman was referring to the fact that Frenchy was known to carry a knife. He was probably trying to send a message to the jury that because Frenchy carried a knife, he probably had a knife with him on the night of the murder, and this made it likely that the knife found at the scene was Frenchy's. This evidence had been excluded.

280. Tr. pp. 868, 869.

281. Tr. pp. 903–906.

282. It is ordinarily improper to call as rebuttal evidence that which the prosecution could have, and should have, introduced in its case in chief. That is to say, sometimes the prosecution sandbags the defense, for want of a better term. In this particular case it was not so much a matter of sandbagging the defense as it was getting a second chance to repeat earlier testimony, for emphasis.

283. Tr. pp. 999–1003.

284. Tr. pp. 1003–1007.

285. Tr. pp. 1008–1011.

286. House's summation appears at Tr. pp. 1006–1089.

287. See the discussion of that case in chapter one of GASLIGHT LAWYERS.

288. Tr. pp. 1090–1091.

289. Wellman would also allude to his arrests, which are not ordinarily admissible. As to improper incitement of bias and prejudice in closing argument, *see* RICHARD H. UNDERWOOD AND WILLIAM H. FORTUNE, TRIAL ETHICS §13.13 (1988). Also, reflected in the press are attitudes of bias and prejudice toward Frenchy's ethnicity ("Ameer is an uneducated Arab, a member of the tribe of Beni Alchi. He is so ignorant that he can hardly write his own name, even in his native language.") NEW YORK WORLD, June 30, 1891; Noting physical appearance, demeanor and poor English language skills—"...the dark skinned prisoner kissed the tips of his fingers...smiling pleasantly and murmuring the compliments of the day in choicest Arabesque." WORLD, June 30, 1891; "...immense ears that stick out wonderfully like those of a flying

fox..."; "He jabbered clasped his long talons together..."; and
"...all the time keeping up a jabber like the chatter of monkeys." World, July 2, 1891.

290. During the defense case in chief, House employed an unusual tactic related to the Frenchy's alleged prior robbery of Jen Ali, previously discussed in the text of this chapter.

291. The only reference to anything like this was the following sentence in Levy's opening statement for the defense, made after the close of the state's case.

> The only persons who know him in this country are two, Genali [Jen Ali?] and...[illegible]...of his own people; of course he may know some others; and these two men, if necessary, may come forward, if we deem it wise to put them on the stand, to testify to the fact that he is a gentle and harmless fellow. (Tr. p. 787.)

292. Tr. p. 843.

293. Tr. pp. 1105–1111.

294. The press reported, "It took the twelve men in the jury box two hours to agree upon [the verdict]." World, July 4, 1891.

295. The jury took five ballots before reaching a verdict. On the first ballot eight voted for second degree murder and four for first degree murder.

296. *Frenchy's Life is Safe—Our Ripper Case Ends in 'Murder in the Second Degree,'* Sun, July 4, 1891. *Ben Ali's Big Luck. The Algerian Made Glad by the Jury's Surprising Verdict. His Life Saved. He Seems to Care for Little Else... Victory for Inspector Byrnes*, World, July 4, 1891.

297. *See Ameer Ben Ali Sentenced*, N.Y. Times, July 11, 1891.

298. N.Y. Times, July 5, 1891.

299. *See* Sun, July 4, 1891.

300. Luck and Opportunity, *supra* note 209, at 80.

301. A reporter for the World is said to have interviewed Juror Rutzky (Juror #8 in the jury box). World, July 4, 1891. According to this World article, Juror Rutzky stated that after a number of ballots "the verdict finally rendered was a compromise verdict...it was evident

that the majority believed the man guilty of something." This article also reports that Rutzky further commented on the prosecution's argument as "showing [Frenchy's] motives, but indicating no premeditation." In other words: "That was the theory of the verdict, Frenchy did not premeditate, but he murdered." *Id.*

302. N.Y. TIMES, July 14, 1893.

303. This from the N.Y. TIMES article.

304. Russell was a socialist and a muckraker. He is best known for his reporting on the Johnstown Flood. Forgotten today is the fact that he was a founding member of the NAACP. His biographer made only a passing reference to his role in the Frenchy case. The biographer reported that the murder involved a young woman (?) and that Byrnes's investigation focused on a "mysterious Dutchman." His notes to the case mostly refer to an unrelated murder. *See* MIRALDI, *supra* note 7, at 51 (2003). In EDWIN BORCHARD's classic work, CONVICTING THE INNOCENT, *supra* note 222, Borchard notes that Russell wrote his assessment of the case in *Old Shakespeare*, THE ILLUSTRATED DETECTIVE MAGAZINE (Oct. 1931).

305. BORCHARD, *supra* note 222 at 71.

306. State of New York, PUBLIC PAPERS OF BENJAMIN B. ODELL, JR. GOVERNOR FOR 1902 at 272–277 (1907). Unless specifically otherwise referenced, all quotations in this section of the text are attributable to the PUBLIC PAPERS OF BENJAMIN B. ODELL, JR., as referenced in this note.

307. *See* FLINT, *supra* note 233, at 518.

308. Tr. pp. 128, 130, 198, 199, 563.

309. VANDERLINDEN, *supra* note 186, cites a report as early as May 2, 1891, saying that reporters on the scene before the body was removed had not noticed the blood trail relied upon by the prosecution. Of course, that does not mean that the blood was not there, but it suggests that the evidence against Ben Ali may have been manufactured. The possibility figured into the pardon. But why did none of the reporters come forward during the trial? We must also consider the fact that many members of the press were hostile to Inspector Byrnes. Vanderlinden also argues that Detective Griffin added to the confusion by twice testifying at the coroner's inquest and at trial that he had seen the blood trail on Saturday, "a day after it had supposedly been chiseled

from the floor." The transcripts of the preliminary hearing (Tr. p. 52) and trial (Tr. p. 217) confirm that Griffin said that. On the other hand, Detective Frink testified (Tr. pp. 545–546) that he and Detective Sergeant Crowley cut the flooring of the hall with a chisel on April 29, 1891, the same day that he took the fingernail scrapings from defendant. This is confirmed by Frink's and Captain McLaughlin's testimony at the coroner's inquest (Tr. pp. 154 and 157), and Inspector Byrnes's testimony that the nail scrapings and some stained floor material from the hall between rooms 33 and 31 were delivered to him on April 29 (Tr. pp. 657–658). The confusion may be attributable to the fact that McLaughlin had taken some material earlier.

310. N.Y. Times, Apr. 17, 1902.

311. Conway, *supra* note 185, at 30.

312. Luck and Opportunity, *supra* note 209, at 80–81.

313. The five victims that Ripperologists agree were committed by the same fiend: Mary Ann Nichols, Annie Chapman, Elizabeth Stride, Catherine Eddowes, and Mary Jane Kelly.

314. The ultimate question being, was there a Jack the Ripper after all. The question is hinted at in Gary Coville & Patrick Lucanio, Jack the Ripper 152–53 (1999).

315. New York State Archives.

316. Tr. pp. 354–550.

317. N.Y. Times, Jan. 17, 1898.

318. *See The Death of Dr. Henry F. Formad*, IV University of Pennsylvania Medical Bulletin 735 (Adams and Wood, eds., Oct. 1891–Sept. 1892).

319. *See* Ignaz Semmelweis, Etiology, Concept and Prophylaxis of Childbed Fever (K. Codell Carter trans. 1983); Sherwin Nuland, The Doctors' Plague: Germs, Childbed Fever, and the Strange Story of Ignaz Semmelweis (reprint ed. 2004).

320. *Justice Smyth Is Dead*, N.Y. Times, Aug. 19, 1900.

321. *See* chapter one of Gaslight Lawyers.

322. *See supra* note 179.

Chapter Five
There Was Something About Maria

323. *Maudlin Sentiment in Parallel*, N.Y. Times, Apr. 28, 1895.

324. The preface to Gaslight Lawyers includes a discussion of the beginnings of my interest in the case and my research process and sources.

325. According to one account, he claimed that Maria was his sixth live-in girlfriend and offered to show her mother pictures. Zacks, *supra* note 23, at 116.

326. In the official report of her appeal, the court reports that he said, "Only hogs marry!" The transcript of Maria's first trial is still available in John Jay's collection. It is listed as Trial #53, 1895/7/8, Reel 15. It is 843 pages long, and the page numbers I cite are handwritten in the upper-right corner. At page 618 Maria testified through an interpreter; it must be remembered that Cataldo's last words were, "The hogs may marry." Later at Tr. pp. 665 and 666 Maria testified "It was not my intention to kill him, but I was in a state of terrible agitation in that moment. I didn't see, myself, what I was doing, and when I heard that ejaculation, that word, 'hog,' I nearly lost consciousness, and I didn't know what I did. ... I lost consciousness, and, physically, my eyesight, in the moment that I heard him say that a hog may marry me. ... It was all in the moment, an irresistible moment, and I followed the impulse of rage, when I heard that a pig had to marry me."

327. Pucci, *supra* note 35, at 8. *Also see*, discussion of Pucci's book in the preface of Gaslight Lawyers.

328. *See* Levy, The Nan Patterson Case, *supra* note 31, at 106.

329. Lloyd Paul Stryker, The Art of Advocacy 67 (1954).

330. Pucci, *supra* note 35, at 45.

331. From the transcript of the first trial, *supra* note 326, at Tr. pp. 573–574.

332. Tr. pp. 574–577.

333. Tr. p. 573.

334. Tr. pp. 680–81.

335. *People v. Barberi*, 149 N.Y. 256, 43 N.E. 635 (1896).

336. *Maria Barberi Is Guilty*, N.Y. Times, July 16,1895.

337. *Id.*

338. *Maria Barbella to Die*, N.Y. Times, July 19, 1895.

339. Mrs. Foster was known as the "Tombs Angel." She will also appear in chapter ten of Gaslight Lawyers.

340. *Maria Barberi Breaks Down—Weeps and Bemoans Her Fate— Called Upon by a Countess and an Italian Priest*, N.Y. Times, July 18, 1895.

341. The firm was assisted by Edward Hymes, who was considered an expert in psychiatric evidence in criminal cases. It is not entirely clear to me why Emanuel Friend has been credited as the author of her defense. Both House and Hymes seem to have done much of the heavy lifting.

342. *Clemency Asked for Maria Barbella—Many Letters Sent to Gov. Morton—Women to Watch Her*, N.Y. Times, July 20,1895; *Many Appeals for Maria Barbella—Surprising Ignorance of Some Who Ask for Executive Clemency*, N.Y. Times, Aug. 16, 1895.

343. A letter to N.Y. Times dated July 24, 1895, laments the fact that "signatures can be obtained to any conceivable petition." *See also The Case of Maria Barberi*, 11 (14) The Literary Digest, Aug. 3, 1895, at (397) 7, which included editorial comments from a number of publications across the country and noted:

> The journals in commenting are pretty generally agreed that a commutation of the sentence to imprisonment would be advisable, but that a pardon would be unjustifiable. The right of a girl to avenge her honor by slaying her betrayer enters into the discussion and has given it more than temporary interest.

344. *Id.*

345. Untitled—N.Y. Times, Sept. 11, 1895.

346. *Maria Barberi a Costly Prisoner—Slowness of Her Case Costs the State Nearly $4,000 a Year*, N.Y. Times, Mar. 13, 1896.

347. N.Y. Times, *supra note 323*.

348. *Woman Suffrage and the Barberi Case*, N.Y. Times, Aug. 8, 1895.

349. The courtroom erupted in applause! *See* Richard H. Underwood, 'Arch and Gordon': *The Crime Behind the Ballad, supra note 47*, at 825, 834.

For the response from the woman from Cape Code *see The Barberi Case and What It Means*, N.Y. Times, Aug. 8, 1895.

350. *Maria Barberi's Father in Poverty—The Poor Tailor's Family Is Now Threatened with Eviction*, N.Y. Times, July 17, 1895.

351. *In Maria Barbella's Behalf*, N.Y. Times, July 24, 1895. See also *In Behalf of Maria Barbella—First of a Series of Proposed Parlor Meetings—Some Favor a Commutation and Some a Pardon*, N.Y. Times, Aug. 1, 1895.

352. *No Appeal Yet for Maria Barbella—Two People Who Want to Die in Her Place*, N.Y. Times, July 31, 1895.

353. Edmund Pearson, *The Sob-Sisters Arise*, New Yorker, Nov. 11, 1933, at 25.

354. Much was made of Maria's tender care of her prison roommate, a pet canary named Cicillo. *See* Zacks, *supra* note 23, at 118.

355. Henry B. Blackwell, *The Case of Maria Barberi*, 10 Woman's Journal 252, Aug. 1895. Maria was thought to be in her early twenties, but she was probably a bit older.

356. 11(14) The Literary Digest, *supra* note 343. For additional editorials and commentary printed in various newspapers across the United States, *see The Case of Maria Barberi*, 19 Public Opinion, A Comprehensive Summary of The Press Throughout the World on all Important Current Topics, July, 1895–Dec.1895, at 169–170.

357. The Literary Digest, *supra* note 343.

358. *Id.*

359. *The Governor and the Barbella Case*, N.Y. Times, Aug. 17, 1895.

360. *To Save Maria Barbella*, N.Y. Times, Apr. 8, 1896. House would end his career as a judge in New York's traffic court.

361. *People v. Barberi*, 3 E.H. Smith 256, 43 N.E. 635 (NY 1896). *See also Recorder Goff's Errors—His Conduct in the Barbella Case Was Not in Good Judgment*, N.Y. Times, Apr. 22, 1896. The news article reports that prosecutor McIntyre was inclined to allow her to plead guilty to manslaughter, but that was not to be.

362. *People v. Barberi*, 43 N.E. at 638.

363. *Id.*

364. *Id.* at 639.

365. *Id.* at 639–640.

366. *Maria Is Told the News*, N.Y. Times, Apr. 22, 1896.

367. *Gathered About Town*, N.Y. Times, Nov. 18, 1896.

368. *Cherry v. Des Moines Leader*, 114 Iowa 298, 86 N.W. 323 (1901).

369. *Gathered About Town*, N.Y. Times, Nov. 18, 1896. In a desperate attempt to make the Cherry Sisters relevant and keep the editors from deleting any reference to them, I note that Newman Levy, the son of Abraham Levy, included the lyrics of a silly song, *The Three Cherry Sisters Karamazov*, in his book Theatre Guyed (1933) (adapted from the folk song *Stenka Razin*).

Chapter Six
There Was Something More About Maria

370. It is reported that this ditty with this ending was offered up to the papers in Maria's defense. Zacks, *supra* note 23, at 117.

371. *See* chapter one of Gaslight Lawyers, discussing the famous *Rose, Thaw,* and *Stephani* cases. On the famous *Thaw* case *see* Emil Pinta, *Examining Harry Thaw's "Brain-Storm" Defense: APA and ANA Presidents as Expert Witnesses in a 1907 Trial*, 79 Psychiatric Q. 83–89 (2008).

372. At one time it had even been advanced that Edgar Allan Poe had suffered from psychic epilepsy. *See Edgar Allan Poe's Tragic Death Explained*, N.Y. Times, Jan. 20, 1907.

373. *See, e.g.,* Joel Peter Eigen, Witnessing Insanity: Madness and Mad Doctors in the English Court (1995); Joel Peter Eigen, Unconscious Crime: Mental Absence and Criminal Responsibility in Victorian London (2003). Long before the *Barbella* case, a curious Kentucky case recognized the defense of somnolentia or somnambulism in a shooting at the Veranda Hotel in Nicholasville, Kentucky (just down the road from my home in Lexington). *Fain v. Commonwealth*, 78 Ky. 183 (1879).

374. Eclectic medicine made use of botanical remedies and physical therapy, and was favored by such savants as Constantine Rafinesque, who noted its debt to Native American medicine. *See* Leonard Warren, Constantine Samuel Rafinesque: A Voice in the American

WILDERNESS (2004). Eclectic medicine would not be approved by the famous *Flexner Report* (1910).

375. Enrico Granieri & Patrick Fazio, *The Lombrosian prejudice in medicine. The case of Epilepsy. Epileptic psychosis. Epilepsy and aggressiveness*, 33(1) NEUROLOGICAL SCIENCES 173–92 (May 2011).

376. *Id.*

377. *See* STEPHEN JAY GOULD, THE MISMEASURE OF MAN (1996).

378. Linda Magaña, *Mr. America's Creator: The Race Science of Dr. Ales Hrdlicka 1896–1943*, Columbia University Academic Commons 2011. *See also*, Douglas H. Ubelaker, *Evolution of the relationship of forensic anthropology with physical anthropology and forensic pathology: A North American perspective*, 4 STUDIES IN HISTORICAL ANTHROPOLOGY, 199–205 (2006) [hereinafter cited as Ubelaker].

379. Published in the 24TH ANNUAL REPORT, MIDDLETOWN STATE HOMEOPATHIC HOSPITAL AT MIDDLETOWN, NEW YORK (1895).

380. *Id.* at 162.

381. Ubelaker, *supra* note 378, at 200–201.

382. Hrdlicka's article on the case of Maria Barbella, cited in *supra* note 30, [hereinafter cited as Hrdlicka study] contains all of the information included in the hypothetical question posed to him during the trial. Hrdlicka seems to have cleaned up his trial report and expanded it with more measurements and commentary on family members. I note that Pucci's reproduction of some data from Hrdlicka's trial report includes measurements using feet and inches, while his scientific publication uses the metric system.

383. McIntyre would later become a New York judge.

384. *Rather A Long Query—It Took Two Hours to Read the Hypothetical Question*, N.Y. TIMES, Dec. 3, 1896.

385. Hrdlicka study, *supra* note 30, at 52.

386. Hrdlicka study, *supra* note 30, at 85–87.

387. Pucci, *supra* note 35, at 260.

388. HAMILTON, RECOLLECTIONS OF AN ALIENIST, *supra* note 33, at 282. He describes Dr. Hrdlicka as "an anthropologist and a craniologist" whose testimony was so "improbable" that he could not resist stopping

by the shop of Dunlop, the hatter, to procure conformateur tracings of distinguished customers, including Vanderbilt and Judge Gildersleeve.

389. *Dr. A.M'L Hamilton, Alienist, Dies At 71*, N.Y. Times, Nov. 24, 1919.

390. Judge Gildersleeve's charge to the jury can be found at 12 N.Y.Crim.R. 89, 12 N.Y.Crim.R. 423, 47 N.Y.S. 168 (1896). *See also Trial of Maria Barberi—Degeneracy, in* 4 Am. Law. 532 (1896) in which the author seems to favor and await a not guilty verdict.

391. When Hamilton died in 1919, the N.Y. Times provided a summary of his career. He testified in more than one hundred murder trials, including those of presidential assassins Guiteau and Czolgosz. The article alludes to three celebrated murder trials—those of Carlyle Harris, Marie Barberi, and Harry Thaw. *See Dr. A.M'L Hamilton, Alienist, Dies at 71, supra* note 389. For more on those cases and others *see* chapter one of Gaslight Lawyers. In an article in the Herald, Oct. 3, 1888, Dr. Hamilton, and the famous brain-collecting Dr. Edward C. Spitzka, hold forth on the likely personality and mental state of Jack the Ripper.

392. *See* Pucci, *supra* note 35, at 270.

393. *Id.*

394. Dr. Hamilton was a graduate of the College of Physicians and Surgeons (Columbia). He may have had a negative opinion of other schools of medicine.

395. Why can't they get the name right?

396. Hamilton, Recollections of an Alienist, *supra* note 33, at 335–336. Maria did in fact marry.

397. Dr. Hamilton was frequently sought out because of his fairness. Although he had criticized Christian science, he was hired by lawyers for Mary Baker Eddy when "a good-for-nothing" son raised an issue of her sanity. He opined in her favor. *See Id.* at 310–324.

398. According to John Ranseen, PhD, Department of Psychiatry, University of Kentucky, "It is possible that a highly charged emotional event will induce a seizure, yet the odds of that leading to an exact outcome, such as slicing the throat of the offending party, is a little hard to swallow (pun intended)." (from an e-mail from Ranseen to Underwood in the author's file)

399. Ira Van Gieson, MD, & Boris Sidis, MA, PhD, *Epilepsy and Expert Testimony, in* CONTRIBUTIONS FROM THE PATHOLOGICAL INSTITUTE OF THE NEW YORK STATE HOSPITALS (1896–1897) at 199.

400. *Id.* at 11.

401. *Id.* at 12.

402. *Id.* at 16.

403. *Id.* at 17.

404. *Id.* at 18.

405. *Id.* at 19.

406. *Id.* at 20.

407. *Id.* at 21.

408. The usual journalistic convention is to refer to lawyers as "prominent" and doctors as "well-respected." Draw whatever conclusion you like.

409. *See also R v. Sullivan* [1983] 2 All ER 673 (HL); [1984] AC 156 (HL).

410. *Psychic Epilepsy Excuses Assault*, N.Y. TIMES, June 28, 1907.

411. In a letter to the editor of the N.Y. TIMES commenting on the *Elliot* case, a physician cited an earlier case in which the defense of psychic epilepsy failed. On Christmas Eve 1896, one Floyd Meyers, described as a lawless character, shot and killed two farmers who lived in his neighborhood. He killed them with no apparent provocation and continued beating their bodies with his shotgun until it fell apart. The letter writer was appointed by the court to address the question of his psychic epilepsy, but the physician was unable to discover any symptoms or history consistent with such a condition. *See "Psychic Epilepsy" in Law—Physician Cites a Case in Which It Failed to Excuse Murder*, N.Y. TIMES, June 29, 1907.

412. *Psychic Epilepsy Defense Justified—Plea Which Won Dr. Elliot's Discharge in Assault Case Sustained by Experts—Disease Long Recognized— Patients Prone to Violence Without Consciousness of Their Acts—Warning Against Impostors*, N.Y. TIMES, July 1, 1907.

413. I claim no medical expertise, but direct the reader to such available modern literature as Granieri & Fazio, *supra* note 378. This article is consistent with Dr. Ranseen's observations, *supra* note 398.

That is to say, "It is very rare…that epilepsy can cause outbursts of violence…" in studies cited "in none of these cases [was] the aggressive action…accompanied by the use of a lethal weapon or blunt objects. … A violent and aggressive action as murder, or other violent crimes, is too complex to be committed by an individual during epileptic automatisms, it needs a series of logic planning of sequential finalized consecutive and prolonged actions with criminal intention, and the use of weapons or other damaging tools is foreseen."

414. *Judge Buys Sleepwalking Defense to Assault Charges*, Lowering the Bar, June 22, 2011, http://loweringthebar.net/2011/06/judge-buys-sleepwalking-defense-to-assault-charges.html. (last visited Jan. 26, 2017). See also, Kevin Martin, "Sleepwalker not Responsible for Brutal Attack," Calgary Sun, June 20, 2011, www.calgarysun.com/2011/06/20/sleepwalker-not-responsible-for-brutal-attack (last visited Jan. 26, 2016).

415. *See* Paul Krassner, *Behind the Infamous Twinkie Defense*, huffingtonpost.com (December 4, 2008, and November 4, 2009). The latest variation is the "Killer Buzz." *See* Wendy N. Davis, *Killer Buzz—Caffeine Intoxication Is Now Evidence for an Insanity Plea*, ABA J., June 2011, at 16.

416. *The Doctor in Court*, N.Y. Times, June 30, 1915; *Value of 'Expert' Evidence*, N.Y. Times, July 13, 1906; *For a Standing Board of Insanity Experts*, N.Y. Times, July 12, 1906.

417. *The Decadence of 'Expert' Testimony*, N.Y. Times, July 16, 1906.

418. Bob Warden, Wilkie Collins's the Dead Alive: The Novel, the Case, and Wrongful Convictions 162–164 (2005). An interesting side note, in 1931 Dr. Hrdlicka was called upon to identify the newly discovered, bullet-riddled skull of Adolph Ruth, who had disappeared while searching for the legendary Lost Dutchman's Gold Mine. He also examined bones thought to be those of Pizarro. After Hrdlicka's retirement J. Edgar Hoover personally recognized his service to the FBI, which Hrdlicka had kept strictly confidential even as to close colleagues. *See*, David Hunt, "Forensic Anthropology at the Smithsonian," 27(1) *AnthroNotes* (Smithsonian, Spring 2006) at 7.

419. *A 'New Journalist's' Plan—He Schemed to Have Maria Barberi After Her Acquittal Sit in the Electric Chair—Wanted a Sunday Article—He*

Asked a Prominent Society Woman to Take the Girl to Sing Sing Prison, Strap Her in the Chair, and Write the Story, N.Y. TIMES, Feb. 7, 1897.

420. JONATHAN GOODMAN, BLOODY VERSICLES: THE RHYMES OF CRIME 26 (1971); *See also* OLIVE WOOLLEY BURT, AMERICAN MURDER BALLADS 55 (1964). I have not been able to determine if this was the same ditty as previously reported at *supra* note 370. Perhaps the first was a fragment.

Chapter Seven
Mr. Howe's Last Case: The Best Show in Town

421. Quotation attributed to William F. Howe by HERALD, Nov. 10, 1897.

422. ROVERE, *supra* note 12, at 126–27.

423. ROVERE, *supra* note 12, at 126–132.

424. ROVERE, *supra* note 12, at 127.

425. ROVERE, *supra* note 12, at 128.

426. ROVERE, *supra* note 12, at 129.

427. ROVERE, *supra* note 12, at 128.

428. ROVERE, *supra* note 12, at 129.

429. ROVERE, *supra* note 12, at 130.

430. ROVERE, *supra* note 12, at 132 (*emphasis added*).

431. Remember Aristophanes?

432. *See* discussion at note 443, and note 461.

433. HERALD, Nov. 9, 1897.

434. HERALD, Nov. 7, 1897.

435. *Id.*

436. HERALD, Nov. 8, 1897.

437. HERALD, Nov. 7, 1897.

438. *Id.*

439. *Id.*

440. HERALD, Nov. 8, 1897.

441. As discussed in chapters five and six of GASLIGHT LAWYERS, Maria Barbella (referred to in the official court records as "Maria Barberi") had been convicted of murdering one Dominico Cataldo and had faced death in the electric chair. But she was found not guilty after a second trial in which lawyer Friend presented a defense of epilepsy.

442. HERALD, Nov. 9, 1897. For the reported opinions in the *Barberi* case, *see People v. Barberi*, 149 N.Y. 256 (1896); *People v. Barberi*, 47 N.Y.S. 168 (N.Y. Sup.Ct. 1896).

443. *Id.*

444. *Id.* Actually, this is consistent with Rovere's report that Howe liked to take the first twelve jurors that came along, so long as there was enough diversity to foster dissension among them later on. ROVERE, *supra* note 12, at 63.

445. *Id.*

446. *Id.*

447. The menu and commentary in the HERALD, Nov. 10, 1897.

448. HERALD, Nov. 9, 1897.

449. *Id.*

450. *Id.*

451. *Id.*

452. *Friend Answers Howe*, HERALD, Nov. 11, 1897.

453. All of this from the HERALD, Nov. 12, 1897.

454. ROVERE, *supra* note 12, at 131.

455. HERALD, Nov. 12, 1897.

456. HERALD, Nov. 10, 1897.

457. *Id.*

458. The testimony is laid out in detail in the HERALD, Nov. 10, 1897.

459. *Id.*

460. HERALD, Nov. 11, 1897.

461. HERALD, Nov. 12, 1897. Later, during the second trial, about the time that the prosecution completed its case, a "morning newspaper"

(apparently not the Herald) carried a story in which Larsen was quoted as having said the following:

> I will say positively that if the case of Martin Thorn had gone to the jury he would either have been acquitted or there would have been a disagreement of the jury. After listening to Mrs. Nack's testimony I would never have assented to the conviction of Martin Thorn for the murder of Guldensuppe. I believe she committed the murder herself, and I would have stayed in the jury room until the day of judgment before I would have cast a vote for the conviction of Thorn. There were at least five others in the jury who held the same opinion, and who would have stuck to it as strenuously as I would.

When confronted with this story by a Herald reporter, Larsen said that every word of the story was false. Herald, Nov. 27, 1897, under the heading "Larsen Explodes a 'Fake'"—Could the "Fake" have been Howe's handiwork?

462. Herald, Nov. 13, 1897.

463. Id.

464. Id.

465. Herald, Nov. 23, 1897.

466. Herald, Nov. 24, 1897.

467. Id.

468. Id.

469. Id.

470. Herald, Nov. 25, 1897.

471. The later theory was entertained by Mrs. Nack's lawyer, Manny Friend.

472. Herald, Nov. 25, 1897.

473. Id.

474. Herald, Nov. 25, 1897.

475. Does the law-trained reader recall being taught something like this? Don't ask a question on cross if you don't know what the answer is

going to be. Don't ask the witness why or give the witness an opportunity to explain.

476. Menu from the HERALD, Nov. 26, 1897.

477. HERALD, Nov. 27, 1897.

478. HERALD, Nov. 28, 1897.

479. HERALD, Nov. 27, 1897.

480. *Id.*

481. *Id.* The jurors seemed surprised as anyone else, and they may have been disappointed on one count. The HERALD's Monday edition would report that the Thorn jurors spend Sunday organizing a "Good Thing Club" and planning annual reunions. The reporter noted that they probably had nothing else to do since billiards and pool were not allowed on Sunday at the Garden City Hotel and, worse still, the bar was closed.

482. These are the words of the HERALD reporter, at least. HERALD, Nov. 30, 1897.

483. *Id.*

484. Do we really need to name trials or defense attorneys?

485. HERALD, Dec. 1, 1897.

486. *Id.*

487. HERALD, Dec. 5, 1897.

488. *Id.*

489. *See People v. Thorn*, 50 N.E. 947 (1898).

490. HERALD, July 31, 1898.

491. HERALD, Aug. 2, 1898.

492. *Id.*

493. *Id.*

494. BROOKLYN DAILY STAR, Aug. 2, 1898.

495. HERALD, Aug. 2, 1898.

496. HERALD, Dec. 2, 1897.

497. HERALD, Aug. 2, 1898.

498. ROVERE, *supra* note 12, at 132–33.

Chapter Eight
Emanuel Friend: "The Best Lawyer in the City"

499. *See* Angelica Gibbs, et al., 1 New York Murders (Ted Collins ed., 1944).

500. *Scharn Girl Strangled—Death Not Caused by Hammer Blows, Dr. Donlin Says—Police Suspect a Woman—Jealousy a Possible Motive—Eisenprice Says Julia Lang Has Quarreled with the Victim,* N.Y. Times, Aug. 21, 1900.

501. *Scharn in the Tombs—Police Seek to Fasten the Murder on the Girl's Brother—Not Satisfied with His Story—Rings Supposed to Have Been Taken from the Victim, Found in a Pawn Shop...* N.Y. Times, Aug. 22, 1900; *The Scharn Boy's Alibi—His Movements on the Night of the Murder Figured Out—The Pawned Watch Stolen—The 'Man in Gray' Out of the Case...* N.Y. Times, Aug. 23, 1900.

502. *Young Scharn Is Silent,* N.Y. Times, Aug. 24, 1900; *Scharn's New Witness,* N.Y. Times, Aug. 25, 1900.

503. *The Scharn Murder Case,* N.Y. Times, Aug. 26, 1900.

504. *Scharn Case Postponed,* N.Y. Times, Sept. 27, 1900.

505. *The Scharn Murder Case,* N.Y. Times, Oct. 11, 1900; *Scharn Murder Mystery,* N.Y. Times, Oct. 12, 1900.

506. *Young Girl Saves Scharn—Her Timely Testimony Clears Him of His Sister's Murder,* N.Y. Times, Oct. 13, 1900.

507. *Frank Farrell Finally Free,* N.Y. Times, Nov. 20, 1901.

508. *Kathryn Scharn, in* New York Murders, *supra* note 499, at 109, 141.

509. For an interesting study of the case, written as a murder mystery by crime novelist Baynard Kendrick, *see The Dolly Reynolds Case, in* New York Murders, *supra* note 499, at 85–108. Detective Arthur Carey, who worked on the case, wrote of the case in his Memoirs of a Murder Man (1930) in a chapter called *The Man in the Straw Hat.*

510. Kendrick, *supra* note 509, at 88.

511. Baynard Kendrick obviously drew from the same sources, but he did not cite his sources.

512. *People v. Kennedy*, 2 Bedell 449, 164 N.Y. 449, 58 N.E. 652 (1900).

513. *Reynolds Murder Case*, N.Y. Times, Aug. 20, 1898. The victim's maid was positive that she had never seen Dr. Kennedy at the victim's home.

514. *Woman Murdered in Hotel—Body of Miss Emeline Reynolds Found in the Grand Hotel, in Broadway—Killed with a Leaden Bar...* N.Y. Times, Aug. 17, 1898.

515. Captain Price would lay all of this out at the first trial. *See Police Against Kennedy*, N.Y. Times, Mar. 28, 1899.

516. *The Grand Hotel Murder*, N.Y. Times, Aug. 18, 1898.

517. *Reynolds Murder Case—Salesman Says He Sold a Straw Hat Monday to the Accused Dentist Kennedy...* N.Y. Times, August 20, 1898.

518. *The Grand Hotel Murder*, N.Y. Times, *supra* note 516.

519. *Kennedy Held for Murder*, N.Y. Times, Aug. 27, 1898.

520. *Kennedy's Life Hangs by Thread—Dentist Indicted for Killing 'Mrs. Reynolds'—Police See 'Ideal Case,'* The Morning Telegraph, Sept. 22, 1898.

521. *Say Kennedy Is the Man—Witnesses Saw Him with Miss Reynolds on the Night of the Murder...* N.Y. Times, Mar. 25, 1899.

522. *Id.*

523. *Police Against Kennedy—Iron Bar That Fitted into the Bludgeon Found at His Home...* N.Y. Times, Mar. 28, 1899.

524. *Kennedy Was in a Trance—Said He Might Have Killed Miss Reynolds While in that State—Told This to a Detective—Chemist Lederle Showed How Materials at the Dentist's Home Fitted the Bludgeon,* N.Y. Times, Mar. 29, 1899.

525. *Kennedy's Defense Opens—Prosecution Rests Its Case in the Reynolds Murder Trial—Trying to Prove an Alibi—Witness Swears He Met Kennedy at the Time It Is Alleged the Latter Was with Dolly Reynolds,* N.Y. Times, Mar. 30, 1899.

526. *Id.*

527. *Dr. Kennedy Found Guilty*, N.Y. Times, Mar. 31, 1899.

528. *Id.*

529. *Kennedy Sentenced to Die—Emeline C. Reynolds's Murderer to Be Executed Late in May—He Blames Police Perjurers...* N.Y. Times, Apr. 1, 1899.

530. *Dr. Kennedy's Appeal—Counsel for Murderer of 'Dolly' Reynolds Argue for New Trial*, N.Y. TIMES, Oct. 5, 1900.

531. *See* note 509, *supra*.

532. *Kennedy Case on Appeal—Defense Accuses Detective Carey of Having Manufactured Evidence*, N.Y. TIMES, Oct. 11, 1900.

533. JOHN JOSIAH MUNRO, THE NEW YORK TOMBS, INSIDE AND OUT! 281 (1909).

534. *Kennedy*, 58 N.E. 652.

535. Under modern doctrine, the admission of this evidence would probably be held to violate the Confrontation Clause of the U.S. Constitution, as well. It may be worth noting that under modern evidence rules the out of court identification by Davis (a prior identification) would be admissible because he testified at trial, although the accompanying commentary injected by Captain Price would be kept out as hearsay "bolstering" Davis. The opinion of the court of appeals suggests that this was not the law at the time. *Kennedy*, 58 N.E. 652, at 655.

536. *Id. See also New Trial for Dr. Kennedy—Court of Appeals Decides Case of Dentist Convicted of Murdering 'Dollie' Reynolds*, N.Y. TIMES, Nov. 21, 1900. The mere fact that an out of court statement was made in the presence of the defendant does not make it admissible. The defendant can only be said to have adopted another person's out of court statement as his own, allowing for an "exception" to the hearsay rule, if he was free to reply if he did not mean to accept what was said.

537. It was suggested that the court had departed from established rules because of opposition to the death penalty. *Kennedy Case Discussed—Court of Appeals Establishes New Precedent—May Affect Molineux Decision—Against Death Penalty*, N.Y. TIMES, Nov. 23, 1900.

538. *Dr. Kennedy Gets the News—Congratulated by Roland B. Molineux and Other Prisoners*, N.Y. TIMES, Nov. 21, 1900.

539. *People v. Kennedy*, 15 N.Y.Crim.R. 351, 34 Misc. 101, 69 N.Y.S. 470 (1901).

540. His point was later rejected in *People v. Molineux*, 6 Bedell 264, 168 N.Y. 264, 61 N.E. 286 (1901).

541. *Witness for Kennedy Suddenly Disappears—Plumber Melville Supposed to be in Florida—Steamship Ticket Said to Have Been Obtained by Police Officer...* N.Y. Times, Feb. 12, 1901.

542. *Dr. Kennedy's Counsel Secures Admissions; Testimony of Dr. Lederle Weakens the Police Theory. Bludgeon May Not Have Been Made of Pipe Found, According to Evidence, in Kennedy's Cellar*, N.Y. Times, Feb. 14, 1901.

543. *Id.* Only the transcript of Kennedy's third trial can be found in the John Jay collection at Trial #261, 1901/05/06, Reels 47–48. Dr. Lederle's testimony can be found at Tr. pp. 988–1032. Lederle tried to take back the concessions he made in the second trial, but Attorney Osborne impeached him with his prior statements.

544. *Id.*

545. *Ex-Juror Aids Kennedy—Believes the State Has Failed to Establish His Guilt... More Handwriting Evidence*, N.Y. Times, May 28, 1901.

546. *Kennedy Expects Acquittal—Elated at Turn Murder Case Has Taken—Mr. Osborne's View of Judge's Ruling on Handwriting Experts*, N.Y. Times, Feb. 16, 1901.

547. Charles Dickens, A Tale of Two Cities *in* II The Annotated Dickens 635 ("The Likeness") (Edward Guiliano & Philip Collins eds., 1986).

548. *New Point for Kennedy—Robbery at Grand Hotel on Night of Dolly Reynolds Murder—Testimony to That Effect by Proprietor Leland—Entrance to Room Possible from Fire Escape*, N.Y. Times, May 15, 1901.

549. *Id.*

550. *Defense in Kennedy Trial Strengthened—Identification of Accused Dentist Weakened by New Evidence—Waiters at the Grand Hotel Admit Uncertainty Regarding Identity of the Man Who Was with Dolly Reynolds*, N.Y. Times, May 16, 1901.

551. N.Y. Times, May 28, 1901, *supra* note 545.

552. *Id.*

553. *Kennedy's Fight Ended*, N.Y. Times, June 14, 1901.

554. *Kennedy Jury Locked Up for the Night—A Failure to Agree After Many Hours of Deliberation—No Verdict Now Expected...*

N.Y. Times, *June 16, 1901; Dr. Kennedy Free—Greeted with Cheers—*
Hurries to His Waiting Wife in Lawyer's Office—An Ovation at His
Home in New Dorp, Where Houses Are Illuminated and Red Fire
Burned, N.Y Times, June 19, 1901.

Chapter Nine:
The Guilty Girl Who Beat The Case

555. On Friend's advice she confessed, made a deal, and got a
fifteen-year sentence. She served nine years and five months. *See*
Mrs. Nack Set Free, Met Here by Mob, N.Y. Times, July 20, 1907.

556. When application was made for Frank's pardon, Friend's
senior partner Frederick House said that he did not know who made
the application. "Frenchy is crazy," he said, "and he is better off where
he is [the State Asylum for Insane Criminals at Matteawan] than were he
at liberty." *Want 'Frenchy' Pardoned—Gov. Flower Asked to Liberate the*
Man Convicted of Killing 'Old Shakespeare' [Carrie Brown], N.Y. Times,
July 14, 1893.

557. *Emanuel M. Friend, The Lawyer, Dead,* N.Y. Times, Nov. 2, 1904.

558. Levy, The Nan Patterson Case, *supra* note 31. Newman
Levy was the son of Abraham Levy and was himself an expert in the
criminal law. He was also a successful writer. Among his papers at
New York University's Fales Library Special Collections is an undated
manuscript relating to "The Frenchy Case." According to the jacket of
his book on the Nan Patterson case, he claims that he possessed the only
existing copy of the trial transcript.

559. *Florodora* was a popular Edwardian musical comedy. The female
stars were courted by and sometimes became married to wealthy men.
Things did not always work out well. Consider the sensational trial of
Harry Thaw for the murder of Stanford White—the femme fatale being
another "Florodora Girl," Evelyn Nesbit, who came to be known as "The
Girl in the Red Velvet Swing." *See* Paula Uruburu, American Eve:
Evelyn Nesbit, Stanford White, the Birth of the "It" Girl and
the Crime of the Century (2008). *See also* discussion in chapter ten
of *Gaslight Lawyers.*

560. This play is presented entirely through courtroom scenes. In his opening statement, the prosecutor, Mr. Galwey, begins by alluding to the Nan Patterson and Harry Thaw cases. *The Trial of Mary Dugan* is thought to have inspired Ayn Rand's *Night of January 16th*, which opened successfully in 1934 in Los Angeles under the title *Woman on Trial*. It may also have inspired a play by Clyde Fitch titled *The Woman in the Case* (1905). See *New Play by Fitch of Absorbing Interest*, N.Y. TIMES, Jan. 31, 1905. A 1948 movie SO EVIL MY LOVE (Paramount British Pictures 1948) may also have taken its ending from the Nan Patterson case. The movie was described as "gaslight noir."

561. *Bookmaker Is Shot in Cab with Actress, 'Caesar' Young Killed and Nan Patterson Held Without Bail—He Was Going to Europe—Wife Waits on Pier Until Liner Sails and News Is Kept from Her—Police Say Former 'Florodora' Singer Had Made Threats*, N.Y. TIMES, June 5, 1904.

562. *Id*. For more of the work up to the first trial see the following: *Will Seek to Indict Nan Patterson To-day—Prosecutor Hopes to Have Eye-Witness of Shooting of Young—Revolver Not Yet Traced—Affecting Meeting in the Tombs of the Imprisoned Actress and Her Father*, N.Y. TIMES, June 8, 1904; *Coroner Says Nan Patterson Guilty—Two New Witnesses Impress Police and Jerome—Point for Her, Thought—A. C. Meyer of Jacksonville Says He Saw Cab Struggle, Young Holding the Pistol*, N.Y. TIMES, June 9, 1904; *Nan Patterson Will Not Answer Questions—Her Lawyers Decline to Accept Grand Jury's Invitation—J. Morgan Smiths Disappear—Pawnbroker from Whom Pistol Was Bought Fails to Identify the Prisoner*, N.Y. TIMES, June 10, 1904; *No Indictment Yet for Nan Patterson—Grand Jury Adjourns Without Action in the Shooting of Young—Search for Morgan Smith On—New Witness Appears—An Actual Witness of Shooting Said to Have Been Found*, N.Y. TIMES, June 11, 1904; *Father Will Stand by Nan Patterson—Could Not Visit Her Sunday, but Waited Long in Corridor—Wanted to Be Near Her—Says He Believes Firmly in Her Innocence—Thinks Morgan Smith and Wife Will Appear*, N.Y. TIMES, June 13, 1904; *Nan Patterson Indicted for Murder of Young—Slain Man's Friend Testifies He Feared the Woman—Prisoner Will Plead To-day—Coroner's Jury Renders Formal Verdict—Missing J. Morgan Smith Said to Be in a Sanitarium*, N.Y. TIMES, June 14, 1904.

563. Indeed, Levy thought that Rand's "haughty" manner was not well received by Recorder Goff when he presided during the second

full trial and that Goff uncharacteristically tended to rule in favor of the defense! *See* RICHARD O'CONNOR, COURTROOM WARRIOR: THE COMBATIVE CAREER OF WILLIAM TRAVERS JEROME, 153, 155 (1963).

564. *Patterson Witnesses Are in Washington—Morgan Smith and His Wife Shadowed by Detectives—Relatives Deny They Called—Man and Woman Resembling Couple Wanted in Young Case Entered House of Actresses Parents,* N.Y. TIMES, June 19, 1904; *Hunt Patterson Witnesses— Local Detectives and Pawnbroker Try to Find J. Morgan Smith and Wife,* N.Y. TIMES, June 23, 1904; *Morgan Smith Said to Have Been Found— Nan Patterson's Lawyers Say They Have Heard from Him—Will Appear at the Trial—According to the Lawyers He Will Testify for Actress in the Young Murder Case,* N.Y. TIMES, June 26, 1904.

565. *Aged Witness Speaks for Nan Patterson—Mr. Hazelton of Oneonta Says He Saw Cab Tragedy—Man Shot Himself He Says—Kept Silent at First, He Declares, Because He Feared Detention as Witness—Is Subpoenaed,* N.Y. TIMES, Nov. 2, 1904; *Witness Corroborates Hazelton's Version—Tombs Prisoner Writes Nan Patterson He Saw Shooting—Says Young Held Pistol—John Latour, and Ex-Convict Awaiting Sentence on New Conviction, Makes the Revelations,* N.Y. TIMES, Nov. 3, 1904.

566. *Skeletons and Cab to Show Young's End—Plenty of the Dramatic Promised in Nan Patterson's Trial—The Case Will Start To-day—Lawyers Laying Stress on Courses of Bullets That Killed Bookmaker—Special Panel Drawn,* N.Y. TIMES, Nov. 15, 1904.

567. *Four Jurors Selected in the Young Case,* N.Y. TIMES, Nov. 17, 1904; *Witness Ill May Halt Nan Patterson Trial, Pawnbroker Who Identified Revolver Confined at Home—Jury Completed at Last—Witness Disclosed by Talesman Saw Shooting from Car... Platform, Lawyer for Defense Says,* N.Y. TIMES, Nov. 19, 1904; *Nan Patterson Gets Stage Offer, Refuses—To Live Quietly with Father if Freed—Story of New Witness—Talesman Tells Trial Justice of a Man He Says Saw Young Shoot Himself,* N.Y. TIMES, Nov. 18, 1904; *Young, Witness Says, Hit Nan Patterson,* N.Y. TIMES, Nov. 24, 1904.

568. N.Y. TIMES, Nov.19, 1904, *supra* note 567.

569. *Nan Patterson Hears the Case Against Her,* N.Y. TIMES, Nov. 22, 1904.

570. *Smith May Be Here for Patterson Trial—Nyack Police Believe Prisoner's Relative Was Found There—Defense to Set Up Alibi—The Pair*

Returned from the Track Too Late to Reach Pawnshop, It Is Said, N.Y. TIMES, Nov. 26, 1904.

571. *Young, Witness Says, Hit Nan Patterson,* N.Y. TIMES, Nov. 24, 1904.

572. *Juror's Illness Halts Nan Patterson Trial,* N.Y. TIMES, Nov. 27, 1904.

573. *Nan Patterson's Trial to Begin Again Monday—Juror Dressler's Illness Necessitates Calling a New Panel—Actress Weeps at News—Badly Disappointed at Breakdown of Case Before Jury She Had Chosen—200 Talesmen Called,* N.Y. TIMES, Nov. 29, 1904.

574. O'CONNOR, *supra* note 563, at 152.

575. *Second Patterson Jury Has Been Completed—Rand Says He Will Explain J. Morgan Smith's Whereabouts,* N.Y. TIMES, Dec. 9, 1904.

576. *Patterson Counsel Witness at Trial—Mr. O'Reilly Testifies That He Knows Missing J. Morgan Smith—Rand's Purpose Not Shown,* N.Y. TIMES, Dec. 10, 1904.

577. *Rand Springs Surprise in Nan Patterson Case—Would Prove That the Morgan Smiths Plotted to Wrong Young—Lawyer Said to Be Involved—Judge Excuses Jury to Hear Argument on New Line of Evidence— Pawnbroker Fails to Identify Defendant,* N.Y. TIMES, Dec. 14, 1904.

578. *Mrs. Young Testifies at the Murder Trial—Nan Patterson Avoided Looking at Bookmaker's Widow—Fight to Introduce Letter—The Prosecution Couldn't Get in Note from Mrs. Smith—Had Another Setback, Too,* N.Y. TIMES, Dec. 15, 1904.

579. *Prosecution Scores in Patterson Trial—Alleged Menacing Letter from Girl's Sister to Young Is Admitted—State Will Close To-day—Defendant's Lawyers Refuse to Say Whether They Will Introduce Testimony—Actress May Take Stand,* N.Y. TIMES, Dec. 16. 1904.

580. *Nan Patterson to Testify? Her Lawyers Agree Upon Their Line of Defense,* N.Y. TIMES, Dec. 18, 1904.

581. *Nan Patterson Swears Young Shot Himself—No Quarrel the Night Before, She Declares on Stand—Good Witness, Rand Admits— Hazelton Tells His Story on the Shooting—Earl of Suffolk on the Bench with Justice Davis,* N.Y. TIMES, Dec. 20, 1904.

582. I am too old to speak of our new cyber-courtroom.

583. THE NAN PATTERSON CASE, *supra* note 31, at 93–97.

584. *Id.*

585. N.Y. TIMES, Nov. 2, 1904, *supra* note 565.

586. N.Y. TIMES, Dec. 20, 1904, *supra* note 581.

587. *Id.*

588. Between the mistrial and Nan's final trial, the press would report other last-minute witnesses that supported Nan's story and whom Rand allegedly ignored. Were they kooks? *See Saw Caesar Young Shot?* N.Y. TIMES, Jan. 2, 1905; *Says He Saw Young Shoot—Rosen Only Recently Read Patterson Story in Jewish Newspaper,* N.Y. TIMES, Apr. 21, 1905; *Story of Cab Shooting—Chicago Man Tells in Detail How He Saw Young End His Life,* N.Y. TIMES, Apr. 22, 1905.

589. *Rand Highly Praised for Closing Address—Never Heard One Like It, Says Nan Patterson's Counsel—Savage Hit at Her Story— Prosecutor Declares It Was Manufactured for Her—Levy's Associate Says He Has New Evidence,* N.Y. TIMES, Dec. 22, 1904. Nowadays there would be an objection and a charge of prosecutorial misconduct.

590. *Nan Patterson Case Results in Mistrial—Jury Six for Acquittal, Six for Conviction to the Last—Girl Collapses in Court—Her Counsel Tells of New Evidence, He Says, That Mrs. Young Always Carried Pistol,* N.Y. TIMES, Dec. 24, 1904.

591. *Id.* It was rumored that the first vote was two for conviction and ten for acquittal. *No Patterson Verdict After Eleven Hours,* N.Y. TIMES, Dec. 23, 1904.

592. *The Nan Patterson Case—Failure of the Jury to Agree Far from an Argument Against New Trial,* N.Y. TIMES, Dec. 30, 1904; *Misdirected Sympathy,* N.Y. TIMES, Jan. 2, 1905.

593. N.Y. TIMES, Dec. 30, 1904, *supra* note 592; N.Y. TIMES, Jan. 2, 1905, *supra* note 592.

594. The story of the pursuit and arrest of the Smiths was a minor epic in itself. Here are the press clippings for the interested reader. *Smith Couple Arrested in Nan Patterson Case—Conspiracy to Extort from Caesar Young, the Charge—Who Bought Fatal Pistol? Cincinnati Police Told Pawnbroker Will See if Smith Purchased It—Detective's Long Chase,* N.Y. TIMES, Mar. 31, 1905; *The Smiths Prepare to Fight Extradition,*

N.Y. Times, Apr. 1, 1905; *Smiths Fight Hard to Get Seized Letters*, N.Y. Times, Apr. 2, 1905; *Smiths Fight to the End*, N.Y. Times, Apr. 3, 1905; *Smiths on Their Way Here*, N.Y. Times, Apr. 11, 1905; *Smiths Locked Up Here*, N.Y. Times, Apr.12, 1905; *Pawnbroker Stern Sees J. Morgan Smith, Rand Refuses to Say Whether He Identified the Man*, N.Y. Times, Apr. 13, 1905; *Give Up Letters, Justice Gaynor Orders*, N.Y. Times, Apr. 16, 1905; *Jerome Surrenders Smith Letters*, N.Y. Times, Apr. 18, 1905.

595. O'Connor, *supra* note 563, at 154–155.

596. *Id.* at 155. I hope my Evidence and Trial Practice students are listening.

597. *Choose Married Men for Patterson Jury*, N.Y. Times, Apr. 19, 1905; *Recorder Goff Fills Patterson Jury Box*, N.Y. Times, Apr. 20, 1905.

598. *Smith Bought Pistol, Declares Mr. Rand—Statement a Blow to Defense in Nan Patterson Trial—Almost Cruses Prisoner—Recorder Orders Windows Opened and Adjourns Court to Give Her the Opportunity to Regain Composure*, N.Y. Times, Apr. 25, 1905.

599. The Nan Patterson Case, *supra* note 31, at 112–113.

600. *Pawnbroker Fails to Identify Smith—Has Rand Something in Reserve in Nan Patterson Case—Riot at Courtroom Door—Women's Clothes Torn and Man Swept from Feet in Struggle to Gain Entrance*, N.Y. Times, Apr. 27, 1905.

601. *Id.*

602. Ada's work on the Nan Patterson case is discussed in Phyllis Leslie Abramson, Sob Sister Journalism (1990) and in Shannon Peterson, *Yellow Justice: Media Portrayal of Criminal Trials in the Progressive Era*, 1:1 Stan. J. of Legal Stud. 72, 88–96 (1999).

603. The Duestrow case is discussed briefly in Carol Ferring Shepley, Movers and Shakers, Scalawags and Suffragettes: Tales from Bellefontaine Cemetery 151–152 (2008).

604. *Shot Wife and Child—Duestrow Says It Was Accidental, But There Are Serious Doubts*, 75:76 San Francisco Call, Feb. 14, 1894.

605. Several medical journals carried articles to the effect that the killing might be attributed to alcoholic epileptic insanity. One doctor wrote that the condition also explained Maria Barbella's conduct! *See*

William Lee Howard, MD, *in* XIX:3 Q. J. of Inebriety, *reprinted in* 12 Am. Medico-Surgical Bulletin (1898).

606. *See A Millionaire to Hang,* 98:37 Alexandria Gazette, Feb. 12, 1897.

607. *The Sanity of Duestrow; An Expert's Analysis of the Murderer's Plea,* N.Y. Times, Feb. 21, 1897.

608. *Dr. Duestrow Convicted: The Verdict is Murder in the First Degree,* 45:115 Los Angeles Herald, Feb. 3, 1896.

609. A detailed summary of the evidence is presented in the opinion of the Missouri Supreme Court, *State v. Duestrow,* 137 Mo. 44, 38 S.W. 554 (1897).

610. *Arthur Duestrow Hanged—The Wealthy Murderer of His Wife and Child Pays the Last Penalty,* N.Y. Times, Feb. 17, 1897.

611. *Duestrow Executed,* Ann Arbor Argus, Feb. 19, 1897.

612. William J. Kuehling, *Letter to the Editor,* Oct. 27, 2005, to the St. Louis B. J. (Winter 2006) at 3. While awaiting execution, Duestrow beat and seriously injured another inmate who taunted him with "Hello, Moneybags," "Hello, Cigarette Fiend," and "Hello, Crazy." *Affray in a Prison—Duestrow, The Condemned St. Louis Murderer, Punished a Tormenter,* N.Y. Times, Jan. 7, 1897. In the early 1900s, before the Civil War, it was believed by many that the cigarette released a "frightening Jekyll-and-Hyde drug." *See* Jennifer Redmond, *In the 1900s, Being a 'Cigarette Fiend' Was a Legitimate Defense for Murder,* Atlas Obscura, (Oct. 5, 2016) http://www.atlasobscura.com/articles/in-the-1900s-being-a-cigarette-fiend-was-a-legitimate-defense-for-murder (last visited Mar. 27, 2017) (despite the title of the story, the defense appears to have failed in the cases cited in the article). For an interesting tidbit *see* engraving *The Fate of the Cigarette Fiend,* by John Held Jr., whooping the progression from the cigarette, to drugs, to prison, to the grave, *in* Frank Shay, More Pious Friends and Drunken Companions: Songs and Ballads of Conviviality 75 (1928).

613. *Miss Duestrow to Be a Nun,* N.Y. Times, Feb. 20, 1897.

614. Abramson, *supra* note 602, at 45.

615. *Stern Failed to Identify Smith,* Lewiston Evening Journal, Apr. 25, 1905.

616. This was a sample known to be the handwriting of Nan Patterson.

617. Chauncey Montgomery McGovern, An Experts Study of the Dreyfus Case: An Interview with D. N. Carvalho, Engaged by Madame Dreyfus to Study the Documents (1899).

618. One wonders whether today the prosecution would be able to provide enough evidence to claim a conspiracy and get the letter in under the co-conspirator's exception to the hearsay rule.

619. *Nan Patterson Wrote to Others Than Young—Letter Introduced by Mr. Rand to Show Mercenary Motives*, N.Y. Times, Apr. 28, 1905.

620. Newman Levy raises the interesting point that the Smiths were supposedly wandering around the country in October 1904. Why would they have returned to New York City on October 7 to pawn items and why to a pawnshop where they would be recognized? *See* Levy, The Nan Patterson Case, *supra* note 31, at 183.

621. *Will Make No Defense in Nan Patterson Case—Decision After Prosecution Offers Striking Evidence—Smith in Pawnshop June 3—Pledged Wife's Jewelry on Day Before Young's Death with Man Who Sold Pistol*, N.Y. Times, Apr. 29, 1905.

622. *Nan Patterson Talks—Confident of Acquittal—Lawyers Busy Preparing for Summing Up*, N.Y. Times, Apr. 30, 1905; *Nan Patterson Case May Go to Jury To-day—Defense in Summing Up Suggests that Young Bought Pistol*, N.Y. Times, May 2, 1905; *Recorder Will Charge Patterson Jury To-day—Prosecutor Rand Closes State's Case with Severe Arraignment—Delay in Verdict Probable—Those Who Have Watched Trial Do Not Believe Jury Will Come to Prompt Decision*, N.Y. Times, May 3, 1905.

623. *Disagreement in Patterson Case—Jury Is Discharged After Deliberating Thirteen Hours—8 to 4 for Manslaughter—Crowds in Streets Jostled Jurymen on Way to Dinner and Cried 'Free Nan Patterson!'* N.Y. Times, May 4, 1905.

624. *Re-Trial Not Probable in Patterson Case*, N.Y. Times, May 5, 1905; *Indictment Against Morgan Smith Quashed—Judge Foster Severely Censures Grand Jury for Its Finding—No Evidence of Conspiracy*, N.Y. Times, May 6, 1905; *Nan Patterson Trial Question Not Settled—District Attorney Jerome Delays His Decision—Consults with Assistants—Letter Threatening to Kill*

the Girl and Avenge Young's Murder Sent to Her Mother, N.Y. Times, May 9, 1905.

625. O'Connor, *supra* note 563, at 156.

626. N.Y. Times, May 17, 1905.

627. *Id.*

628. *Nan Patterson Free: Jerome Blames Press,* N.Y. Times, May 13, 1905.

629. *The Repentance of Jerome,* N.Y. Times, May 14, 1905.

630. Oddly enough, this rather obvious possibility "hardly entered into [Jerome's] calculations. ... He was convinced that Nan shot Young—how could it have been otherwise?...Jerome considered [Nan] an immoral creature and believed her case should be prosecuted to the hilt." O'Connor, *supra* note 563, at 154.

631. *Nan Patterson Held Pistol—Justice Davis Says He Believes Majority of People Hold That Opinion—His Theory of the Case—Thinks She Exhibited Pistol and Young Was Killed When He Seized It,* N.Y. Times, May 16, 1905.

632. *See, e.g., The Indiscretions of a Judge,* N.Y. Times, May 17, 1905; *The Nan Patterson Case Again—from* Saturday Review (London), June 1, 1905 ("Even in court it is considered a mistake for an English Judge to express a disagreement with the jury, and it would be felt to be inexcusable if he carried the controversy outside."); *The Nan Patterson Murder Trial—Extraordinary after Proceedings,* XXXVI: 156 Auckland Star, July 1, 1905, at 13 ("Such an expression of opinion after the case has been entirely disposed of is surely in the worst possible taste from such a quarter.").

633. XII:1, The Bar, Jan. 1905. Note that the case generated interest as far away as West Virginia.

634. The same story was repeated on the front page of the Los Angeles Herald, May 18, 1905.

635. Arthur Train, Courts and Criminals 26 (no date). This may be the same book as Arthur Train, Courts, Criminals, and the Camorra (1912).

636. *See Nan Patterson Murder Trial—Extraordinary After Proceedings,* XXXVI:156 Auckland Star, July 1, 1905, at 13.

637. Levy, The Nan Patterson Case, *supra* note 31, at 226.

638. At the time, Goldfield, the county seat of Esmeralda County, was the largest town in Nevada. There was no Las Vegas. Besides the gold mines and the big fight, the town was known for a brief stay by Wyatt and Virgil Earp in 1904. Virgil had been hired to be a deputy sheriff, but he died shortly thereafter of pneumonia. Wyatt moved on. The town is nearly a ghost town now. *See* Charles LeDuff, *Grizzled Nevada Sentinel Watches as Town Withers*, N.Y. Times, June 26, 2004.

639. William Gildea, The Longest Fight: In the Ring with Joe Gans, Boxing's First African American Champion (2012). Gans won when Nelson threw a foul punch.

640. Bernie S. Jacobson, *When All Goldfield Was Aglitter*, Sports Illustrated Vault, Aug. 5, 1968.

641. *See Can't Bar Nan Patterson—Efforts to Prevent Her Appearance on Wilkes Barre Stage Fails*, N.Y. Times, May 29, 1905; *Nan Patterson Quits—Fails to Draw Profitable Houses and Returns to Washington*, N.Y. Times, June 5, 1905.

642. N.Y. Times, June 4, 1905.

643. *Nan Patterson Bride of Former Husband—Becomes Mrs. Leon Gaines Martin Again in Washington—Divorced Five Years Ago—First Minister Requested to Reunite Them Refused, but Another Consented Willingly*, N.Y. Times, Sept. 17, 1905. It seems that Jerome was still dogging her. *See Nan Patterson Moves—Jerome Is Said to Have Suggested Her Leaving Pittsburg*, N.Y. Times, Mar. 11, 1907.

644. One not so famous case, but an interesting one, involved Mrs. Caroline Fitzhugh, known in the press as "The Woman of Mystery." Mrs. Fitzhugh was accused of thefts from churches. Levy took her case and advised her to plead guilty, but she discharged him. In the end she broke down before Judge Swann in the court of general sessions and pleaded guilty anyway. *See Mrs. Fitzhugh Guilty—So Pleads After Refusing to Take the Advice of Her Counsel*, N.Y. Times, June 17, 1913; *Mystery Woman Confesses Two Church Thefts*, World, June 16, 1913.

645. For a report of official proceedings relating to the case *see People v. Moore*, XIV N.Y.Crim.R. 387 (Court of General Sessions, Nov. 1899).

646. May Churchill Sharpe, Chicago May, Her Story (1928).

647. *See* Nuala O'Faolain, The Story of Chicago May (2005). Justice Davis, who presided over Nan Patterson's last trial, was invited to sit on the bench with the English judges during Chicago May's trial for the attempted murder of her former lover Eddie Guerin. *See "Chicago May" Case Attended by Jurist of American Court—Davis Was Judge in Patterson Case*, Washington Times, July 27, 1907, Last Edition, at 12.

648. *See Fayne Moore, Champion Badger Game Dame—1898*, The Unknown History of Misandry, July 27, 2011, http://unknownmisandry. blogspot.com/2011/07/fayne-moore-champion-badger-game-dame.html (last visited January 30, 2017).

649. *Moore 'Badger' Case Closed*, N.Y. Times, July 11, 1901.

650. *Moore Guilty of Robbery... Fayne Moore Will Be Defended by Benjamin H. Hill and Will Take the Stand in Her Own Defense*, N.Y. Times, Dec. 17, 1898.

651. *Moore Trial About Ended; Benjamin Hill Makes an Eloquent Appeal for His Client*, N.Y. Times, Dec. 24, 1898.

652. *Mistrial in Moore Case*, N.Y. Times, Dec. 26, 1898.

653. *Moore Jurors Very Angry—Incensed at McIntyre's Statement that They Were 'Fixed,'* N.Y. Times, Dec. 7, 1898.

654. *Fayne Moore May Go Free*, N.Y. Times, Feb. 26, 1899.

655. *Mahon May Be in Washington—Much-Wanted Witness in Fayne Moore Trial Said to Have Left Philadelphia for the Capital*, N.Y. Times, Feb. 28, 1899.

656. *Mrs. Fayne Moore Set Free—She Leaves the Tombs for the Home of Her Mother*, N.Y. Times, Apr. 2, 1899.

657. *Mrs. Fayne Moore's Divorce*, N.Y. Times, May 9, 1902; *Moore of Badger Game Fame Gets Divorce and Maiden Name*, Milwaukee Journal, May 9, 1902.

658. *Fayne Moore, supra* note 648, *citing Mrs. Moore's Eyes Dazzle a Court—Assistant District Attorney McIntyre Compels Her Retirement from Jury's View*, Boston Globe, Dec. 1, 1898. *Fayne Moore, supra* note 648, *citing* Ward Green, *Why Beautiful Fayne Moore Comes Back to America—The Extraordinary Life of the Principal Figure in a*

Notorious "Badger Game" Trial, Now Married to "The Diamond King," NEWSPAPER FEATURE SERVICE, Aug. 9, 1919.

659. *O'Reilly to Testify in His Own Defense—Prosecutor's Case Against the Lawyer Ends and Friends Testify as to His Character,* N.Y. TIMES, May 20, 1911. *Former Assistant District Attorney John F. McIntyre represented him on appeal. See McIntyre for O'Reilly—Former Associate of Convicted Lawyer Succeeds Levy as Counsel,* N.Y. TIMES, June 10, 1911. The disgraced and disbarred O'Reilly dies at age 44. *See Daniel J. O'Reilly—Lawyer Dies at 44—His Death Hastened by Imprisonment in Bancroft Bond Theft and Disbarment,* N.Y. TIMES, Nov. 7, 1913.

660. *Ida Rogers to Deny She is Responsible—Collapses on Hearing She Will Be Prosecuted for Killing Her Two Babies,* N.Y. TIMES, Jan. 13, 1915.

661. *Mrs. Rogers Insane Is Murder Defense,* N.Y. TIMES, Apr. 25, 1916; *Mrs. Rogers Freed; Insane Says Jury; Verdict of Acquittal Based on Mental Condition When She Poisoned Her Two Babies,* N.Y. TIMES, Apr. 27, 1916.

662. It appears that Levy got all three counts in the indictment dismissed, although one count was held to be good on appeal. *See People v. Rogers,* 183 App. Div. 604, 37 N.Y.Cr.R. 13, 170 N.Y. Supp. 825 (First Department 1918). Both Levy and the trial judge were not happy with the overreach in the indictment. Some amusing repartee between the judge and the prosecutor was reported. *See Martin Resents Sarcasm,* N.Y. TIMES, Feb. 6, 1915. "Mr. Levy…accused District Attorney Martin of making public evidence submitted to the Grand Jury. Mr. Martin resented this hotly, exclaiming:

> "I want to make a statement in the presence of the court"—
> "And the newspaper reporters," Justice Brady added.
> Mr. Martin continued:
> "I'm glad they are here, because I never make a statement"—
> "Unless they are present," the Justice added again.

"Rapid-fire repartee continued until Mr. Martin declared that if he continued to be the subject of attack he would place the whole case before the governor."

663. *Gay Life of Broadway Lured Her to Death,* EVENING INDEPENDENT (St. Petersburg, Florida) Mar. 23, 1917.

664. *Sternberg Is Set Free*, N.Y. Times, June 30, 1917.

665. *Holds That Chapin Was Legally Sane—Commission Finds That Editor Killed His Wife Under Fear of Disgrace*, N.Y. Times, Dec. 15, 1918.

666. *Chapin Confesses He Planned Murder—Editor Decided As Long As Four Years Ago to Kill His Wife and Himself—Lost Heavily in Stock—After Crime He Said He Was at Point of Shooting Himself in Park but Concluded to Surrender*, N.Y. Times, Sept. 18, 1918.

667. *Id. See also Blond Woman Is Being Sought in Murder Mystery*, Pittsburgh Press, Mar. 19, 1917. There are apparently one or more photos relevant to the case in an archive that only recently became available to the public. *See* Sam Roberts, *In Black and White, a Gritty History of New York Crime*, N.Y. Times, May 11, 2012.

668. James M. Morris, The Rose Man of Sing Sing: A True Tale of Life, Murder, and Redemption in the Age of Yellow Journalism (2005).

669. Attributed to Andy Logan, a correspondent for New Yorker.

670. *Abraham Levy, Lawyer, Dies at 58—Counsel for Defense in Many Famous Criminal Trials Underwent Two Operations*, N.Y. Times, Dec. 18, 1920.

Chapter Ten:
The "Reformer"

671. Munro, *supra* note 533, at 213.

672. True Stories of Crime from the District Attorney's Office 313 (1926).

673. O'Connor, *supra* note 563, at 114–145; Rovere, *supra* note 12; Arthur Train, *A Flight into Texas*, in True Stories of Crime, *supra* note 672, at 283–313.

674. *People v. Hummel*, 21 N.Y.Crim.R. 162, 119 A.D. 153, 104 N.Y.S. 308 (1907).

675. O'Connor, *supra* note 563, at 143.

676. *See, e.g.,* Rick Geary, Madison Square Tragedy: The Murder of Stanford White (2013); Gerald Langford, The Murder of Stanford White (1962, 2011); Paula Uruburu, *supra* note 559; Deborah Paul, Tragic Beauty: The Lost Memoirs of Evelyn Nesbit (2006); Suzannah Lessard, The Architect of Desire: Beauty and Danger in the Stanford White Family (1997); Michael McDonald Mooney, Evelyn Nesbit and Stanford White: Love and Death in the Gilded Age (1976); Benjamin H. Atwell, The Great Harry Thaw Case (1907).

677. There are accounts of the case on the web pages of two law schools. See Richard F. Hamm, *The Prosecutor and the Show Girl,* www.albany.edu/faculty/hamm/ahis292z/thaw (last visited Jan. 30, 2017); Douglas O. Linder, *The Harry Thaw Trials for the Murder of Stanford White,* (2009) http://law2.umkc.edu/faculty/projects/ftrials/thaw/ Thawaccount.html (last visited Jan. 30, 2017).

678. *Want Expert View on Thaw's Sanity—Commission Will Hear Story of Dr. Hamilton, Who Quit the Defense,* N.Y. Times, Mar. 30, 1907.

679. *See* chapter two of Gaslight Lawyers.

680. A copy of the chilling affidavit can be found at http://law2. umkc.edu/faculty/projects/ftrials/thaw/evelynstory1.html (last visited Jan. 30, 2017).

681. O'Connor, *supra* note 563, at 227–228.

682. *Say Thaw Affidavit Must Be a Forgery—Defense Declares Evelyn Nesbit Didn't Sign an Attack on Him,* N.Y. Times, July 10, 1906. For its part, the prosecution claimed the affidavit was in her handwriting and had been "interlined" by White. *Miss Nesbit's Affidavit Interlined by White,* N.Y. Times, July 7, 1906.

683. O'Connor, *supra* note 563, at 229.

684. *Thaw Is Sane Says Board—Jerome Will Take an Appeal Against Its Pronouncement,* N.Y. Times, Apr. 5, 1907. Dr. Hamilton stuck to his position that Thaw was hopelessly insane. *See* N.Y. Times, Mar. 30, 1907, *supra* note 678.

685. Hamilton, Recollections of an Alienist, *supra* note 33, at 399.

686. O'Connor, *supra* note 563, at 235.

687. *Id.* at 209. Detective Arthur Carey, mentioned in connection with another case, was also involved. *See* Albert Borowitz, *Packaged Death," in Crimes Gone By, Collected Essays of Albert Horowitz*, 29 Legal Stud. F. 631, 636 (2005).

688. *People v. Molineux*, 168 N.Y. 264 (1901); Randolph N. Jonakait, *People v. Molineux and Other Crime Evidence: One Hundred Years and Counting*, 30 Am. J. Crim. L. 1 (2002).

689. *See* the discussion of Frenchy's case and the discussion of the Charles Becker case, where the jury was surely influenced by the prosecution's charges of Becker's grafting, *infra* note 754 and accompanying text.

690. *See People v. Littlejohn*, 23 Misc.3d 1127 (A), 889 N.Y.S.2d 507 (Table), 2009 WL 1392605 (N.Y.Supp.), 2009 N.Y. Slip Op. 50958 (U). This opinion involved the admission of other crimes evidence in the prosecution for the rape and murder of Imette St. Guillen, a John Jay College of Criminal Justice graduate student.

691. *People v. Molineux*, 168 N.Y. 264, 334 (1901).

692. Rev. Munro tells of his discussion with the two men in The New York Tombs, Inside and Out!, *supra* note 533, at 281.

693. *Id.*

694. *Molineux's Second Trial Is Started*, N.Y. Times, Oct. 14, 1902.

695. *Molineux Free Receives Ovation—Verdict of Acquittal Reached by Jury in a Few Minutes*, N.Y. Times, Nov. 12, 1902. This article gives a detailed history of the case and reports the views of the jurors who set Molineux free.

696. Munro, *supra* note 533, at 281.

697. The room with a little door was the death row at Sing Sing, which had a total of eight cells.

698. Schechter, The Devil's Gentleman, *supra* note 210, at 444.

699. *See* O'Connor, *supra* note 563, at 168–170; Arthur Train, *A Murder Conspiracy, in* True Stories of Crime from the District Attorney's Office 249–280 (1926).

700. James A. Baker Sr., was a partner in his father's firm—we now know it as Baker & Botts. James A. Baker's grandson is James Addison Baker III who was President Ronald Reagan's Chief of Staff.

701. *Patrick Defense Opens—Counsel Will Try to Show That Rice Was Not Murdered—Witnesses to Be Produced to Testify That Millionaire's Death Resulted from Dropsy of the Lungs*, N.Y. Times, Mar. 7, 1902.

702. *People v. Patrick*, 20 Bedell 131, 182 N.Y. 131, 74 N.E. 843 (1905). This very long opinion is worth reading for its detailed statement of the case.

703. *Higgins Saves Patrick from the Death Chair*, N.Y. Times, Dec. 21, 1906.

704. Had Patrick and Jones been charged with attempted murder, the question would have been whether there is such a thing as "impossible attempt," one of the conundrums of the criminal law. *See* Leo Katz, Bad Acts and Guilty Minds—Conundrums of the Criminal Law 15–16, 284–286 (1987).

705. *People v. Patrick*, 74 N.E. 843 (1905). The press carried stories undermining Jones's credibility. *See, e.g., Jones's Friend Says Valet Cleared Patrick—Called His Confession Mere Lies—Affidavit Declares Doctors Say Chloroform Didn't Kill Rice*, N.Y. Times, Feb. 1, 1906. For a recent work accepting that a murder took place *see*, William Marsh Rice and His Institute: The Centennial Edition (Randall L. Hall and Sylvia Stallings Morris eds. 2012). For a work raising all the questions *see* Martin L. Friedland, The Death of Old Man Rice: A True Story of Criminal Justice in America (1996).

706. *Patrick Still Hopeful, Compliments Osborne… Mr. Jerome Says Valet May Go Free*, N.Y. Times, Mar. 28, 1902.

707. *Twelve Year Fight That Won Freedom—Story of One Man's Undaunted Struggle After Conviction of Cruel Murder—Used Every Legal Device*, N.Y. Times, Nov. 28, 1912.

708. There was some suggestion in the record that Florence's father may have been abusive. *See Mrs. Brooks Faints on the Witness Stand*, N.Y. Times, Mar. 16, 1902.

709. *Florence Burns's Threat—Mother of Man She Is Held for Killing Tells of Girl's Words—Says That Young Woman Threatened While Walter Brooks Was Ill to Kill Him If He Did Not Marry Her*, N.Y. Times, Feb. 21, 1902.

710. *Id.*

711. *Id.*

712. To add to the confusion, it was reported that "Miss Dunn resembles the prisoner, and her presence yesterday in the District Attorney's office caused a sensation. It was rumored that a 'double' for Florence Burns had been found." *Witnesses in Burns Case*, N.Y. Times, Mar. 13, 1902.

713. *The Burns Examination—Girl to Be Presented in Court Today on Murder Charge—Her Little Sister May Be Put on the Stand to Prove Her Alibi*, N.Y. Times, Feb. 22, 1902.

714. *Id.*

715. *Id. See also Florence Burns's Alibi—Conductor Weibles Says He Saw Her on Night of Murder—This Was at the Time She Says She Was at Home—Bellboy Again Identifies the Young Woman*, N.Y. Times, Feb. 23, 1902.

716. *Florence Burns Very Cool*, N.Y. Times, Feb.18, 1902.

717. *Conduct of the Burns Girl*, N.Y. Times, Mar. 17, 1902.

718. *Id.*

719. *Case of Florence Burns*, N.Y. Times, Feb. 20, 1902.

720. *Florence Burns in Court*, N.Y. Times, Feb. 19, 1902.

721. She was not the first "Tombs Angel," and she would not be the last. The first was Mrs. Ernestine Schaffner. Being a widow of some means, she furnished bonds bail to many unfortunate prisoners in the Tombs. In fact, she set up a law office of sorts on Centre Street. The sign on the office read "Free advice to the poor and the innocent accused." *A Thoroughly Good Woman*, N.Y. Times, Feb.11, 1890. She seems to have been taken advantage of by many unworthy types, and Recorder Smyth sometimes refused to take her bond to protect her from lying crooks. She died "in poor circumstances." *See* Munro, *supra* note 533, at 248–249. Munro had been the chaplain of the Tombs. For a tribute to Mrs. Schaffner *see Mrs. Ernestine Schaffner*, N.Y. Times, June 22, 1902.

722. There are several interesting articles about her in the N.Y. Times archives. She frequently appeared in court to plead for dismissal or lenient sentences in cases brought against young women— especially first offenders. She was respected even by the notorious Recorder Goff. *See Tombs Angel Overcome—Mrs. Foster Faints After*

Securing a Girl Prisoner's Release, N.Y. TIMES, Jan. 19, 1901. There is
also a short article reporting Mrs. Foster's efforts on behalf of burglar
George Foster, a homeless man. George Foster received a sentence of one
year and after thanking Judge Foster for his clemency and Mrs. Foster
for her kindness was led out by Officer E. D. Foster of the Tombs Prison.
See *Lots of Fosters in this Case—Judge, Accuser* [Officer Foster], *Accused,
Turnkey, and "Tombs Angel" Have Same Name*, N.Y. TIMES, Feb. 1, 1900.
Of course, sometimes the first offenders went on to repeat their crimes.
See, *Still a Thief in Her Old Age—Carrie Roche Robs Three Employers
in About a Month*, N.Y. TIMES, Aug. 19, 1894. For a description of her
activities *see Little Stories of the Tombs Angel*, N.Y. TIMES, Mar. 2, 1902.

723. MUNRO, *supra* note 533, at 253.

724. *Rigid Inquiry to Place the Blames… The Tombs Angel's Fate*,
N.Y. TIMES, Feb. 23, 1902; *The Tombs Angel*, N.Y. TIMES, Feb. 24,
1902. *Tributes to Mrs. Foster—Services Held at the Tombs in Memory
of Her—Labor Unions Praise Her*, N.Y. TIMES, Feb. 24, 1902; *Funeral
of "Tombs Angel"—The Services at Calvary Church Were Largely
Attended—Clergymen, Judges, and Lawyers Sit Side by Side with
Ex-Prisoners—Internment in Greenwood Follows*, N.Y. TIMES, Feb. 26,
1902. Among the attendees was a young woman dressed "shabbily in
black," who was identified as "Marie Barberi." Mrs. Foster would be
succeeded as "Tombs Angel" by Miss Ada Elliot, who would serve
as the probation officer for the court of special sessions. *See "Tombs
Angel's" Successor*, N.Y. TIMES, Mar. 22, 1902; *New York's New
"Tombs Angel" and Her Work*, N.Y. TIMES, Oct. 23, 1904.

725. N.Y. TIMES, Feb. 23, 1902.

726. *Burns Case Is Continued—Only Two Witnesses Testified Before
Judge Mayer—Accused Girl Enjoyed Tilt Between Her Lawyer and Mr.
Jerome and Laughed at Bellboy's Testimony*, N.Y. TIMES, Feb. 27, 1902.

727. *Florence Burns's Alibi*, N.Y. TIMES, Feb. 23, 1902, *supra* note 715.

728. *Case of Florence Burns—New and Voluntary Testimony in
Her Favor—Man Who Knows Her Declares She Was Not on Conductor
Weibles's Train on the Night of February 14*, N.Y. TIMES, Feb. 25, 1902.

729. *Miss Burn's Mother Gone—Said to Have Left State to Avoid
Testifying at Examination—District Attorney's Office Perturbed—Girl's*

Lawyer Says Parents Will Be Produced at Proper Time, N.Y. Times, Feb. 28, 1902.

730. *Burns Case Is Continued*, N.Y. Times, *supra* note 726.

731. *Evidence in the Burns Case*, N.Y. Times, Mar. 2, 1902.

732. *Says Miss Burns Asked About a Pistol*, N.Y. Times, Mar. 9, 1902.

733. *Witnesses in Burns Case*, N.Y. Times, Mar. 1, 1902.

734. N.Y. Times, Mar. 9, 1902, *supra* note 732.

735. *Says Miss Burns Asked About a Pistol—Detectives Testimony Against Girl Accused of Murder—He Also Says She Described Money Brooks Had with Him—Judge Denounces Police Identification Methods*, N.Y. Times, Mar. 9, 1902.

736. *Mrs. Brooks Faints on the Witness Stand*, N.Y. Times, Mar. 16, 1902.

737. *Court Causes Surprise in the Burns Case—Doubtful About Admissibility of Detectives' Testimony*, N.Y. Times, Mar. 19, 1902.

738. *Id.*

739. *Veracity of Witness in Burns Case Challenged—Eyre Alleged to Have Said Brooks Was Sole Authority for His Statement About the Girl's Threats*, N.Y. Times, Mar. 17, 1902.

740. *Court Causes Surprise in the Burns Case*, N.Y. Times, *supra* note 737.

741. *Florence Burns Free, Leaves the Tombs*, N.Y. Times, Mar. 23, 1902.

742. *Jerome on Burns Case—"I Still Believe Girl Guilty, but Can't Prove It," He Says.—Declares that "There Has Been a Miscarriage of Justice," but Will Not Rearrest the Girl*, N.Y. Times, Mar. 25, 1902.

743. *Brooks Inquest Begins*, N.Y. Times, May 15, 1902.

744. *Says Brooks Killed Himself—Florence Burns's Counsel at Inquest Gives Reasons for Suicide Theory—Two New Witnesses Heard*, N.Y. Times, May 16, 1902.

745. *Florence Burns a Bride*, N.Y. Times, Nov. 29, 1902.

746. *Florence Burns on the Stage*, N.Y. Times, Feb. 15, 1903.

747. *Florence Burns Gets Delay—Magistrate Gives Her and Brooks Till To-day to Answer "Badger" Charge*, N.Y. Times, Sept. 22, 1910.

748. *Id.; See also Florence Burns in Bold "Badger" Game... Aged Father Weeps at News,* N.Y. Times, Sept. 21, 1910; *Florence Burns Again in the Hands of Police—Woman Involved in Murder Case Arrested with Man Who Is Held for Blackmail,* N.Y. Tribune, Sept. 21, 1910.

749. *Florence Burns's Accuser Found Dead... Had Spoken of Threats—Feared Friends of Woman and Man He Had Sent to Jail, He Told Uncle—Drowned, Says Coroner,* N.Y. Times, Sept. 2, 1911.

750. *Florence Burns Guilty—Admits Threatening Police with Revolver During Raid,* N.Y. Times, Feb. 16, 1922.

751. *Florence Burns Held After Police Raid—Woman Acquitted of Walter Brooks Murder Is Accused of Threatening to Use Pistol,* N.Y. Times, Jan. 27, 1922.

An Afterthought

752. Lardner & Reppetto, *supra* note 37, at 97.

753. *See also* O'Connor, *supra* note 563, at 152.

754. *See* Andy Logan, Against the Evidence: The Becker-Rosenthal Affair (1970); Mike Dash, Satan's Circus: Murder, Vice, Police Corruption, and New York's Trial of the Century (2008).

755. J. Edward Lumbard, *Mr. Justice Frankfurter,* 56 J. Crim. L. & Criminology 138, 139 (1965).

756. Lardner & Repetto, *supra* note 37, at 162.

Selected Bibliography

Court Records and Official Documents

District Attorney Collection (New York County),
  People v. Patterson (1904–1905)

Indictment file, *People v. Carlton* (November 1888)

Indictment file, *People v. Frank* (May 1891)

Indictment file, *People v. Nelson* (February 1891)

Indictment File, *People v. Stephani* (June 1890)

Indictment File, *People v. Unger* (February 1887)

Indictment File, *People v. Walden* (November 1891)

Pardon File for Criminal Prisoner/Defendant: George Frank,
  1891 Request for Pardon to Governor Odell

Trial Transcript, *People v. Barberi*, Trial #53 (1895)

Trial Transcript, *People v. Considine*, Trial #64 (1896)

Transcript of the Coroner's Inquest, *People v. Frank* (1891)

Trial Transcript, *People v. Harris*, Trial #21 (1892)

Trial Transcript, third trial, *People v. Kennedy*, Trial #261, (1901)

Trial Transcript, *People v. Nelson*, Trial #15 (1891)

Court Opinions

Cherry v. Des Moines Leader, 114 Iowa 298, 86 N.W. 323 (1901)

Fain v. Commonwealth, 78 Ky. 183, 1879 WL 6704 (Ky. 1879)

In re Stephani's Estate, 159 Misc. 43, 288 N.Y.S. 486 (1936)

Michelson v. United States, 335 U.S. 469 (1948)

People ex rel. Stephani v. North, Medical Sup't, etc., 91 Misc 616,
  155 N.Y.S. 595 (1915)

People v. Barberi, 3 E.H. Smith 256, 149 N.Y. 256, 43 N.E 635 (NY 1896)

People v. Barberi, 47 N.Y.S. 168 (N.Y. Sup.Ct. 1896)

People v. Hummel, 21 N.Y.Crim.R. 162, 119 A.D. 153, 104 N.Y.S. 308 (1907)

People v. Kennedy, 15 N.Y.Crim.R. 351, 34 Misc. 101, 69 N.Y.S. 470 (1901)

People v. Kennedy, 2 Bedell 449, 164 N.Y. 449, 58 N.E. 652 (1900)

People v. Littlejohn, 23 Misc.3d 1127 (A), 889 N.Y.S.2d 507 (Table), 2009 WL 1392605 (N.Y.Supp.), 2009 N.Y. Slip Op. 50958 (U)

People v. Molineaux, 61 N.E. 286 (N.Y. 1901)

People v. Molineux, 168 N.Y. 264 (1901)

People v. Moore, XIV N.Y.Crim.R. 387 (Court of General Sessions, Nov. 1899)

People v. Patrick, 20 Bedell 131, 182 N.Y. 131, 74 N.E. 843 (1905)

People v. Thorn, 50 N.E. 947 (N.Y. 1898)

People v. Zackowitz, 254 N.Y. 192 (1930)

R v. Sullivan [1983] 2 All ER 673 (HL); [1984] AC 156 (HL)

Sidis v. F-R Publishing Corp., 113 F.2d 806 (2d. Cir. 1940)

State v. Duestrow, 137 Mo. 44, 38 S.W. 554 (1897)

Special Collections and Archives

City Museum of New York

Criminal Trial Transcripts of the County of New York County Collection (1883–1927), Lloyd Sealy Library, John Jay College of Criminal Justice, The City University New York

Library of Congress, Chronicling America

Library of Congress, Prints and Photographs Division

New York City Municipal Archives, Department of Records and Information

New York Public Library

New York State Archives

New York State Library

The New York Times Article Archives

Books

Abramson, *Sob Sister Journalism* (1990)

Asbury, *All Around the Town* (1st ed. 1934, 2003)

Asbury, *The Gangs of New York* (1928)

Atwell, *The Great Harry Thaw Case* (1907)

Blaine, *The Midnight Band of Mercy* (2004)

Borchard, *Convicting the Innocent* (1932)

Boswell and Thompson, *The Carlyle Harris Case* (1961)

Boyer, *Max Steuer: Magician of the Law* (1932)

Browder, *The Wickedest Woman in New York: Madame Restell, the Abortionist* (1988)

Burt, *American Murder Ballads* (1964)

Byrnes, *Professional Criminals of America* (1886; reprint 2000)

Campbell, *The Year That Defined American Journalism: 1897 and the Clash of Paradigms* (2006)

Carey, *Memoirs of a Murder Man* (1930)

Cohn and Chisholm, *Take the Witness!* (1934)

Conway, *The Big Policeman* (2010)

Dash, *Satan's Circus: Murder, Vice, Police Corruption, and New York's Trial of the Century* (2008)

Dickens, *A Tale of Two Cities in II The Annotated Dickens* (Edward Guiliano & Philip Collins eds., 1986)

Eigen, *Unconscious Crime: Mental Absence and Criminal Responsibility in Victorian London* (2003)

Eigen, *Witnessing Insanity: Madness and Mad Doctors in the English Courts* (1995)

Fitch, *The Woman in the Case* (1905)

Fowler, *The Great Mouthpiece* (1931)

Freeland, *Automats, Taxi Dances, and Vaudeville* (2009)

Friedland, *The Death of Old Man Rice: A True Story of Criminal Justice in America* (1996)

Galloway, *The Servant Girl Murders: Austin,Texas 1885* (2010)

Geary, *Madison Square Tragedy: The Murder of Stanford White* (2013)

Gibbs, et al., *1 New York Murders* (Ted Collins ed., 1944)

Gildea, *The Longest Fight: In the Ring with Joe Gans, Boxing's First African American Champion* (2012)

Gilfoyle, *A Pickpocket's Tale: The Underworld of Nineteenth-Century New York* (2006)

Goodman, *Bloody Versicles: The Rhymes of Crime* (1971)

Goodman, *The Killing of Julia Wallace* (1969)

Gould, *The Mismeasure of Man* (1996)

Hamilton, *A Manual of Medical Jurisprudence with Special Reference to Diseases and Injuries of the Nervous System* (1890)

Hamilton, *Recollections of an Alienist—Personal and Professional* (1916)

Hamilton, *The Social Misconstruction of Reality: Validity and Verification in the Scholarly Community* (1996)

Hamilton, *Types of Insanity: An Illustrated Guide in the Physical Diagnosis of Mental Disease* (1883)

Homberger, *The Historical Atlas of New York City* (2005)

Howe and Hummel, *In Danger; Or Life in New York. A True History of a Great City's Wiles and Tempatations. True Facts and Disclosures* (J.S. Ogilve & Co., Chicago, 1888)

Huffman, *A Yankee in Meiji Japan: The Crusading Journalist Edward H. House* (2003)

Jesse, *Trial of Madeline Smith* (1949 reprint from Notable British Trials Series)

Katz, *Bad Acts and Guilty Minds—Conundrums of the Criminal Law* (1987)

Keller, *Scandalous Lady: The Life and Times of Madame Restell, New York's Most Notorious Abortionist* (1981)

Langford, *The Murder of Stanford White* (1962, 2011)

Lardner and Reppetto, *NYPD: A City and Its Police* (2000)

Lessard, *The Architect of Desire: Beauty and Danger in the Stanford White Family* (1997)

Levy, *The Nan Patterson Case* (1959)

Levy, *Theatre Guyed* (1933)

Logan, *Against the Evidence: The Becker-Rosenthal Affair* (1970)

McGovern, *An Experts Study of the Dreyfus Case: An Interview with D. N. Carvalho, Engaged by Madame Dreyfus to Study the Documents* (1899)

Miraldi, *The Pen Is Mightier: The Muckraking Life of Charles Edward Russell* (2003)

Mohr, *Abortion in America: The Origins and Evolution of National Policy* (1978)

Monkkonen, *Murder in New York City* (2001)

Mooney, *Evelyn Nesbit and Stanford White: Love and Death in the Gilded Age* (1976)

Morris, *The Rose Man of Sing Sing: A True Tale of Life, Murder, and Redemption in the Age of Yellow Journalism* (2005)

Mueller and Kirkpatrick, *Evidence* (2d ed., 1999)

Mueller and Kirkpatrick, *Evidence* (5th ed., 2012)

Munro, *The New York Tombs, Inside and Out!* (1909)

State of New York, *Public Papers of Benjamin B. Odell, Jr. Governor for 1902* (1907)

Nuland, *The Doctors' Plague: Germs, Childbed Fever, and the Strange Story of Ignaz Semmelweis* (reprint ed. 2004)

O'Connor, *Courtroom Warrior: The Combative Career of William Travers Jerome* (1963)

O'Faolain, *The Story of Chicago May* (2005)

Pathological Institute of the New York State Hospitals, *Vols. I and II Contributions from the Pathological Institute of the New York State Hospitals* (1896–97)

Paul, *Tragic Beauty: The Lost Memoirs of Evelyn Nesbit* (2006)

Pucci, *The Trials of Maria Barbello* (1997)

Rand, *Night of January 16th* (1934)

Rice, *Counselor-at- Law* (1931)

Rice, *Street Scene* (1929)

Rome, *Destry Rides Again* (1959)

Rome, *I Can Get It for You Wholesale* (1962)

Rome, *Pins and Needles* (1936)

Rovere, *Howe & Hummel: Their True and Scandalous History* (New York: Farrar, Straus 1947)

Russell, *Edgar Lee Masters: A Biography* (2001)

Sante, *Low Life: Lures and Snares of Old New York* (1991)

Schechter, *The Devil's Gentleman* (2008)

Semmelweis, *Etiology, Concept and Prophylaxis of Childbed Fever* (K. Codell Carter, trans. 1983)

Sharpe, *Chicago May: Her Story* (1928)

Shay, *More Friends and Drunken Companions: Songs and Ballads of Conviviality* (1928)

Shepley, *Movers and Shakers, Scalawags and Suffragettes: Tales from Bellefontaine Cemetery* (2008)

Spitzka, *Treatise on Insanity, Its Classification, Diagnosis and Treatment* (1883)

Srebnick, *The Mysterious Death of Mary Rogers* (1995)

St. John, *Final Verdict* (1962)

Stashower, *The Beautiful Cigar Girl: Mary Rogers, Edgar Allan Poe, and the Invention of Murder* (2006)

Steuer, A., *Max D. Steuer, Trial Lawyer* (1950)

Stevens, *Sensationalism and the New York Press* (1991)

Stryker, *The Art of Advocacy* (1954)

Tanford, *The Trial Process: Law, Tactics and Ethics* (3d ed. 2002)

Train, *Courts, Criminals, and the Camorra* (1912)

Train, *True Stories of Crime from the District Attorney's Office* (1926)

Trope, *Once Upon a Time in Los Angles: The Trials of Earl Rogers* (2001)

Underwood and Fortune, *Trial Ethics* (1988)

Uruburu, *American Eve: Evelyn Nesbit, Stanford White, the Birth of the "It" Girl and the Crime of the Century* (2008)

Van Emery, *Sins of New York: As "Exposed" by the Police Gazette* (1930)

Veillier, *The Trial of Mary Dugan* (1928)

Wallace, *The Prodigy: A Biography of William James Sidis, America's Greatest Child Prodigy* (1986)

Walsh, *Midnight Dreary: The Mysterious Death of Edgar Allan Poe* (1998)

Warden, *Wilkie Collins's the Dead Alive: The Novel, the Case, and Wrongful Convictions* (2005)

Warren, *Constantine Samuel Rafinesque: A Voice in the American Wilderness* (2004)

Wellman, *The Art of Cross-Examination* (4th ed. 1936)

Wellman, *Gentleman of the Jury* (1924)

Wellman, *Luck and Opportunity: Recollections* (1938)

Wellman, *Success in Court* (1941)

Whyte, *The Uncrowned King: The Sensational Rise of William Randolph Hearst* (2009)

William Marsh Rice and His Institute: The Centennial Edition (Randall L. Hall and Sylvia Stallings Morris eds. 2012)

Winkler, *William Randolph Hearst: A New Appraisal* (1955)

Zacks, *An Underground Education* (1997)

Articles and Book Chapters

Asbury, "That Was New York—The Escape of William J. Sharkey," 39 *The New Yorker* (March 7, 1931)

Borowitz, "Packaged Death," in "Crimes Gone By, Collected Essays of Albert Horowitz," 29 *Legal Stud. F.* 631 (2005)

Burrell, "The Strange Fate of Whitman's Brain," 20 *Walt Whitman Quarterly Review* 107 (2003)

"The Case of Maria Barberi," 11(14) *The Literary Digest* 7 (August 3, 1895)

"The Case of Maria Barberi," 19 *Public Opinion, A Comprehensive Summary of the Press Throughout the World on all Important Current Topics*, 169–170 (July–December 1895)

"The Case of Maria Barberi," 10 *Woman's Journal* 252 (August 1895)

Davis, "Killer Buzz—Caffeine Intoxication Is Now Evidence for an Insanity Plea," 16 *ABA Journal* (June 2011)

Fatout, "Mark Twain, Litigant," 31 *American Literature* 30–45 (1959)

Flint, "Reminiscences of the 'Frenchy' Murder Case," *New York Medical Journal* 514–518 (July 26, 1902)

Flint, "Some Medico-Legal Points in the 'Frenchy' Murder Trial," *New York Medical Journal* (July 19, 1891)

Formad, "Comparative Studies of Mammalian Blood, with special reference to the Microscopical Diagnosis of Blood Stains in Criminal Cases," 51 (IX:3) *Journal of Comparative Medicine and Surgery* (Philadelphia: A.L. Hummel, 1888)

Granieri and Fazio, "The Lombrosian prejudice in medicine. The case of Epilepsy. Epileptic psychosis. Epilepsy and aggressiveness," 33(1) *Neurological Sciences* 173–92 (May 2011)

Hapgood, "The Foreign Stage in New York: III The Italian Theater," 11 *The Bookman* 545-553 (August 1900)

Hrdlicka, "Contribution to the General Pathology of the Insane (Physical Examinations and Measurements)," *24th Annual Report, Middletown State Homeopathic Hospital at Middletown, New York* (1895)

Hrdlicka, "The Medico-Legal Aspects of the Case of Maria Barbella," *Contributions from the Pathological Institute of the New York State Hospitals* (1896-1897), *Surgical Bulletin* (1898)

Hunt, "Forensic Anthropology at the Smithsonian," 27(1) *AnthroNotes* 6–12 (Smithsonian, Spring 2006)

Jacobson, "When All Goldfield Was Aglitter," *Sports Illustrated Vault* (August 5, 1968)

Jonakait, "People v. Molineux and Other Crime Evidence: One Hundred Years and Counting," 30 *Am. J. Crim. L.* 1 (2002)

Kendrick, "The Dolly Reynolds Case," in Angelica Gibbs, et al., 1 *New York Murders* (Ted Collins ed., 1944)

Keppel, Weis, Brown and Welch, "The Jack the Ripper Murders: A Modus Operandi and Signature Analysis of the 1888–1891 Whitechapel Murders," 2(1) *Journal of Investigative Psychology and Offender Profiling* 1–21 (January 2005)

Leonard, "In Defense of the Character Evidence Prohibition: Foundations of the Rule Against Trial by Character," 73 *Ind. L.J.* 1161 (1998)

Liebling, Annals of Crime: The Case of the Scattered Dutchman, *The New Yorker* (September 24, 1955)

Lumbard, "Mr. Justice Frankfurter," 56 *J. Crim. L. & Criminology* 138, 139 (1965)

Mortimer, "Rumpole and the Younger Generation," in *The First Rumpole Omnibus* (1983)

Pearson, "The Sob-Sisters Arise," *The New Yorker*, 25 (November 11, 1933)

University of Pennsylvania, *The Death of Dr. Henry F. Formad*, IV UNIVERSITY OF PENNSYLVANIA MEDICAL BULLETIN 735 (Adams and Wood eds., October 1891–September 1892)

Peterson, "Yellow Justice: Media Portrayal of Criminal Trials in the Progressive Era," 1:1 *Stan. J. of Legal Stud.* 72, 88-96 (1999)

Pinta, "Examining Harry Thaw's 'Brain-Storm' Defense: APA and ANA Presidents as Expert Witnesses in a 1907 Trial," 79 *Psychiatric Quarterly* 83-89 (2008)

Portnoy, "Jewish Abortion Technician," *Tablet Magazine* (August 20, 2009)

Ramsey, "Public Responses to Intimate Violence: a Glance at the Past," 121(4) *Public Health Reports* (July–August 2006)

Rovere, "Profiles: 89 Centre Street, Part I—Can Lawyers Be Honest?" 36 *The New Yorker* (November 23, 1946)

Rovere, "Profiles: 89 Centre Street, Part II—The Weeper," 44 *The New Yorker* (November 30, 1946)

Royal Microscopical Society, "The Kentucky Meat Shower," in "Progress of Microscopical Science," 314 *The Monthly Microscopical Journal* (December 1876) in XVI *The Monthly Microscopical Journal Transactions of the Royal Microscopical Society, and Record of Histological Research at Home and Abroad* (Harry Lawson, MD, MRCP, FRMS, ed., 1876)

Russell, "Old Shakespeare," *The Illustrated Detective Magazine* (October 1931)

Scientific American, Supplement No. 30 (July 22, 1876)

Spitzka, "The Whitechapel Murders: Their medico-legal and historical aspects," *The Journal of Nervous & Medical Disease* (1888)

Thurber, "Where Are They Now? April Fool." *The New Yorker*, 22–26 (August 14, 1937) (under the pseudonym of Jared Manley)

"Trial of Maria Barberi—Degeneracy," 4 *Am. Law.* 532 (1896)

Ubelaker, "Evolution of the relationship of forensic anthropology with physical anthropology and forensic pathology: A North American perspective," 4 *Studies in Historical Anthropology*, 199–205 (2006)

Underwood, "Arch and Gordon": The Crime Behind the Ballad, 31 *Legal Stud. F.* 825 (2007)

Underwood, "Mr. Howe's Last Case," 31 *Legal Stud. F.* 801 (2007)

Vanderlinden, "The New York Affair—Part 1," *The American Journal for Ripper Studies* (July 2003)

Vanderlinden, "The New York Affair—Part 2," *Ripper Notes, The American Journal for Ripper Studies* (January 2004)

Van Gieson and Sidis, "Epilepsy and Expert Testimony," *Contributions from the Pathological Institute of the New York State Hospitals* (1896–1897)

Thesis

Magana, "Mr. America's Creator: The Race Science of Dr. Ales Hrdlicka," 1896–1943 (Thesis for Department of History, Columbia University 2011)

Newspapers

Alexandria Gazette (Virginia)

The Anaconda Standard (Montana)

The Ann Arbor Argus (Michigan)

The Auckland Star (New Zealand)

The Boston Globe (Massachusetts)

The Columbian (Pennsylvania)

Lewiston Evening Journal (Maine)

Los Angeles Herald (California)

The Milwaukee Journal (Wisconsin)

The Morning Telegraph (New York)

The New York Herald (New York)

The New York Times (New York)
New-York Tribune (New York)
The North American (Pennsylvania)
The San Francisco Call (San Francisco)
Saturday Review (London, U.K.)
The Sun (New York, New York)
The Washington Times (Washington, DC)
The World (New York)

Video Recordings

Frankenstein (Universal Pictures 1931)
Gangs of New York (Miramax Films 2002)
Godfather II (Paramount Pictures 1974)
So Evil My Love (Paramount British Pictures 1948)

Illustration Credits

Numbers in *italics* refer to illustration numbers in the inserts.

Asylum Projects: *22*
Author's Private Collection: *1, 39*
Folger Shakespeare Library: *5*
Geographicus Rare Antique Maps, Brooklyn, New York: Map on
    front and back endpapers
Library of Congress: *2, 3, 4, 24, 26, 27, 28, 30, 37*
Museum of the City of New York: *7, 8, 40* (Richard Hoe Lawrence
    for Jacob August Riis [1849–1914])
New York City Archives: *11, 12, 35, 36, 38*
New York Public Library: Frontispiece, *6, 9, 13, 15, 16, 17, 18, 19,
    20, 29, 33, 34*
New York State Archives: *23, 25*
University of Alabama: *10, 14*
University of Kentucky Libraries: *21, 31, 32*
University of Michigan: *41*

Index

Note: Photographs, drawings and documents are indicated by figure number "(fig 1)." Note content is indicated by an italic *"n"* and note number. All locations are in New York City or New York State unless otherwise indicated.

A Note About the Author

Richard H. Underwood is the W. L. Matthews Professor of Law at the University of Kentucky College of Law. He is the author of *CrimeSong: True Crime Stories from Southern Murder Ballads* and the co-author of several books on evidence, trial technique, and legal ethics. He has published numerous articles on the law, legal history, perjury, famous trials, and true crime. Richard has lectured and presented papers on diverse subjects at conferences across the United States and in London and Amsterdam.